MW00897855

Show Me Your Ways

Making Sense of the Seasons of Your Life
A Journey to Maturity through Psalm 119

Ken Eberly

Partnership
Publications

www.H2HP.com

Show Me Your Ways
Making Sense of the Seasons of Your Life - A Journey to Maturity through Psalm 119
by Ken Eberly

© 2017 by Ken Eberly

Partnership Publications
A Division of House to House Publications
www.H2HP.com

ISBN 13: 978-1542611800
ISBN 10: 1542611806

All rights reserved.

Unless otherwise noted, all scripture quotations in this publication are taken from the New King James Version. Copyright © 1982 by Thomas Nelson, Inc. Used by permission. All rights reserved."

Permission to make photocopies or to reproduce by any other mechanical or electronic means in whole or in part of any designated* page, illustration, or activity in this book is granted only to the original purchaser and is intended for noncommercial promotion, advertising or sale of a product or service. Sharing of the material in this book with other churches or organizations not owned or controlled by the original purchaser is also prohibited. All rights reserved.

Printed in the United States of America

Cover Design by Jamie Eberly

Dedication

This book is dedicated to:

My dear wife and best friend, Betty, who stood by me through almost forty years of ministry, and kept me encouraged in this endeavor;

My children, Kendra, Chad, Krystal, Kordel and Kyle, all who love the LORD and have honored me as their father. I love them dearly and pray often that they would know the fullness of the Abundant Life in *Yeshua*.

Acknowledgements

My deepest gratitude is reserved for my Lord and Savior, *Yeshua* the Messiah, who has been the True Vine from which my life has been drawn, and who has surrounded me with godly and supportive men and women who have loved me and helped me in my journey.

I thank Betty and the children for their support of, and contribution to, the call of God on my life for ministry.

I thank all our intercessors and for their investment in prayer, aimed at seeing this book become a reality – especially Ann, who helped keep me on course and helped to formulate the questions that appear at the end of each chapter.

I thank Ruth Ann, who spent hours poring over the early versions of the book, helping with wording and punctuation. Her encouragement helped to keep me going.

I also thank Donna for her hours of work in helping with the Hebrew letters and ancient pictographs at the beginning of each chapter. The ancient pictograph of each Hebrew letter comes from the work of Dr. Frank T. Seekins in his Hebrew alphabet workbook.[1]

Contents

Foreword

overview

Psalm 119 has tremendous lessons for our walk with Christ. This very unique psalm provides a progression into spiritual maturity that helps us identify and understand the ways and dealings of God as He forms us into His image. Psalm 119 helps us know God's ways and make sense of the seasons of our lives so that we can cooperate with Him in the process of spiritual growth.

God the Father committed Himself to a massive undertaking with mankind: conforming every believer into the image of His Son *Yeshua*, the "pattern Son."

The process of hearing a *rhema* word and allowing that word to work a transformation within us is experiential in nature. It takes time to convert a rebellious soul into an obedient spirit. No one can cross the Red Sea, which is the beginning of our faith walk, and also cross the Jordan River, which is the fullness of our faith walk, at the same time. We are on a journey to become like our Master Himself, but the journey itself is a requirement in that process. Transformation is not instantaneous.

Psalm 119, the story of that journey in the life of our psalmist, presents a form of Hebrew poetry. It is an acrostic psalm, divided into twenty-two sections of eight verses each, one section for each of the twenty-two letters of the Hebrew alphabet. Each verse of any given section begins with the letter of the Hebrew alphabet, which identifies that respective section.

Each of the twenty-two sections of Psalm 119 has a dominant theme, and the first Hebrew word or phrase of any given section often identifies that theme. Likewise, Psalm 119:1 identifies the over-arching theme of the entire psalm: *The Blessed Life.* "Blessed (happy) are the undefiled in the way, who walk in the law (*torah*) of the LORD."

This book, a manual for maturity, is not for the faint of heart. It should be read devotionally, along with an open Bible. It is designed to allow you, the reader, to meditate on and prayerfully ponder key words, phrases and themes.

Moses prayed in Exodus 33:13, "Show me now Your way, that I may know You and that I may find grace in Your sight." As we study and meditate on the truths in this psalm, I pray that it can be a guide that will help us know the ways God, even as our Heavenly Father works to conform each one of us into the image of His Son.

Let this be your prayer as you embark on this journey along with our psalmist.

Chapter 1

Conformed into the Image of His Son: Journey to Maturity

Christ-likeness Is the Ultimate Goal

The goal of a believer's life is to be Christ-like, or to be conformed into the image of His Son (Romans 8:29). *Yeshua* is the One whom we are to love, admire and desire to be like, both in character (fruit of the Spirit) and in power (gifts of the Spirit). This is "the prize of the upward call of God in Christ Jesus" that the Apostle Paul spoke of pressing toward in Philippians 3:14-15. Paul labored to "present every man perfect (mature) in Christ Jesus" (Colossians 1:28); he wanted believers to grow up!

The progression into spiritual maturity seen in Psalm 119 is certainly not the only such journey found in scripture. Numerous journeys into spiritual maturity can be seen in the Bible. Through studying them, we can begin to understand God's work in man, bringing us into the image of *Yeshua* according to His own purpose. These progressions include the Psalms of Ascents (Psalms 120 to 134), the forty-two treks of the children of Israel as they journeyed from Egypt to Canaan (Numbers 33), the Song of Solomon and others. All of these progressions culminate with fallen humans becoming redeemed and sanctified in order to become like the Master, *Yeshua*. They have become those "of whom the world was not worthy" (Hebrews 11:38). They "love not the world neither the things that are in the world" (1 John 2:15). Rather they love the Lord their God with all their heart, with all their soul and with all their mind and their neighbor as themselves (Matthew 22:37-39). These have "set their affection on things above and not on things of the earth" (Colossians 3:2). They have become pilgrims whose treasure is in heaven. The cry and longing of their hearts is for Christ: "Even so, Lord Jesus, come."

Law and Grace: Old Testament and New Testament?

The relationship between law and grace is a huge subject that is discussed and taught relentlessly. It is not our main purpose in this study to examine the debate between law and grace. However, the brief overview of the debate below will provide some helpful orientation to this study.

Translating the Hebrew word *torah* as law seems unfortunate because such a translation can give the impression that God's word is cold or unyielding. The word *torah* is more accurately translated as instruction or teaching, that being a father's instruction to the son or daughter he loves. This is explained further in the next chapter.

Salvation is always the gift of God that comes by grace through faith, not of works (Ephesians 2:8-9). The cross is an eternal reality, because *Yeshua* was "the Lamb slain from the foundation of the world" (Revelation 13:8). Consider the following:

1. Abel accessed the provision of the cross as recorded in Genesis 4:4. See also Hebrews 11:4.

2. "But Noah found grace in the eyes of the LORD" (Genesis 6:8).

3. Israel was first brought out of Egypt, saved by grace through faith in the Passover Lamb, and later given the *torah* (law) at Sinai. The law teaches us how to walk with God, how to represent Him on earth and how to remain in His blessing. The law is not intended to be about salvation through works.

We have access by faith into this grace in order to rejoice in hope and glory in tribulation (Romans 5:2-3). Grace is not a license to live in bondage to sin and yet remain in God's favor (see Romans 6:1-2; Jude 1:4). Rather, it is the power to walk as *Yeshua* walked (1 John 2:6). *Yeshua* spoke often about loving God and keeping His commandments (John 14:15, 21, 23, 24; 15:10 and others). When giving His final instructions to His disciples, *Yeshua* said, "teaching them to observe all things that I have commanded" (Matthew 28:20).

The New Covenant gives the substance that the Old Testament pointed to through types and shadows. For example, Moses' tabernacle was a shadow picture of *Yeshua* as the tabernacle of God. From it, we learn what is required in order to become the dwelling place of God on earth and have communion with Him. Grace is available through our faith to live in God's presence. While ritual fulfillment of a set of laws without faith and love in our hearts never pleases the Lord, neither does it work to claim to have faith and love while violating the same laws that embody that faith and love.

Legalism promotes the idolization of law but prevents wholesome and healthy relationships. Law, when used as a means to an end, creates healthy boundaries that provide for healthy relationships. Law defines what love is. For example, in marriage there are rules—laws, if you will—that guide the way we relate to a spouse. While we do not promote a loveless marriage that is based on sterile adherence to a set of laws, neither can we violate these laws without violating love.

1. The law is not the end or goal, but it leads us to the goal, just as maps and signs help us stay on the right course. The purpose is reaching the destination, not the trip.

2. Dallas Willard writes in his book, *The Divine Conspiracy,* "While the law is never the source of life in the kingdom, it is forever the course of it."[1] It was not given as the way to holiness, but as a revelation of God's character, holiness and the ways of the kingdom of God. Hence the law is a schoolmaster to bring us to Messiah (Galatians 3:24).

3. It is not helpful to talk about sinless perfection as being our goal. That only causes us to focus on our sins and sinful flesh, making the fulfillment of the law the final goal. Instead, we are to fix our eyes on *Yeshua* and define ourselves as He does, according to our new nature. Our weak flesh does not define us. More on this explanation will appear later in the book.

4. Mature Christ-likeness is the more scriptural idea. This makes *Yeshua* the end and allows for a process of coming to fullness. "Be perfect (*teleios*) as your Father in heaven is perfect *(teleios)*" (Matthew 5:48). The Greek word *teleios* refers to being of full age or mature, having reached the goal toward which one has been pressing. Nowhere in scripture are we told to what extent we can be like the sinless *Yeshua* in this age. But we are instructed to "be transformed" by the renewing of our minds (Romans 12:2). Furthermore, John wrote his epistle so that "you may not sin" (I John 2:1). We can therefore conclude that substantial, if not full, Christ-likeness is available to us, and expected of us, in this present age, even though we continue to live in our mortal bodies—within which an entity called "sin" still operates.

    Note: Stumbling because of the weakness of our flesh is not the same thing as living in rebellion and disobedience or being controlled by sinful passions (see James 3:2).

Romans 10:4 says, "Messiah (Christ) is the end (*telos:* consummation or purpose) of the law for righteousness to everyone who believes." This does not refer to the termination of the law, but is about the outcome, end goal, purpose, aim or consummation of the law.

The law is a schoolmaster to bring us to Messiah. Once Messiah is formed in us, the law is irrelevant because we have it written upon our hearts. We have become "word made flesh" if you will, and are no longer under the law because Messiah lives in and through us to fulfill all of God's will for our lives (Galatians 3-4; Romans 8:4).

A famous story from the Talmud[2] about a pagan who was interested in Judaism has been told and retold many times. The version I am familiar with goes like this: "A pagan went to a great rabbi named Shammai and said, 'Teach me the entire law while standing on one foot.' Shammai grew angry and said it was impossible, because there were 613 commandments in the *Torah* and each must be learned and mastered with all of its derivations before one can begin to understand and live the law. So the pagan went away. Eventually, this same pagan came to Hillel and made the same request of him. Hillel without hesitating stood on one foot and said, 'And you shall love the LORD your God with all your heart and with all your soul and with all your might' (Deuteronomy 6:5), and 'you shall love your neighbor as yourself' (Leviticus 19:18); the rest is commentary, go and learn.'" Based on this answer, the pagan was converted to Judaism.

"Go and learn" implies a journey or a process over time. A quote from Preston Eby's writings on spiritual maturity helps us understand the nature of this journey:

"NATURE is inherited; CHARACTER is developed! No one is born possessing character. Every child of Adam is born into this world with a sinful (flesh) nature. But that precious little infant does not yet have a sinful character. As the child grows the character is formed progressively out of the nature. The nature gradually manifests itself through the actions of the child as character. In the same way, we have by regeneration been made partakers of the divine nature."[3]

Certainly, character is never formed instantaneously. Through our faith in *Yeshua* as the Messiah, we have been "born. . . of God" (John 1:13) through the "incorruptible seed" of the word of God (I Peter 1:23) and have become part of the family of God. We have become partakers of the divine nature (2 Peter 1:4), but now that nature needs to become manifest through the formation of our character.

Ponder this excerpt from a message by Francis Frangipane on Christ-likeness:

"When people think of their destiny, they often think of something they will do for God, a task that involves the visible demonstration of a unique gift. But neither our gifts nor a specific calling represent the core reality of our destiny. That destiny is to be Christ-like."[4]

If we believe that becoming Christ-like is the reason we exist, we will be in obvious pursuit of that transformation.

Frangipane continues: "We have seen ministry leaders whose gifts and callings were so powerful, so captivating, that they seemed capable of bringing heaven itself to earth. Then, to our shock, we discovered later that these same individuals were secretly in the grip of the most disgraceful sins. How could such things occur? When our primary goal is the development of our gifts or calling rather than character, we become increasingly vulnerable to satanic deception."[5]

Becoming like *Yeshua* is why we exist. When we pursue the image of Messiah, we possess the meaning of life.

This is the journey of our psalmist through the verses of Psalm 119.

As we join him on the journey, with Bible open and heart attuned, may we meditate on the key words, prayerfully consider the themes, and come to know the ways of God more deeply.

Notes

1. All Hebrew and Greek word definitions begin with or include the definitions from the *Enhanced Strong's Lexicon*. Around these basic definitions I have filled in many of the nuances of meaning from my own understanding which have come from my years of reading and meditating on the scriptures, hearing the scriptures taught by others, and teaching them myself. As a reader, I encourage you to be like the Bereans in Acts 17:11, who "searched the scriptures daily to find out whether these things were so."

2. All scriptures are quoted from the *New King James Version* (NKJV) unless otherwise noted.

3. In keeping with a more Hebraic flavor to this study from the Hebrew Scriptures:

    *   Jesus is referred to according to His Hebrew name, *Yeshua*, except in quotations and printed scriptures from the NKJV.

    *   Christ (Greek for the Anointed One) will most often be rendered Messiah (Hebrew for the Anointed One) except in the word "Christ-likeness."

    *   "The church" will often be referred to as "the congregation" or "the community of faith" or "the Body of Messiah."

    *   The covenant Name of God, "I AM WHO I AM" (Exodus 3:14), commonly thought in Christian circles to be Jehovah, will be transliterated from the four Hebrew letters, yood-hey-vav-hey, as YHVH.

4. The first page of each chapter shows the respective letter of the Hebrew alphabet corresponding with that section of the Psalm, followed by the ancient pictograph for the same.

Chapter 2

Introduction to Psalm 119: *The Blessed Life*
Conformed to the Image of His Son

Authorship

Some consider this psalm an abridgement of David's life in which he expresses the stages of his life journey. It shows the trials and persecutions, as well as the assistance and encouragement, that he received along the way. Others perceive in it the morality of the Gospel, and as a description of rules that would guide man's conduct. Some believe it was written in Babylon during Israel's exile.

I believe Psalm 119 to be Davidic. Whether written by King David himself or compiled from his writings by someone else in Babylon, it certainly depicts the heart of David. It displays David's great love for God and His word, and it corresponds with the stages and events of David's life.

Structure

As noted in the introduction, Psalm 119 contains twenty-two sections that have eight verses in each. It employs a form of Hebrew poetry, with each section being assigned one of the twenty-two letters of the Hebrew alphabet. The first verse of each section provides the theme of those eight verses as it begins with the respective Hebrew letter.

Dominant Themes in Each Section

A dominant theme can be found in each of the twenty-two sections of Psalm 119. The first Hebrew word or phrase of any given section often identifies that theme. For example, verse 25, the first line of the fourth section (*dalet*) says, "My soul clings to the dust." That line identifies the theme of this specific eight-verse section as the psalmist acknowledges the struggle within his members, between his flesh and his spirit (see Galatians 5:17).

Likewise, Psalm 119:1 identifies the over-arching theme of the entire psalm: *The Blessed Life*. "Blessed (happy) are the undefiled in the way, who walk in the law (*torah*) of the LORD." This is a major truth! To be happy, or blessed, in life, one must live blamelessly, just as *Yeshua* did (see 1 John 2:6). Yet we are instructed to do this while sinful passions burn within our flesh, and while living in a fallen world in which sin and offenses easily beset us. On this point, *Yeshua* and the New Testament writers agree:

1. Matthew 5:8, "Blessed (happy) are the pure in heart for they shall see God."

2. Philippians 2:14-15, "Do all things without murmuring . . . that you may become blameless . . . children of God without fault in the midst of a crooked and perverse generation."

3. 1 Thessalonians 3:13, "That He may establish your hearts blameless in holiness. . . ."

4. 1 John 2:6, "He who says that he abides in Him (*Yeshua*) ought himself also to walk just as He (*Yeshua*) walked."

Also, the meaning of the Hebrew letter at the head of each section sometimes seems to play a role in identifying the dominate theme of a given section. For example, verses one through eight each begin with the Hebrew letter, *aleph*. *Aleph*, signified by the ancient pictograph of an ox, speaks of authority, strength, gentleness and servant-hood, offering us a type of Messiah, the perfect Servant, into whose image we are to be conformed. The question in that opening section is this: Will I say "yes" to the Lord? Will I receive with meekness (like the ox) the implanted word (James 1:21), and submit to His authority and to His dealings? Or, will I remain content with my distance from God, lack of impact, and status quo faith that is filled with unnecessary troubles, all of which flow out of immaturity and lack of being like the Messiah?

The Word of God

Of the 176 verses in Psalm 119, all but three of them (v. 90, 122, 132) have a direct reference to the word of God. We know that *Yeshua's* name is called "The word (*logos*) of God" (Revelation 19:13; John 1:1, 14), hence He is the sum total of God's communication and revelation to humans. The writer of Hebrews says that God has "in these last days spoken to us by His Son" who is "the brightness of His glory and the express image of His person" (Hebrews 1:2-3). *Yeshua*, the Messiah, is the revelation of the Father. Consider the following quotations from John's gospel:

1. "If you have seen Me, you have seen the Father" (John 14:9).

2. "I and My Father are one" (John 10:30).

3. "I have declared to them Your Name" (John 17:26).

Yeshua, who is the Word, will employ the word of God in order to "sanctify and cleanse her (His bride, the church) with the washing of water by the word (rhema)." He will nourish and cherish His bride with these words (Ephesians 5:26, 29). He is both the Message and the Messenger.

The word of God has many functions related to our conversion and journey to maturity.

1. It washes (Ephesians 5:26).

2. It nourishes and feeds—Yeshua is the "Bread of Life" (Matthew 4:4; John 6:35).

3. It is good seed—there is life in the seed (Mark 4:14; 1 Peter 1:23; 1 John 3:9; James 1:18).

4. Everything exists by the word of God (Genesis 1; Hebrews 1:3; 11:3; Psalm 33:6).

5. It is powerful, alive and active (Hebrews 4:12).

6. It heals (Psalm 107:20; Matthew 8:8).

7. It can make "wise unto salvation through faith." It corrects, instructs, and rebukes (2 Timothy 3:15-16).

8. It is light to our path (Psalm 119:105, 130; 2 Peter 1:19).

9. It is life to us and prolongs our days (Deuteronomy 32:47; John 6:63).

10. It is a weapon, "the sword of the Spirit which is the word of God" (Ephesians 6:17).

11. Faith comes through the word of God (Romans 10:17).

12. The word of God is truth (1 Kings 17:24; Psalm 33:4; 119:43, 160; John 1:14; 17:17).

    This list could go on and on!

Nine different Hebrew words are employed in Psalm 119 as synonyms for the word of God. Here below, they are listed according to the English transliteration of the Hebrew word, followed by the English word which is employed in the NKJV, together with a brief definition. Each word portrays a different facet of the word of God, like facets of a diamond. These nine facets of the word of God are really nine dimensions of *Yeshua*, who is both the Message and the Messenger: "The Word of God." They reflect both who He is in His person and His ministry to us through the word. Just as "the worlds were framed by the word of God" (Hebrews 11:3), so Messiah will be formed in us by that word.

1. *Torah*—translated law from the root, *yarah*, meaning to teach or to instruct. Literally, *torah* is instruction or teaching and it speaks of teaching, guiding, directing and instructing. This word occurs twenty-five times in the psalm.

    •   The root word, *yarah*, is often translated teach, but actually means to shoot (as an arrow), cast or throw. This word is translated archer five times in scripture. These two concepts together form the idea of teaching that is given with the aim of hitting the mark. *Chata*, the primary Hebrew word for sin, is "to miss the mark."

- *Torah* is really the instruction, correction and direction of a father who wants his son to be blessed. *Torah* is not a dictator's list of rules, but has to do with learning the ways and wisdom of our heavenly Father.

- The law (*torah*), being sound, complete and utterly dependable, serves to turn us away from our self life and toward *Yeshua*. It is perfect, converting (turning) the soul from sin and the world to the kingdom of God and to His righteousness (Psalm 19:7).

2. *Eduth* and *edah* are translated testimonies. *Eduth* is a revelation, a testimony, a witness, a reiteration, or an attestation. It represents or repeats something that took place at a different time or existed in a different place. Testimony (*eduth*) hints at a fresh revelation or communication from God to us—something experiential or manifest from heaven and represented on the earth. This family of Hebrew words is employed twenty-three times in the psalm.

   - "The testimony (*eduth*) of the LORD is sure (trustworthy) making wise the simple" (Psalm 19:7). The testimony of God in His Son is like the steadfast fostering of a little child by a trustworthy parent who faithfully duplicates what God is like.

   - "The testimony of *Yeshua* is the spirit of prophecy" (Revelation 19:10).

   - The ark of the testimony (*eduth*) testified of God's presence and power (Exodus 25:16).

   - The two tablets of the testimony testified of God's character and nature (Exodus 31:18).

   - *Yeshua* is a trustworthy earthly witness or testimony of what God in heaven is like. Yeshua is an accurate and full representation or duplication of God on the earth (Colossians 2:9; Hebrews 1:1-3; John 1:18; 14:9). This God can be experienced, touched and spoken to (1 John 1:1-3). He reveals to us God Himself, and by His life demonstrates the will of God for our lives.

3. *Piqqudim* or *piqqud*, translated precepts, means to place in trust, to take notice (or care) of a thing, to attend to, appoint, visit, take oversight of or superintend. This word occurs 21 times in the psalm. God's precepts are ever present to care for us and preside over our lives. They are authorized by a righteous and loving Father to attend to our lives and produce a cause and affect related to our choices, so that we are helped to stay on the right path. While our greatest rewards may be realized in the age to come, there are also rewards (and consequences) related to our choices in this life, which encourage us stay on the path of life.

   - "The statutes and precepts (*piqqud*) of the LORD are right, rejoicing the heart" (Psalm 19:8). God's precepts provide the consistent presence, oversight and boundaries that allow His children to feel secure and joyful. For example, what would happen to you if gravity, which is always attending to you as a kind of precept, would arbitrarily fluctuate? You would always be uneasy, not sure of what could befall you.

- This *piqqudim* presence or visit is like an audit that reveals both righteousness and lawlessness.

- *Piqqud* seems to be about cause/affect, consequence/reward, sowing/reaping, blessings/curses: the inviolable laws of life and covenant regulations that guide our relationship with the Lord.

- "All His precepts (*piqqud*) are sure. They stand fast forever and ever and are done in truth and uprightness" (Psalm 111:7-8).

4. *Chukkah* or *choq* is translated statutes. Literally, it is an enactment or an appointment, as if by the royal command of a sovereign ruler. The word occurs twenty-two times in the psalm and its root meaning is to cut into, hack, engrave, or carve. It emphasizes that which is established, unchanging, permanent and definite.

- In Job 26:10, God established the boundary (*choq*) for light and darkness.

- In Job 38:10-11, God fixed the limit (*choq*) for the sea saying, "This far you may come, but no farther, and here your proud waves must stop" (see Proverbs 8:29).

- This word hints at the great promise of the New Covenant—the law of God engraved upon the human heart (see Hebrews 10:16).

- The emphasis is on permanence—that which is unchanging. "I am the LORD, I do not change" (Malachi 3:6).

5. *Mitzvah*, translated commandment, occurs twenty-two times in the psalm and comes from the root *tsavah* which means to command. It is a divine imperative, a decree or an order, as in Noah being ordered to build an ark. Commands are imposed by God's absolute authority and reveal His will for us.

- Psalm 19:8 "The commandment (*mitzvah*) of the LORD is pure giving light to the eyes." Some commandments in scripture apply to all men. Some commandments apply only to certain groups of people such as kings, priests, men, women, children, foreigners and so forth. God's commands are pure because they are for our benefit and fullness, rather than for His own self-serving agenda.

- Then there are those *mitzvah* which are peculiar to each man's calling. Moses was commanded one thing, Abraham another, Noah another and Elijah yet another. These commandments were callings that gave purpose to each life and a unique significance in the kingdom of God such as light to the eyes (Psalm 19:8). God's *mitzvah* determines what we do with our lives and how we live before Him and each other.

- *Mitzvah* can also be a prohibition as in forbidding Adam to eat of the tree of the knowledge of good and evil.

6. *Mishpat* is translated as a judgment that is connected with government, such as a judicial sentence that decrees a decision or verdict. It can be favorable or unfavorable, depending upon whether or not one is in the right when the ruling is given. In *The Scriptures* translation of the Bible, the word is translated as right rulings, which is exactly what it is—the right rulings of a king who decrees a thing that is right. Mishpat occurs twenty-two times in the psalm.

- Kings in Israel were said to judge (*shaphat*, the verb form of *mishpat*) Israel (1 Samuel 8:5-6, 20). "And all Israel heard of the judgment (*mishpat*) which the king (Solomon) had judged (*shaphat*); and they feared the king, for they saw that the wisdom of God was in him to administer justice (*mishpat*)" (1 Kings 3:28).

- When a righteous king decrees a thing and thereby renders a verdict or judgment, things are set in motion to put wrong things right and to make a distinction between the righteous and the wicked (Exodus 11:6-7). The oppressed are released and the oppressors punished. Peace (*shalom*) is the result of righteous government as both the wicked and the righteous are rewarded rightly.

- The Lord, the righteous Judge, is unrelenting in His war against sin. He wants to destroy sin within us as any father would want to destroy a disease that is killing his son whom he loves.

- We are not under the judgment of God, but the sin to which we cling remains under judgment. God's judgments are meant to help us "judge ourselves (so that) we would not be judged (by God). For when we are judged, we are chastened by the Lord, that we may not be condemned with the world" (1 Corinthians 11:31-32).

- Hebrews 4:12 tells us that the word of God is living, powerful and sharp as it pierces, divides and is "a discerner (judge) of the thoughts and intents of the heart."

- Hebrews 5:13-14, "For everyone who partakes only of milk is unskilled in the word of righteousness, for he is a babe. But solid food belongs to those who are of full age, that is, those who by reason of use have their senses exercised to discern (judge) both good and evil."

- *Mishpat* can also refer to the rights belonging to someone (Exodus 23:6).

7. *Dabar,* translated word, occurs twenty-four times. It is similar in meaning to the Greek word *logos.* The root means to discourse or utter one's sentiments in an orderly manner. It is therefore the articulation of God's will to men. It is the spoken word, which, like the oracles of God in 1 Peter 4:10-11, are set down for us in order to give us the knowledge of God and point us to God.

8. *Imrah*, also translated word, is a saying, a thing or a speech. The word occurs nineteen times in Psalm 119 and speaks of something communicated orally—words by which a revelation is imparted. *Imrah* differs little from *dabar,* but seems to be an immediate oracle delivered by God for our instruction at a point in time whereas *dabar* seems to be more about the entirety of God's word. Imrah seems to be in the Hebrew what *rhema* is in the Greek.

9. *Derek*, translated way, means walking or going, hence a journey, path or course of action. *Derek* occurs thirteen times and points to the course of action marked out by God's word.

   - All of Israel saw the acts of God, but God made known His ways (*derek*) to Moses. In other words, Moses understood the "why" behind the "what" of God.

   - Here are two powerful prayers from scripture.
     Moses' prayer: "Show me now your way (*derek*) that I may know You" (Exodus 33:13)
     David's prayer: "Show me Your ways, O LORD; Teach me Your paths" (Psalm 25:4).

The word of God is central to and the very basis of our walk with the Lord. We eat the *logos* (written word of God) through diligent study and meditation. We hear the *rhema* (spoken word of God) through the Holy Spirit and by faith as we walk in relationship with the Lord. Both are necessary to this journey to maturity.

Lionel Cabral explains further: "The process of hearing a *rhema* word and allowing that received *rhema* word to work a transformation within us is experiential. It occurs as we advance on our journey as pilgrims (1 Peter 2:11), trekking through a hazardous, to our natural man, wilderness which extends from the Red Sea to the Jordan River" (see Numbers 33). "It takes time to convert a rebellious soul into an obedient spirit. . . . No one can cross the Red Sea which is the beginning of our faith walk and also cross the Jordan River which is the fullness of our faith walk at the same time. No one, including *Yeshua*, has ever done so."[1]

We are on a journey to become like our Master Himself, but the journey itself is a requirement in that process. Transformation is not instantaneous.

Chapter 3

The Blessed Life: Pursuing Happiness

ALEPH

¹Blessed are the undefiled in the way,
Who walk in the law of the LORD!
²Blessed are those who keep His testimonies,
Who seek Him with the whole heart!
³They also do no iniquity;
They walk in His ways.
⁴You have commanded us
To keep Your precepts diligently.
⁵Oh, that my ways were directed
To keep Your statutes!
⁶Then I would not be ashamed,
When I look into all Your commandments.
⁷I will praise You with uprightness of heart,
When I learn Your righteous judgments.
⁸I will keep Your statutes;
Oh, do not forsake me utterly!

Aleph—Beginning the Journey: Psalm 119:1-8

The original pictograph of this first Hebrew letter *aleph* depicts an ox. An ox speaks of strength, preeminence and authority. The Hebrew word *aluph* (derived from the very name of this letter) means Master or Lord. Great questions face David in this segment: Who will be your master? To whom or what will you submit your life? What will you give your life to?

The first word of our psalm, blessed, introduces the subject, not only of this section, but of the entire psalm: *The Blessed Life*. But what is *The Blessed Life*? Who can experience it?

First, we will study the Hebrew word *esher,* which is translated blessed, and thereby establish a launching pad for our journey.

J. Alec Motyer, in his commentary, *The Prophecy of Isaiah: An Introduction and Commentary,* suggests three shades of meaning for *esher.* The first is divine favor, the second is personal fulfillment, and the third is total rectitude. [1]

Esher occurs only twice in this entire psalm, and both occurrences are here in *aleph* (v. 1-2). This distinguishes this first section from every other. *Esher* occurs forty-five times throughout the Hebrew Scriptures and simply means happy or happiness. It is translated happy by the KJV in many places. Consider the following verses:

1.   "Happy are the people who are in such a state (of obedience and blessing); happy is that people whose God is the LORD" (Psalm 144:15).

2.   "Happy is the man who has his quiver full of them (children)" (Psalm 127:5).

3.   "Happy is the man who fears the LORD, who delights greatly in His command-ments" (Psalm 112:1).

4.   "O taste and see that the LORD is good. Happy is the man who trusts in Him" (Psalm 34:8). See also Deuteronomy 33:29; 1 Kings 10:8; Psalm 128:1-2; 146:5; Proverbs 3:13; 16:20.

Happiness: what a powerful theme for the next 176 verses. But does happiness not seem to be a bit self serving? Many times we detect a subtle suspicion within us and from others that we should repent of our desire to be happy. Yet this is impos-sible. No one has ever successfully accomplished this because happiness is part of the in-built and undeniable image of God in humans. The question is not whether we will or will not pursue happiness—we all pursue it—but rather HOW will we pursue it, and to what or whom we will turn in our quest for it.

Yeshua is not opposed to happiness. The Greek word, *makarios*, used by *Yeshua* as He begins His discourse from the mountain in Matthew 5:1-12, means happy. He employed the word nine times in nine verses, explaining who it is that is happy or blessed. *Makarios*, translated blessed in many Bible versions, is also rightly translated happy in *Young's Literal Translation* as well as in several other modern translations and paraphrases of the Bible.

Happiness and hardship are not mutually exclusive. Many of us have sought and discovered the joy of the Lord despite difficult circumstances. However, endurance through trials, pain, suffering, self-denial, and sacrifice is always framed in scripture in the context of receiving an incomparable reward. James 1:12 provides a classic example of such a promise: "Blessed (*makarios*) is the man who endures temptation; for when he has been approved, he will receive the crown of life which the Lord has promised to those who love Him."

Missionary martyr Jim Elliot's famous quote hints at the same principle: "He is no fool who gives up what he cannot keep in order to gain that which he cannot lose." Inevitably, we pursue many avenues in our pursuit of happiness, only to discover emp-tiness until we turn to the Lord. Hence, the pursuit of happiness should include one's willingness to deny himself and take up his cross for the sake of finding life (Matthew 16:24-25) as well as future reward.

God's highest priority is not to make us happy in some kind of shallow, earthly sense which is dependent upon pleasant circumstances. However, the truth is that happy, fulfilled believers glorify God. Likewise, believers who are "undefiled in the way," (v. 1) are happy and fulfilled people who enjoy God and glorify Him in their lives.

A working definition of *The Blessed Life*, derived from this study of *esher* and the true meaning of happiness, could go something like this: *The Blessed Life* is a life under God's rule (kingdom) that is characterized by fullness and joy (enjoying God). It experiences and showcases, on earth, the favor, goodness and power of an invisible God, thereby drawing others into the same pursuit.

This is the life *Yeshua* lived. He knew great pain and He knew great joy. His life was compelling, drawing many to follow Him. His life is the light of men (John 1:4). Many were drawn to His light and, taking up their crosses, followed Him in their own pursuit of true happiness.

Here in *aleph*, our first eight-verse segment, it is as if the biblical shepherd-king David is hearing the proclamation of, or witnessing a demonstration of *The Blessed Life*. David is drawn by the promise of this blessed life, but, as we will see, it would seem that he has also been confronted with *Yeshua's* words, "Repent, for the kingdom of heaven is at hand" (Matthew 4:17). Now David needs to make a decision as to how he will pursue happiness in life.

We will outline the eight verses of *aleph* as follows:

- Verses 1-2: *The Blessed Life* is announced and demonstrated. David witnesses the proclamation and demonstration of the good news of *The Blessed Life*.
- Verses 3-4: Response is required. Repent for the kingdom of heaven is at hand.
- Verses 5-6: Conviction of sin. David becomes aware of sin, feels shame and wrestles with God's command to repent.
- Verses 7-8: Faith and obedience. Faith that this blessed life is possible causes David to respond in obedience by saying, in essence, "Lord, I will follow you!"

Let's join David on his journey as he is confronted with the good news of *The Blessed Life*. In these passages, we discover that David realizes those who are blessed are those who are without sin. But how can he attain that position? He laments his own failures but resolves that he will follow God, no matter what.

The Blessed Life Announced and Demonstrated

"Blessed *(esher)* are the undefiled in the way, who walk in the law of the LORD. Blessed are those who keep *(natsar)* His testimonies, who seek Him with the whole heart" (v. 1-2).

1.   "Blessed" (*esher*). Blessed means happy. Every human on earth is in some way pursuing happiness. The crucial difference relates to whom or to what we will turn during our quest. This world promises happiness when it actually cannot deliver it, so our quest must turn to the Lord who created us. When we find our life and purpose in Him, we begin to experience true happiness.

    • Consider Psalm 16:11, "You will show me the path of life; In Your presence is fullness of joy; at Your right hand are pleasures forevermore."

    • Our working definition of *The Blessed Life* remains, "A life under God's rule (kingdom) that is characterized by fullness and joy (enjoying God). It experiences and showcases, on earth, the favor, goodness and power of an invisible God, thereby drawing others into the same pursuit."

2.   Who are the happy ones? Those who are undefiled in the way. The Hebrew word *tamiym,* rendered undefiled, means entire, complete, whole or sound. The root word means to be complete, perfect or mature.

    • We know that *Yeshua* was without sin, but t*amiym*, rather than suggesting sinless perfection or even being pure from defilement, says more about a life of integrity and maturity. *Tamiym* points us in two directions:

    To Integrity—A life without duplicity, pretense or hypocrisy suggests unity of our spirit, soul and body. In other words, the heart is undefiled by impure motives which may lie behind our outward actions.

    To maturity (Christ-likeness)—See scriptures like John 6:40; 17:23; 1 Corinthians 2:6; 14:20; Ephesians 4:13; Philippians 3:12, 15; Colossians 4:12; Hebrews 6:1. In Colossians 1:28 Paul writes, "Him we preach, warning every man and teaching every man in all wisdom, that we may present every man perfect in Christ Jesus."

    • Integrity is ultimately about the heart. In everyday language integrity indicates that we are the same all the way through: inside and out, today and tomorrow, in private and in public, with the client or with the supervisor. In all contexts, we are the same person. This person is not afraid to have his way of life, or walk, examined. He is willing to have the Lord test his thoughts and motives.

"Search me O God and know my heart. Try me and know my thoughts. See if there be any wicked way in me" (Psalm 139:23-24).

"Teach me Your way O LORD; I will walk in Your truth; Unite my heart to fear Your Name" (Psalm 86:11).

- To what can we attribute this confidence for examination? It comes because people of integrity walk in His ways, without pretense, and with nothing to hide. Consider the words from 3 John 4, "I have no greater joy than to hear that my children walk in truth."

- Maturity, becoming like our Master, is our journey from carnality to spirituality. Paul writes in 1 Corinthians 3:1, "And I, brethren, could not speak unto you as to spiritual, but as unto carnal, even as babes (immature) in Christ" (KJV). Hence, maturing in Messiah has to do with purifying our lives from the defilement of carnality.

- *Yeshua* is called "faithful and true" (Revelation 19:11). He was known as one whose teaching was true. Who He was and all that He did and said were true; there was no duplicity. His eye was good and His whole body was full of light (Matthew 6:22).

3. "Who walk (*halak*: go, come or walk) in the law (*torah*, or teaching) of the LORD." This person of integrity walks in the teachings of his heavenly Father. The *torah* (as truth) is the measure or standard by which we know how to walk in truth. It is not difficult to understand why those who walk in integrity are blessed (happy)—they have nothing to hide. They are free to be who they are without pretense, with no need to project and sustain a false image, or to be perceived in a certain way.

4. "Blessed (*esher*) are those who keep (*natsar*) His testimonies" (v. 2). The Hebrew word *natsar*, translated here as keep, means to guard, watch, watch over, or keep something that is precious and is susceptible to attack or theft.

- Although keeping His testimonies leads to obedience, "keep" does not actually mean "obey." It means to keep something as if it is very precious but vulnerable to loss.

- Why would the Lord's testimonies need to be guarded as something targeted by an enemy? Must they be guarded from theft? In the parable of the sower and the seed, it was the seed of the word of God which was sown. And it was that seed that was under constant attack (Mark 4:1-20). See Addendum 1 for a more in-depth discussion on this priority of keeping the word.

- Those who live *The Blessed Life* will treasure (keep as precious) the testimonies of the Lord so as to keep (watch, guard, protect) them from theft. Read Proverbs 2:1-5.

5. "Who seek Him with the whole heart." This blessed person who is undefiled in the way and who walks in the law (teaching) of the Lord is a seeker of the Lord. Seek is the Hebrew word *darash*, and it means to tread, to frequent, to follow in search of, to enquire, to seek with care, to resort to or beat a path to.

- He values the word of God as he daily beats a path to it in search of the Lord.

- With the whole heart—this is not a one-day-a-week show of piety. This person seeks the Lord no matter who he is with or where he is. He is true, through and through, with no need to pretend.

Three values, which order the lifestyle of one whose life is blessed by God, are now evident:

- He esteems the Lord's testimonies as precious, guarding them from the enemy.

- He daily "beats a path" to the Lord for intimacy.

- He does these two things with his whole heart (with integrity versus for show or pretense).

Response Required: Repentance

"They also do no iniquity. They walk in His ways. You have commanded us to keep Your precepts (*piqqud*) diligently" (v. 3-4).

1. "They do no iniquity. They walk in His ways."

- No iniquity: Iniquity hints at moral evil or perverseness within a person that leads to violent deeds of injustice, or injustice in general (visible acts of sin).

  o   To do justly, according to Micah 6:8, is to treat others rightly.

  o   In other words, violence toward others flows out of moral evil within.

- The hint is this: The person walking this walk responds to those around him with kindness and self-control. There is no overflow of wickedness pouring from prejudices or wounds within his soul. This is a powerful testimony to any onlooker. James 1:21 says, "Therefore lay aside all filthiness and overflow of wickedness, and receive with meekness the implanted word, which is able to save (*sozo*: heal) your souls."

- Note the role of the word of God in the healing of the soul.

- Again, this is not so much about sinless perfection as it is about being in love with *Yeshua* and being free on the inside from compulsive sin.

- "They." It is as if our psalmist is not yet one of those who "do no iniquity," but is looking with longing toward those who do not sin, or perhaps with conviction concerning his own sinfulness.

- For those trapped in sinful passions such as anger, greed, lust or bitterness, it is inconceivable that a person can be truly and happily free from sinful compulsions.

2. "You have commanded us." Not only is this a compelling invitation to become blessed by God, it is a command to repent (turn from our ways to God and His ways). Consider Acts 17:30, "Truly, these times of ignorance God overlooked, but now commands all men everywhere to repent" (turn from idols to the living God). God requires repentance.

3. "Diligently" (*m\eod*): To do something exceedingly, with force or to do it with vehemence and passion.

    - The Hebrew structure allows for this diligence or passion to be either God's passion in the commanding, or our passion in the responding. The command of God certainly comes to us with His own passion and urgency. Our heavenly Father is not willing that any perish. He greatly desires all to repent and to be reconciled to Himself (1 Timothy 2:5-6; 2 Peter 3:9; 2 Corinthians 5:19).

    - However, our response to His commands is also to be with diligence and passion. Verse four shows that our response is required. We are to commit to keeping His precepts, exceedingly and with passion. This is the wholehearted response to God that shows He is worthy! How will our psalmist respond?

There is something compelling about a righteous person who walks uprightly and with integrity. But *The Blessed Life* concerns more than showcasing excellence of character and integrity; it also showcases the favor and power of God on the earth. Acts 10:38 talks about "how God anointed Jesus of Nazareth with the Holy Spirit and with power, who went about doing good and healing all who were oppressed by the devil, for God was with Him." *The Blessed Life* is a supernatural life. The Father was with the Son in a manifest way, and He powerfully backed up the prayers of His Son on earth. He wants to do the same for all of His sons and daughters.

David has heard the proclamation of the good news of *The Blessed Life*, and understands what is required to walk it out. In verse five, it is as if David himself begins to speak. Let's join him as he wrestles with God's command and the conviction of his own lack. Will he accept the invitation to repent in order to become like this one whose life is blessed?

Conviction of Sin

"Oh, that my ways were directed (firmly established) to keep Your statutes! Then I would not be ashamed (*buwsh:* to put to shame, be ashamed, be disconcerted, be disappointed) when I look into all Your commandments" (v. 5-6).

1. "Oh, that my ways were directed." Can you sense the power of what is happening in David's heart? Can you perceive the longing, the conviction or the shame of falling short of the righteous standard as the light shines upon his life?

   - What a cry from the heart! The desire to be like the Master has been awakened!

   - Directed: A Hebrew word meaning firmly established. The hint is that this walk may not be easy. Sinful passions lurk within, while temptations assail us from without, and it is the overcomers who get the reward (Revelation 2:7, 11, 17, 26; 3:5, 12, 21). *The Blessed Life* will ultimately include the aspect of warfare against sin.

2. "Then I would not be ashamed" (*buwsh*). The Hebrew word for shame, transliterated *buwsh*, primarily has to do with falling into disgrace. It includes the ideas of shame, pain, humiliation and terror. All of this is connected to the disapproval of the One whose commandments we have not kept. Several things can serve to highlight our own lack:

   - Someone more righteous than ourselves, who by the excellence of his life in contrast to ours, serves to call attention to our lack. Our psalmist is aware of his own lack and is recognizing the need for repentance.

3. "When I look into all Your commandments." Reading the word of God also serves to reveal our lack and shame. See scriptures like James 1:25-26, Galatians 3:24 and Psalm 19:11-12. This, in fact, is our psalmist's confession here in verse six.

   - Also, the Holy Spirit convicts us "of sin and of righteousness" (John 16:8).

Faith and Obedience

"I will praise You with uprightness of heart, when I learn Your righteous judgments. I will keep Your statutes; Oh, do not forsake me utterly!" (v. 7-8).

In these two verses, faith comes to David's heart. These verses confirm that "faith comes by hearing and hearing by the word of God" (Romans 10:17).

1. "I will praise (*yadah*) You." *Yadah* literally means to use or hold out the hand. It occurs only here and verse 62 of our psalm. By extension, *yadah* means to give thanks, laud, praise, revere or worship (especially with extended hands). The emphasis is a thankful heart of humility that bows in devotion and adoration to God, thus publically deflecting praise to God for the manifest successes of my (blessed) life.

2. "With uprightness of heart." There is a massive "uprightness of heart" theme throughout Scripture which suggests that, though "we all stumble in many ways"

(James 3:2), we do not necessarily have an evil heart. Ponder scriptures such as 1 Kings 3:6; 1 Chronicles 29:17; Job 33:3; Psalm 7:10; 11:2; 32:11; 36:10; 64:10; 94:15; 97:11; 125:4.

3.   "When I learn Your righteous judgments (*mishpat*: right rulings)." Faith has come and convinces David that he can, in fact, learn God's ways. This is a strategic use of *mishpat* (right rulings) as the word of God. Our psalmist is about to allow the word of God to measure his life and separate out, by judicial verdict, everything that is offensive to the Lord, our righteous judge. Read the introduction again for a fuller understanding of *mishpat.*

4.   "I will keep Your statutes." What a strong declaration of faith and obedience! Basically, David says, "Okay, I'll do it. I will 'follow the Lamb everywhere He goes'" (Revelation 14:4). Faith and obedience always go together in the word of God. This is clearly demonstrated in Romans 1:5; 16:26; Titus 3:8; James 2:14-25.

5.   "Oh, do not forsake me utterly!" David suddenly sobers up as he recognizes, to some extent at least, the magnitude of the journey that he has just committed to undertake. The truth is that David has just said "yes" to something that is humanly impossible. He has said "yes" to living and being like *Yeshua*, the Son of God. Remember, "He who says he abides in Him ought himself also to walk just as He walked" (1 John 2:6). David can never hope to walk this walk unless God is with him.

    •   As you join David in this journey, remember that God's number one commitment to every servant of His—to Abraham, Isaac, Jacob, Moses, Joshua, *Yeshua*, and everyone was, "I will be with you."

    •   God sends us as sheep among wolves! He sends Moses to Pharaoh, Joshua against giants, Abram to a land not known, Elijah to confront King Ahab, Paul and Barnabas to pagan cities, et cetera, and all He promises is "I will be with you."

    •   We learn in Acts 10:38 the secret of *Yeshua's* compelling example of *The Blessed Life* – God was with Him. "How God anointed *Yeshua* of Nazareth with the Holy Spirit and with power, who went about doing good and healing all who were oppressed by the devil, for God was with Him."

    •   We must hear God say these words to us again if we are to face the days ahead. See Matthew 28:20; Hebrews 13:5; Psalm 121:1-8; Joshua 1:9.

Concluding Thoughts

The truth is that God is asking something of us that is humanly impossible, but if the Uncreated God who made the heavens and the earth is with us, that changes everything. The next section will show us more about how this life actually is possible.

Questions to Ponder

1. Can you recall a time when observing the excellence of someone else's life awakened within your heart a longing to pursue that same excellence?

2. How would you describe the difference between sinless perfection and integrity?

3. Have you made the commitment of verse eight: "I will keep your statutes?" In other words, have you said "yes" to the ways of the Lord?

4. Describe an area of your life where you identify with the psalmist in knowing the right thing to do and actually longing it do it, yet not doing it because your weaknesses seem too overwhelming. Write down your thoughts so that in the succeeding chapters you can learn how to move from frantically asking God not to forsake you to attaining His strength to do the right thing.

Chapter 4

This One Thing: Build a House

BET

⁹How can a young man cleanse his way?
By taking heed according to Your word.
¹⁰With my whole heart I have sought You;
Oh, let me not wander from Your commandments!
¹¹Your word I have hidden in my heart,
That I might not sin against You.
¹²Blessed are You, O LORD!
Teach me Your statutes.
¹³With my lips I have declared
All the judgments of Your mouth.
¹⁴I have rejoiced in the way of Your testimonies,
As much as in all riches.
¹⁵I will meditate on Your precepts,
And contemplate Your ways.
¹⁶I will delight myself in Your statutes;
I will not forget Your word.

Bet—Psalm 119:9-16

With the final words of our opening section, "Oh, do not forsake me utterly," David says "yes" to the *torah* (teachings) as his way into *The Blessed Life*. He responds to the Lord's command to keep His precepts diligently (v. 4). However, it is as if he instinctively knows that he is embarking on "mission impossible." The truth is that no one can walk this walk unless God is with him.

Having made the commitment to submit to the Father's leadership, our psalmist now asks the question, "How can a young man cleanse his way"? In other words, having accepted the invitation to be among those who are undefiled in the way, and therefore blessed, David wonders where to begin and how this new way of living and walking in God's kingdom actually works.

The answer that follows in *bet* is surprisingly simple. If God's commitment to us is that He will be with us (as discussed in *aleph*), then our commitment to God needs to be that of hosting God's presence in our house or temple. In fact, the ancient pictograph for the Hebrew letter, *bet*, depicts a tent or house. It speaks of entering someone's house for a face-to-face encounter.

In 1 Corinthians 6:18-20, we learn that believers are the temple (house) of God. The miracle and wonder of the New Covenant is that our bodies have become the temple of the Holy Spirit. The "Genesis 1 God" lives inside of the believer. He desires and is looking for a resting place on the earth (Isaiah 66:1; Psalm 132:13-14). He moves into our house when we respond, in obedience and faith, to the message of the gospel. This premier privilege of communion with God is restored to us in the cross of Messiah. It is accessed through our faith, not our perfection or maturity (see James 4:8; Hebrews 10:19-22; Romans 5:1-2).

In 1 Corinthians 3:16-17, the apostle Paul adds these words: "If anyone defiles the temple of God, God will destroy him. For the temple of God is holy, which temple you are." Paul includes the instruction to flee sexual immorality in 1 Corinthians 6:18-20, because it is a sin against the body, which is His temple, where God dwells and meets with us. The opening question of our section implies the necessity of being pure: "How can a young man cleanse his way?"

If David is to walk this walk of *The Blessed Life*, he will first and foremost need to prepare his life as a house in which both he and God can live together and have relationship.

The Number One priority of David's life, rather than focusing on the rules for holy living detailed in the law of a holy God, is to focus upon God Himself. The truth is that no one can walk this walk except God Himself. Hence, to host God's presence and walk with Him is the key to *The Blessed Life*. He will do in and through me what I cannot do on my own. So, how can a young man cleanse his way? By building his life into a house or dwelling place for God.

The foremost and highest priority in one's life will most shape a person's lifestyle. David said in Psalm 27:4, "One thing I desired of the LORD, that will I seek: That I may dwell in the house of the LORD." This "one thing" determines our lifestyle. It affects our coming and going. It will determine what we say "no" and "yes" to. It controls our checkbooks. This priority of hosting God's presence allowed our biblical heroes to walk in friendship with God (not sinless perfection), and consequently, God did in and through them what they could not possibly do on their own.

For additional meditation on God's passion to dwell among men, on the place of His dwelling which is Mount Zion, and on man's premier privilege of hosting God's presence, see Addendum 2.

Let's join David and look at some of the values of a life which prioritizes the presence of the Lord—a life which gives Him preeminence. These verses display seven "planks" or "building blocks" to the temple of God. Although we cannot humanly walk this walk, and thus merit *The Blessed Life*, we can do these seven things in order to prepare a sanctuary within our own soul for the Lord. He can then do in us what we cannot do in our own strength. The verse by verse outline is:

- Mission impossible: The question—How can a young man cleanse his ways? (v. 9)

- Mission possible: Build the house of God in your life using the seven planks described in verses 10-16:

    1. Seek the face of the Lord with your whole heart (v. 10).

    2. Hide God's word in your heart by memorizing scriptures (v. 11).

    3. Worship, and allow the Lord to enjoy your presence (v. 12).

    4. Declare aloud God's redemptive acts of judgment and right rulings (v. 13).

    5. Ascribe to the word of God its true value and worth (v. 14).

    6. Meditate on God's word and contemplate His ways (v. 15).

    7. Exercise your will; tell your soul what to delight in (v. 16).

Mission Impossible

"How can a young man cleanse (*zakah*: moral purity) his way? By taking heed according to Your word" (v. 9).

1. Ponder the real question: How can a young man at the pinnacle of human passion, zeal, ambition, vision, and strength—one who may be idealistic and not yet tempered by fire—one who has sinful passions within and who lives in a sinful world that is filled with seductions and offenses on every side—how can this man cleanse his way from all that is carnal and of the flesh? How can he be free from the bitterness of offense and from the mixtures inherent in the lack of Christ-likeness? How will this man remain undefiled in the way?

2. The general answer is surprisingly simple. "By taking heed (*shamar*) according to Your word" (*dabar*). The Hebrew action word here is *shamar*, a synonym of *natsar* (studied in verse two) and is the primary word in the Hebrew Scriptures for keep as in keeping the word. Broadly speaking, the answer is simply this: by guarding the word of God and keeping it as great treasure!

    See Addendum 1 for more thoughts about keeping the word.

3. An entity called sin operates within every believer. Romans 7:17-18 says, "But now, it is no longer I who do it, but sin that dwells in me. For I know that in me (that is, in my flesh nature) nothing good dwells; for to will is present with me, but how to perform what is good I do not find." That sin within attaches to the seductions

and stimuli of a sinful world without, so that Paul cries out in verse 24, "Who will deliver me from this body of death?"

4. God requires that we walk undefiled in the way, in the law of the Lord. His standard is His Son *Yeshua* of Nazareth!

    •   1 John 2:1, "My little children, these things I write to you, so that you may not sin."

    •   1 John 2:6, "He who says he abides in Him ought himself also to walk just as He walked."

    •   *Yeshua* said in Matthew 5:48, "Therefore you shall be perfect (complete, of full age), just as your Father in heaven is perfect."

5. Here is the deal: God is requiring the impossible from you (v. 8). Furthermore, He allows no excuse for not fulfilling it. How can He do this? Because, if we build a house to host Him, He will do in us what we cannot do. "I will be with you!" Hence the cry of David in verse eight, "Oh, do not forsake me utterly." This goal is not unreasonable after all.

6. He presents "mission impossible," requiring us to be undefiled in the way, but then He points us in another direction—that of building a house. Rather than focusing with all of our might on being undefiled or on walking in sinless perfection, we are to build God a house. It is as if God is saying, "Don't focus on the standard of the law and on avoiding sin. Focus instead on My presence and on building a house for Me. I will do in and through you what you cannot do on your own."

Mission Possible: Seven planks to the temple of God in one's life

Plank 1: Set your heart to seek the LORD with your whole heart.

"With my whole heart I have sought You: Oh, let me not wander from your commandments" (v. 10).

1. "With my whole heart" (*leb*). The words "whole heart" appear six times in our psalm, and are the key to a life of integrity: being "undefiled in the way." Let's ponder just a few truths concerning the heart of man.

    •   The heart (*leb* or *lebab* in the Hebrew Scriptures) is the center of the human being as a free moral agent. Though they do connect, *lebab* is not so much the seat of emotions and feelings, as we might understand it to be in English. *Lebab* is more the seat of a person's thoughts, intellect, will, and intentions or motives. You think in your heart, and your heart shapes your character, choices, and decisions.

- The pure in heart shall see God (Matthew 5:8; Psalm 24:3-4).

- We are commanded to love God with all of our heart (Deuteronomy 6:5; 11:13; Matthew 22:37).

- God is greater than the deceitful heart of man and is committed to giving us a new one: a good, noble and pure heart that thinks God's thoughts, loves what God loves and hates what He hates—a heart that chooses rightly. (See 1 John 3:20; Jeremiah 31:33-34; Ezekiel 11:18-20; 36:26; Deuteronomy 30:6; Hebrews 8:10; 10:16).

- For a more extensive meditation on the human heart see Addendum 3.

2. "I have sought (*darash:* beat a path to) You." This echoes verse two. David has sought an intimate encounter with God. Many are the promises to those who sincerely seek God.

    - Jeremiah 29:13-14, "And you will seek Me and find Me, when you search for Me with all your heart. I will be found by you, says the LORD." See also Deuteronomy 4:29.

    - The perfect tense of the verb seek indicates that David has in the past (v. 2), is now, and will continue to seek this encounter of intimacy with the Lord. He has set his heart on this one thing—the presence of God—as a lifelong pursuit. We need a deep devotional commitment to and passion for the presence and power of the Holy Spirit in our lives, or we will descend from a plane of Holy Spirit life to a human plane of natural living. Galatians 5:16 says, "Walk in the Spirit, and you shall not fulfill the lust of the flesh." (Read again Psalm 27:4; 42:1; 63:1-2; 84:2).

    - God's house is vitally a house of prayer (Isaiah 56:7). *Yeshua* said, "My house shall be called a house of prayer" (Matthew 21:13). God's house on earth is the place where man seeks encounter and communion with God by way of a life of prayer.

3. "Oh, let me not wander from Your commandments." What a cry! Our psalmist is aware of a fatal tendency within his heart—that of distraction and a propensity to wander from wholeheartedly following the Lord.

    - The irony is that while God does not need us but still wants us, we desperately need God. But we do not really want Him much of the time. Proverbs 4:23 admonishes us well: Keep your heart with all diligence, for out of it spring the issues of life.

    - Let's stop deceiving ourselves; we have as much of God as we want. We are as close to Him as we want to be. Hebrews 4:16 invites us to "come boldly to the throne of grace." Hebrews 10:19 says, "Therefore, brethren, having boldness to enter the Holiest by the blood of *Yeshua*." The devil is not our problem, people are not our problem, circumstances are not our problem—our hearts are our problem.

- I am not advocating some kind of dead-end introspection in search of every selfish or mixed motive and every wrong attitude. Hebrews 4:12 tells us that the word of God will do that for us. "For the word of God is living and powerful, and sharper than any two-edged sword, piercing even to the division of soul and spirit, and of joints and marrow, and is a discerner of the thoughts and intents of the heart." Furthermore, the Spirit of truth has come; He will guide you into all truth (John 16:13). We are to be focused upon hosting the Lord's presence and looking for righteousness, not sin. "God is greater than our heart" (1 John 3:20).

- Even so, a believer who has been born of the Spirit needs to be humbly aware of the sin that dwells within his members. A believer needs to be ready to confess sin when it is detected. See Addendum 3 for more discussion on the heart of man.

This first plank is foundational to the house we are building for God's presence. Pray for hunger that seeks God. Pray for the Holy Spirit to help and teach you. You do not want the pretense of religion—you want Him! The words, "Let me not wander" acknowledge our propensity to stray from passionate pursuit of God and His ways. The Holy Spirit is drawing us. God's grace is abounding. We need to make a decision in light of God's grace and order our lives around one thing: seeking His face with our whole heart. As with the tabernacle in the wilderness, God's house must be built from the heart.

Exodus 25:2, 8 says, "Tell the Israelites to take for Me an offering; from all whose hearts prompt them to give you shall receive the offering for Me. . . . And let them build Me a sanctuary, that I may dwell among them." See Exodus 35:21 for the people's overflowing response.

Here are some scriptures to pray over your heart: Jeremiah 31:33-34; John 6:45; 14:26; 1 Thessalonians 4:9; Psalm 86:11; Ezekiel 11:18-20; Hebrews 10:16; Psalm 25:3-9.

God will do His part, but we must do ours. Decide, as David did, to make *Yeshua's* presence your Number One priority.

Plank 2: Memorizing Scripture.

"Your word I have hidden in my heart, that I might not sin against You" (v. 11).

1.   "Your word I have hidden in my heart." Memorizing scripture may sound trite or even religious. Memorizing scripture may benefit us very little if we limit it to an

exercise of our minds, but for those who truly desire to grow, we have a promise from God: "This is the covenant that I will make with them. I will put My laws into their hearts, and in their minds. I will write them on their hearts" (Hebrews 10:16). God certainly wants the words of scripture to dwell in our minds and hearts. He energizes these words by the power of His Spirit in order to change our hearts. Consider the following:

- Deuteronomy 6:6, "And these words which I command you today shall be in your heart."

- Deuteronomy 11:18, "You shall lay up these words of mine in your heart and in your soul."

- Deuteronomy 32:46-47, "Set your hearts on all the words which I testify among you today . . . all the words of this law . . . because it is your life, and by this word you shall prolong your days in the land which you cross over the Jordan to possess."

- John 6:63, "The words that I (*Yeshua*) speak to you are spirit, and they are life."

If the words of scripture are in us, it makes sense to keep (*shamar*) them guarded as precious treasure. Hidden (*tsaphan*) means to lay up as treasure, hide or store up.

How precious is the word of God? Without it nothing would exist. "By faith we understand that the worlds were framed by the word of God" (Hebrews 11:3).

Messiah will be formed within every believer by that same word.

2.   "That I might not sin against You." We must recall *Yeshua's* victory over the devil in the wilderness (Matthew 4:4, 7, 10). When His identity as the Son of God was challenged, *Yeshua's* answer was, "It is written. . . ." He employed the scriptures that were in His mind and heart to overcome the temptation.

- How about Proverbs 7:1-5? "My son, keep my words, and treasure my commands within you . . . that they may keep you from the immoral woman." I cannot overcome lust, but the word in me can. What I can do is hide God's word in my heart, which keeps me from sinning.

- Hebrews 4:12, "For the word of God is living and powerful, and sharper than any two-edged sword, piercing even to the division of soul and spirit, and of joints and marrow, and is a discerner of the thoughts and intents of the heart."

- I am not able to keep from sinning through mere human effort, but the word that lives within me cannot sin. I cannot walk this walk, but the word in me can.

- o   Negatively, the focus is to *not* sin, but the goal instead should be a positive focus: to choose God instead of sin. To sin is to fall short of glorifying God. Romans 3:23 says, "For all have sinned and fall short of the glory of God." James 1:12-16 clearly shows us that a primary way to show our love for God is to resist sin. James begins verse 12 with these words, "Blessed is the man who endures temptation; for when he has been approved, he will receive the crown (*stephanos*: an overcomer's wreath) of life which the Lord has promised to those who love Him."

- o   The irony is that a focus on not sinning is still a focus on sin.

- o   Positively, the ultimate goal of life is to focus on the word of God and glorify God by choosing and enjoying Him forever.

Plank 3: Worship—Enjoy the Lord and allow Him to enjoy you.
"Blessed are You, O LORD. Teach me Your statutes" (v. 12).

1.   "Blessed are You, O LORD!" What is this eruption of worship about? What just happened? This may seem like a stretch, but I believe that David has just experienced an encounter with the Lord that produced a big "I love You" in his heart. God really does want to meet with us and speak to us (Exodus 25:8, 22). David has barely begun to build his sanctuary when the Lord suddenly shows up.

- •   Blessed (*barak*): This is a different Hebrew word from the opening word, *esher*. It occurs 331 times in the Hebrew Scriptures but only once in this psalm. *Barak* means to kneel, to bless in adoration. It is the primary Hebrew word for:

  - o   Men blessing the Lord. "Bless the LORD O my soul and all that is within me bless His holy name" (Psalm 103:1). "I will bless the LORD at all times. His praise shall continually be in my mouth" (Psalm 34:1).

  - o   The Lord blessing men. "The LORD bless you and keep you" (Numbers 6:24; Psalm 67:6-7). In this scripture, it seems as if the Lord just blessed (*barak*) David, and now David is returning the blessing.

- •   Adoration flows both ways. What if God adores you? What if He loves your presence as much as you love His? Many scriptures reveal the Lord's desire for and enjoyment of humans. Here are a few:

  - o   Psalm 45:11, "The King greatly desires your beauty." See also Isaiah 62:5.

  - o   Psalm 149:4 "For the LORD takes pleasure in His people." See also Zephaniah 3:17.

- o   In Hebrews 12:1-3, you were "the joy that was set before Him" at the cross.

- o   In Exodus 31:17, God is refreshed when His people keep Sabbath.

2.   "Teach me Your statutes." Can you hear a cry of "More, Lord" in this prayer? David's love for God's word is legendary. He often asks to be shown the ways of God (Psalm 25:4; 27:11). A great part of the promise of the New Covenant is knowing God.

- •   "No more shall every man teach his neighbor, and every man his brother, saying, 'Know the LORD,' for they all shall know Me" (Jeremiah 31:34).

- •   "It is written in the prophets, 'And they shall all be taught by God'" (John 6:45).

- •   Song of Songs 2:4 is a premier example of mutual enjoyment between God and man. "He brought me to the banqueting house and his banner over me was love. Sustain me with cakes of raisins, refresh me with apples, for I am lovesick." If this is all true, why not dial down from a mindset in which we perform for God, then choose to sit quietly and invite Him to enjoy you? What kind of friendship or marriage is it, really, if one partner is always working, serving, or doing something for the other? Maybe the other partner is patiently waiting for a time to just be together.

If this interpretation of verse twelve seems like too much of a stretch, one thing is for sure, this plank is about worship. Look up the scriptures where men are blessing the Lord in worship. Begin to worship Him also. An atmosphere of worship in your house certainly invites His manifest presence (see Psalm 22:3).

Plank 4: Declare out loud the redemptive acts of the Lord recorded in scripture.

"With my lips I have declared (*caphar*) all the judgments of your mouth" (v. 13).

1.   "Declared (*caphar*)." This Hebrew word means to recount, scribe, enumerate, relate, rehearse, tell or show. Many scriptures speak of declaring (*caphar*) His mighty acts. See scriptures such as Psalm 9:1; 26:7; 40:5; 44:1; 66:16; 73:28; 75:1; 78:4; 96:3; 107:22; 118:17; 145:6.

- •   Psalm 9:1, "I will praise You, O LORD, with my whole heart; I will tell of all Your marvelous works."

- •   Psalm 26:7, "That I may proclaim with the voice of thanksgiving, and tell of all Your wondrous works."

- Psalm 44:1, "We have heard with our ears, O God, Our fathers have told us, the deeds You did in their days, in days of old. . . ."

- Psalm 66:16, "Come, hear, all you who fear God, I will declare what He has done for my soul."

- Psalm 73:28, "But it is good for me to draw near to God; I have put my trust in the LORD God, that I may declare all Your works."

- Psalm 75:1, "We give thanks to You, O God, we give thanks! For Your wondrous works declare that Your name is near."

- Psalm 96:3, "Declare His glory among the nations, His wonders among all peoples."

- Psalm 107:22, "Let them sacrifice the sacrifices of thanksgiving, and declare His works with rejoicing."

- Psalm 145:6, "Men shall speak of the might of Your awesome acts, and I will declare Your greatness."

2. "All the judgments (right rulings) of your mouth." Here we are to declare the judgments (*mishpat*: right rulings) of God's mouth.

   - The Hebrew word for mighty acts is *pala'*, which means to be marvelous, wonderful, surpassing, extraordinary, and separate by distinguishing action. These *pala'* include ALL of God's works: from creation in Genesis 1, the administration of His government through history, redemption, and all the supernatural display of His power and wisdom through signs and wonders in the earth.

   - Out of all His *pala'*, *mishpat* focuses on those acts which were redemptive in nature such as the dramatic deliverance of Israel from Egypt. When a king issues a right ruling, things are set in motion to set wrong things right. For more than four hundred years, Israel was in the iron furnace of Egypt (Deuteronomy 4:20). Then, the King of kings issued a ruling (judgment) to bring them out, and everything changed. Consider Exodus 11:6-7: "Then there shall be a great cry throughout all the land of Egypt, such as was not like it before, nor shall be like it again. But against none of the children of Israel shall (even) a dog move its tongue, against man or beast, that you may know that the LORD does make a difference between the Egyptians and Israel."

   - When we recount the great deliverances of God throughout the scriptures, faith comes for our own deliverance from difficulty. God is the same yesterday, today and forever.

Throughout the Psalms, David often recounts the plagues of Egypt, the parting of the Red Sea and other miraculous events. Inevitably he would end up worshipping and believing God for his own deliverance. Try it. Recount with your lips the judgments of God in history which turned the tables on the wicked and delivered the righteous from oppression.

Plank 5: Ascribe proper value and worth to the word of God.

"I have rejoiced (exulted) in the way of your testimonies, as much as in all riches" (v. 14).

1. "I have rejoiced." Our psalmist is exulting (rejoicing with glee) in "the way of your testimonies" as one who has discovered buried treasure and is suddenly wealthy. Recall from the introduction that the word testimonies (*eduth*) hints at a fresh revelation or communication from God to us—something experiential. Nothing is as exhilarating or life-changing as an encounter with the Lord!

2. "All riches." Ponder this familiar quote by *Yeshua*: "Where your treasure is, there will your heart be also" (Matthew 6:21). Our heart follows our treasure. Obviously, God is not against His people being wealthy, but money can be a powerful seduction that leads our hearts astray. Many are the warnings in scripture concerning the love of money (1 Timothy 6:10-11; Matthew 6:24; 16:26).

   - Read Proverbs 2:1-5 again. Psalm 19:10, "More to be desired are they (the words of God) than gold, yea, than much fine gold."

   - It is quite possible that this is the point where the psalmist began to obey the Lord in the tithe (first-fruits) and in offerings (generosity). Learning to trust God in the area of finances is certainly one of the first lessons in this journey.

Plank 6: Meditation on God's word and God's ways.

"I will meditate on Your precepts, and contemplate Your ways" (v. 15).

Note the following Hebrew definitions:

1. "Meditate" (*siyach*): to put forth (thoughts), meditate, muse, commune, speak, sing, converse (with oneself aloud), mutter.

2. "Contemplate" (*nabat*): to look intently at, regard (with pleasure), look upon, pay attention to.

3. "Ways" (*orach*): This Hebrew word hints at the ways of God manifest throughout history in His administration and leadership among men and nations.

A great source of wonderment lies in this truth: In all of God's dealings with humanity, He always brings forth His purposes at precisely the right time without violating the free-will of a single person.

Biblical meditation is a vast subject that we cannot examine fully here, but let's make a few observations:

- First, it is not just about pondering something in your mind or heart. It is an oral, audible interaction with scripture that includes reading it aloud regularly, or "day and night," to use the language of Joshua 1:8 and Psalm 1:2, two primary texts on biblical meditation.

- The meditation that scripture commends seems to focus specifically on: 1) the character of God (Psalm 63:6; 145:5a); 2) the works of God (Psalm 77:12; 143:5; 145:5); 3) the word of God (Joshua 1:8; Psalm 1:2; 119:15).

- Destiny Image writer Don Nori writes this regarding biblical meditation: "Contrary to the passivity-inducing, mind-emptying technique of eastern religions, biblical meditation actively focuses the mind and heart on the God of Scripture in a way that fully engages the faculties of memory and speech."[1]

- Simply reading scripture aloud to yourself is a powerful practice, because "faith comes by hearing, and hearing by the word of God" (Romans 10:17).

Scripture memorization (v. 11) provides a well to draw from when contemplating the ways of God. Add to that the declaration of His redemptive acts (v. 13) and mix it with the manifestation of His ways (sovereign leadership) in history as He righteously brings forth His purposes without violating the free will of man. Now gaze intently (*nabat*) and with pleasure at God in wonderment and begin to worship (Joshua 1:8; Psalm 1:2).

Plank 7: When your mind wanders, bring it back.

"I will delight myself in Your statutes; I will not forget Your word" (v. 16).

1. "I will" means to take charge over your desires and tell your soul what to delight in. This is about the power of the human will to choose. We see David taking charge of his soul in many scriptures (Psalm 42:5, 11; 43:5; 103:1; 104:1). Many scriptures speak of taking our thoughts captive and teach us what to think upon. We typically act out of our emotions which in turn flow from our thoughts, that is, we follow this sequence: think, feel, act. Changing our thoughts is our responsibility. It is God's commitment to change our hearts.

2. "Delight" (*sha'a*). This Hebrew word suggests the idea of constant fascination or obsession with something. Philippians 4:8 exhorts: "Whatever things are true,

whatever things are noble, whatever things are just, whatever things are pure, whatever things are lovely, whatever things are of good report, if there is any virtue and if there is anything praiseworthy—meditate on these things."

- Paul speaks of "bringing every thought into captivity to the obedience of Christ" (2 Corinthians 10:5).

3.   "I will not forget (ignore or wither) Your word." In other words, "I will not wither in my commitment, but will remain focused." David said it this way in Psalm 16:8: "I have set the LORD always before me; because He is at my right hand I shall not be moved."

- Remaining focused on God's word is not that difficult if you are in love with the Lord. What or who you love is always on your mind.

Concluding Thoughts

In Colossians 1:26-27, the Apostle Paul referenced a mystery of God that was being revealed among the Gentiles in his day. That mystery was, "Christ in you, the hope of glory." The only hope we have of living *The Blessed Life*, and thus showcasing the glory of God in our lives, is to have Messiah living His life in and through us.

According to Psalm 27:4, David had one consuming desire—to be in the presence of the Lord! "One thing I have desired of the LORD, that will I seek: That I may dwell in the house of the LORD all the days of my life, to behold the beauty of the LORD." Let's join David in allowing this "one thing" to determine our lifestyle. As we seek to host His presence, He will do in and through us what we cannot do ourselves.

Questions to Ponder

1.   Name the highest priority in your life. How does your priority shape your lifestyle?

2.   How healthy is your desire for the presence of the Lord? Here again is that list of scriptures to look up and pray over your heart: 1 John 3:20; Jeremiah 31:33-34; Ezekiel 11:18-20; 36:26; Deuteronomy 30:6; Hebrews 8:10; 10:16.

3.   Have you known what it is to host the presence of God in the temple of your body?

4.   What areas of your life are changed because you committed yourself to memorizing the word of God and meditating upon that word? How have you experienced the cleansing power of God's word?

5.   On what occasion in your life has Messiah *in* you done something *through* you that was beyond your own power to do?

Chapter 5

Collision of Kingdoms—Weaned

GIMEL

¹⁷Deal bountifully with Your servant,
That I may live and keep Your word.
¹⁸Open my eyes, that I may see
Wondrous things from Your law.
¹⁹I am a stranger in the earth;
Do not hide Your commandments from me.
²⁰My soul breaks with longing
For Your judgments at all times.
²¹You rebuke the proud—the cursed,
Who stray from Your commandments.
²²Remove from me reproach and contempt,
For I have kept Your testimonies.
²³Princes also sit and speak against me,
But Your servant meditates on Your statutes.
²⁴Your testimonies also are my delight
And my counselors.

Gimel—Psalm 119:17-24

The Hebrew letter *gimel* depicts a camel. It has the sense of lifting up or reward. It can be a lifting up in pride, but *gimel* mostly points to being "lifted up in revelation" or being "exalted" (in a good sense).

One mounts a camel as it is lying on the ground. The camel then stands up on its long legs, lifting you up, as it were, into another realm. Ephesians 2:4-6 tells us that "He (God the Father) made us alive together with Christ and raised us up together, and made us sit together in the heavenlies in Christ Jesus." As believers in *Yeshua*, we are lifted into the heavenly realm and the supernatural things of the Spirit. *Yeshua* is our door to the heavens.

It is also true that *Yeshua* is dwelling in the believer—we are His door to the earth. This constitutes the meeting of two realms, heaven and earth, which have opposing values and agendas. The earth itself is not evil, because God said that it was good. But the earth is the place where an enemy has set up his kingdom. 1 John 5:19 says that "the whole world lies under the sway of the wicked one." The conflict between these two realms is about which of the two governments will rule the earth.

So then, we are in Him, seated in the heavenlies. He is in us on the earth, for the purpose of conquest as well as for the extension of His kingdom on earth. In Genesis 28:12, 17, we see these two realms connected by a ladder: "Behold, a ladder set up on the earth, and its top reached to heaven; and there the angels of God were ascending and descending on it." How awesome is this place! This is none other than the house of God, and this is the gate of heaven. The ladder depicts *Yeshua*, the Son of Man (John 1:51), opening the gate of heaven to advance heaven's interests on earth. This is our calling too, which means we are in a great battle.

Our psalmist has had a running start and is hungry for more of God. He has encountered the presence of the Lord (in the heavenly realm) and he wants more. He is delighting in his new relationship with and connection to the Creator. He has tasted and has seen that the Lord is good (Psalm 34:8). He has been lifted into the realm of the Spirit (the heavenlies) and has experienced the presence of the Lord and aspects of the supernatural realm. Hebrews 6:4-5 speaks of those "who were once enlightened, and have tasted the heavenly gift, and have become partakers of the Holy Spirit, and have tasted the good word of God and the powers of the age to come."

For David, it is as if his delight in the Lord spills over into his encounters with others and he can't help but speak about the things he has seen and heard (see Acts 4:20). His life opens the gate of heaven, and brings heaven into contact with earth. As with the apostles of *Yeshua* in Acts 4, David's excitement and testimony stirs up a hornet's nest of criticism, false accusation and persecution. He collides violently with that lower realm, the world and its value system—"the proud—the cursed who stray" (v. 21). David finds himself in the center of the war between two kingdoms. Is he ready for it?

This eight-verse section is outlined in a 4 – 4 pattern as follows:

- Verses 17-20: Lifted into the heavens—Tasting the goodness of the LORD
- Verses 21-24: Collision with the world—Disdained by the wicked

Lifted into the heavens–Tasting the goodness of the LORD in the realm of the Spirit (v. 17-20)

"Deal bountifully with Your servant, that I may live and keep Your word" (v. 17).

1. "Deal bountifully" (*gamal*): to treat or deal with a person fully (for well or ill), recompense or reward, benefit, to wean a child.

    - Our psalmist is basically saying, "More, Lord. I have tasted your goodness, now deal bountifully, deal fully, and give me a full portion. I want it all so that I may truly live the resurrected life of the Spirit and keep Your word."

- *Gamal* is employed ten times in the Hebrew Scriptures referring to the weaning of a child from its mothers breast and onto solid food. See Psalm 131 for an example. There David suggests that the source of our hope that brings peace to the soul needs to be shifted (weaned) from one source to another. We need to be weaned from the world and onto the Lord, from the flesh to the Spirit. The turbulence of this weaning process actually occurs in David's life in the next segment, *dalet*, as he struggles with his own flesh. Here in this section, he will encounter the enmity of others who persecute him because of his testimony.

"Open my eyes, that I may see wondrous things from Your law" (v. 18).

1. "Open my eyes, that I may see." What a prayer! The spiritual realm is invisible to the natural eye. We need revelation to see what is unseen so that we can live in relationship with an unseen God. This is like the prayer of Ephesians 1:16-20, which opens the door to all the spiritual blessings enumerated in the first fourteen verses of Ephesians 1. Paul's prayer for the believers is this: "That the God of our Lord Jesus Christ, the Father of glory, may give to you the spirit of wisdom and revelation in the knowledge of Him, the eyes of your understanding being enlightened; that you may know what is the hope of His calling, what are the riches of the glory of His inheritance in the saints, and what is the exceeding greatness of His power toward us who believe" (Ephesians 1:17-18).

2. "Wondrous things" (*pala'*): to be marvelous, wonderful, surpassing, extraordinary, or to separate by distinguishing action. This is the same Hebrew word used for the wonders, marvels and signs that God did in Egypt (Exodus 3:20; Psalm 106:7; 98:1) as He showcased His power when He delivered Israel from slavery. *Pala'* occurs thirty-one times in the Psalms, almost exclusively describing the mighty acts of God which showcase His power in the earth—two realms interacting again.

3. "From Your law *(torah)*." Not only does *torah* record the mighty acts of God in history, it is filled with prophetic shadow pictures of the Messiah Himself. *Yeshua* said that "the law prophesied (pointed to Messiah) until John" (Matthew 11:13).

   - Romans 10:4 does not refer to doing away with the law when it says, "Christ is the end (*telos*: completion, aim, outcome, purpose, consummation) of the law." It means, rather, that Messiah is the end to which the *torah* aimed—the fulfillment of the *torah*. Reading *torah* is a virtual treasure hunt for the Messiah, the One whose name, according to Isaiah 9:6, is "Wonderful" (*Pele'*: a derivative of *pala'* which means wonder or marvel). That is *Yeshua*.

Read 1 Corinthians 2:9-14. These verses powerfully portray what is happening in David's life. Ponder verses 9 and 10: "Eye has not seen, nor ear heard, nor have entered into the heart of man the things which God has prepared for those who love Him. But God has revealed them to us through His Spirit." The passage goes on to explain that the natural man cannot receive the things of the Spirit. It requires a Holy Spirit escort into the depths of God to see what is invisible to the natural eye. It requires revelation.

Let's face it: we are created with a desire to see and experience the supernatural. Whether by encountering God's presence through spiritual experiences (such as hearing His voice, dreams, visions) or by seeing the power of God released through us and into the earth realm via miracles and answered prayers, we were made for the supernatural. The last part of Paul's prayer for the body of Messiah at Ephesus is that they would know (experientially) "what is the exceeding greatness of His power toward us who believe, according to the working of His mighty power which He worked in Christ when He raised Him from the dead."

Our psalmist has not yet attained to any significant maturity, passed any major tests or engaged in any fruitful ministry. He has only said "yes" to the journey (the same is true of the Shulamite in Song of Solomon 2:4-5). This initial encounter with the Lord is critical. It is about first receiving freely of the goodness of God, without the merit of having attained to anything. Our hope of attaining to anything or giving anything to the Lord is to first receive freely from the Lord. We cannot give Him something that He did not first give us. Consider the following scriptures:

- *Yeshua* said, "Freely you have received, freely give" (Matthew 10:8).

- 1 John 4:19 says, "We love Him because He first loved us."

- In 1 Chronicles 29:12-15, King David has just taken up an enormous offering toward the temple that his son Solomon was to build. His prayer is enlightening: "Both riches and honor come from You, and You reign over all. In Your hand is power and might; In Your hand it is to make great, and to give strength to all. Now therefore, our God, we thank You and praise Your glorious name. But who am I, and who are my people, that we should be able to offer so willingly as this? For all things come from You, and of Your own we have given You. For we are aliens and pilgrims before You."

- Notice the aliens and pilgrims idea which shows up in the next verse of our psalm (v. 19).

This flow of the goodness of God serves to get us hooked on Him so that we do not easily renounce our faith when trials come. For David, our psalmist, the trouble begins in verse 21.

"I am a stranger in the earth; Do not hide Your commandments from me. My soul breaks with longing for Your judgments at all times" (v. 19-20).

1. "Stranger"(*ger*): sojourner or alien who is temporarily dwelling in a location. This word implies the idea of passing through one place on the way to another destination. Our psalmist is from another realm. His citizenship is now in heaven (Philippians 3:20; Psalm 84:5), the interests of which he now represents on earth. He is beginning to long for that which is eternal and of the Spirit. The things of this world no longer satisfy.

   • Our psalmist is becoming like Abel, Enoch, Noah, Abraham and Sarah who "confessed that they were strangers and pilgrims on the earth. For those who say such things declare plainly that they seek a homeland. And truly if they had called to mind that country from which they had come out, they would have had opportunity to return. But now they desire a better, that is, a heavenly country" (Hebrews 11:13-16).

   • As he learns to walk by the Spirit, David is beginning to experience something else that is new—he no longer fits in. He is in the world but not of the world. He has been chosen (by *Yeshua*) out of the world, to be sent into the world, and therefore the world hates him (John 15:18-20; 17:14-18). His connection to the Lord is a threat to the world and its value system.

2. "Do not hide Your commandments (*mitzvah*) from me." David desires the commands of God. He is actually asking for orders. Reread the explanation of *mitzvah* in the introduction. In this place of reveling in God's presence, it is as if David is saying, "I just want to please You, LORD. I'll do anything You want." It is not unnatural or abnormal for a child to seek to please his parents and to derive pleasure from having done so.

3. "Longing for Your judgments." The word judgments employs *mishpat*: a right ruling by the King. Basically David is saying, "More, Lord" as he revels in the Lord's goodness. He could also be saying, "I am Yours, LORD. Search me, O God, and know my heart. Try me and know my thoughts: And see if there be any wicked way in me" (Psalm 139:23-24).

   • See Addendum 4 for an extensive treatment of the judgments (*mishpat*) of God. David's longing for God's judgments (right rulings) could mean a desire for:

      o The kingdom of God to advance in his own life and heart: God's word must first come as judgments to discern and judge the sin yet operating in our own flesh. Judgment must begin in the house of God. This is certainly the primary aspect of God's *mishpat* which is needed at this point in David's journey. His hunger for God must include this aspect of God's *mishpat*.

o   The kingdom of God to advance in the earth as God releases His judgments: "For when Your judgments are in the earth, the inhabitants of the world will learn righteousness" (Isaiah 26:9).

o   Personal vindication: Having become a stranger and now bearing reproach (v. 22), David's longing may include a desire for God to vindicate him before his persecutors. Divine vindication may prove David right and his detractors wrong, but this would likely not be for David's ultimate good at this point.

o   Retribution for the proud: David may want to see his persecutors (the proud) rebuked by the LORD (v. 29). The longing for this aspect of God's judgments is premature at best, and is certain, at this early stage, to be laced with untempered zeal or worse. "Punish them, God" is not a good option. That would be like James and John wanting to call fire down on the Samaritans for rejecting them in Luke 9:54-55.

Collision with the world—Disdained by the wicked (v. 21-24)

"You rebuke the proud—the cursed, who stray from Your commandments. Remove from me reproach and contempt, for I have kept Your testimonies. Princes also sit and speak against me, but Your servant meditates on Your statutes" (v. 21-23).

1.   "You rebuke the proud." The collision is taking place. Our excited psalmist, who has just humbled himself to pursue the Lord, is encountering the pride of man in his world. Having the humble live among the proud is like placing sheep among wolves. There are seasons in which the proud prevail over the humble and the wicked prosper over the righteous while God seems to do nothing. We need to know that ultimately, the meek will inherit the earth and the proud will be rebuked. Many are the scriptures which show that the LORD will set everything right in the end (see Job 40:9-13; Psalm 73; 92; 94; 125).

2.   "The proud—the cursed, who stray from Your commandments." For now, the LORD waits because He is working in our psalmist's heart and drawing David to Himself

•   Pride: This can be called the "taproot vice" from which all vice flows in the enemy's kingdom. Humility is "taproot virtue" from which all virtue flows. There are two wisdoms—two moral orders— two governments with opposing values and agendas in conflict:

o One wisdom lives for the self, its own preservation and advantage. This natural wisdom celebrates human pride, strength, knowledge, success and innovation.

o God's wisdom is the wisdom of the cross—self-sacrifice. It lives for another at the expense of the self-life. *Yeshua* pleased the Father without regard for Himself, even unto death. God's wisdom overcomes the world through that which seems weak, foolish and lowly (see 1 Corinthians 1:18-31; James 3:13-18).

4. "Remove from me reproach and contempt." These words include the idea of being scorned, shamed, taunted, despised or disdained. Our psalmist is experiencing the suffering of the righteous although he has kept the Lord's testimonies. To identify with *Yeshua* in a sinful world puts us at risk of being hated (or perhaps loved, for that matter). It is no accident that *Yeshua* had to warn us in Mark 8:38, "For whoever is ashamed of Me and My words in this adulterous and sinful generation, of him the Son of Man also will be ashamed when He comes in the glory of His Father with the holy angels."

5. "Princes (nobles, rulers, chiefs) also sit and speak against me." This refers in particular to those in high places, who have a vested interest in the world system, who are speaking against the psalmist. *Yeshua* said, "If they persecuted Me, they will also persecute you" (John 15:20).

- We know that not everyone persecuted *Yeshua*. Many loved Him and accepted His words. Likewise for us, many will love us and accept our testimony.

- It is interesting to note that in the great end-time drama that is upon the earth, it is the kings of the earth who assemble together against the LORD in Psalm 2:1-3.

- It was the leaders (princes) in *Yeshua's* day who were threatened by His popularity. He was crucified because of envy (Matthew 27:18). The gospel of the kingdom is about *Yeshua's* conquest of all the kingdoms of the earth (Revelation 11:15). Hence princes, who have a vested interest in this world's system, either economically (Acts 19:24-27), politically (Matthew 2:16), socially, religiously, or in any other way, are threatened by this gospel. *Yeshua* said, "It is easier for a camel to go through the eye of a needle than for a rich man (a prince?) to enter the kingdom," but He adds that with God all things are possible (Matthew 19:24, 26).

- Moses chose "rather to suffer affliction with the people of God than to enjoy the passing pleasures of sin, esteeming the reproach of Christ as greater riches than the treasures in Egypt; for he looked to the reward"

(Hebrews 11:25-26). There is a reproach we bear when the fragrance of Messiah is upon our lives. Those who are being saved love us, but those who are perishing hate us. This is what is happening to David. "We are to God the fragrance of Christ among those who are being saved and among those who are perishing. To the one we are the aroma of death leading to death, and to the other the aroma of life leading to life" (2 Corinthians 2:15-16).

- Psalm 123 speaks of "the contempt of the proud," and it speaks of keeping our eyes on the Master when we are being scorned.

6. "Your servant meditates on Your statutes (*choq*)." *Choq* emphasizes that which is unchanging and eternally true. Our psalmist holds himself steady in the face of persecution by meditating upon eternal truth. Living in the light of eternity will hold him steady when it seems that the wicked might prevail over the righteous.

"Your testimonies also are my delight and my counselors" (v. 24).

Our psalmist is stirring up a hornet's nest with his new life in the Lord. He is already manifesting in the earth something of heaven's aroma and excellence. What holds him steady in persecution and reproach are the Lord's testimonies, fresh-breaking words from heaven. They are both:

- His delight or object of enjoyment; and

- His counselors by guiding his decisions and responses. David is listening to the Holy Spirit for direction on how to respond to his persecutors.

Having so tasted the goodness of God, and become hooked on the Lord, our psalmist cannot easily despise God's word by reacting in the flesh.

Concluding Thoughts

As we shall see in the next section, it seems that the rigors of this conflict may have brought to the forefront all of David's own carnality issues. Pride still operates within his life. Maybe, in spite of all of these great confessions, he actually damaged his testimony by giving a sharp retort to the people who are "proud–the cursed who stray." Or perhaps he performed some kind of compromising act of self-preservation. We don't know for sure, but we do know that David now, in *dalet*, enters a fierce struggle with his own flesh.

Questions to Ponder

1. We learn from *Yeshua's* words in Matthew 4:4 that "Man shall not live by bread alone, but by every word that proceeds from the mouth of God." In what ways have you experienced being weaned from this world as your source of food and life and becoming dependent upon the Lord?

2. How strongly is the cry of David in verse eighteen sounding within your heart? Take a moment and pray "that the God of our Lord Jesus Christ, the Father of glory, may give to you the spirit of wisdom and revelation in the knowledge of Him, the eyes of your understanding being enlightened; that you may know what is the hope of His calling, what are the riches of the glory of His inheritance in the saints, and what is the exceeding greatness of His power toward us who believe" (Ephesians 1:17-19).

3. How have you encountered reproach for the name of Messiah? What persecution have you encountered that put your heart and your faith to the test?

Chapter 6

The War Within: Which Way?

DALET

²⁵My soul clings to the dust;
Revive me according to Your word.
²⁶I have declared my ways, and You answered me;
Teach me Your statutes.
²⁷Make me understand the way of Your precepts;
So shall I meditate on Your wonderful works.
²⁸My soul melts from heaviness;
Strengthen me according to Your word.
²⁹Remove from me the way of lying,
And grant me Your law graciously.
³⁰I have chosen the way of truth;
Your judgments I have laid before me.
³¹I cling to Your testimonies;
O LORD, do not put me to shame!
³²I will run the course of Your commandments,
For You shall enlarge my heart.

Dalet—Psalm 119:25-32

"My soul clings to the dust" (v. 32).

After a running start, our psalmist suddenly encounters the earthly realm, or the carnality, operating within his own soul. These issues were probably exposed by the offenses of the preceding stage, *gimel,* where he encountered reproach and contempt for his faith possibly as the result of a failure of some kind such as a sharp retort or a self-preserving response toward one of his persecutors. At any rate, David is suddenly awakened to the fact that it is not only "the proud and the cursed, who stray from Your commandments" (v. 21) but that the propensity to stray from the right way is alive and well even within his own soul (see verse ten).

The ancient pictograph of our Hebrew letter *dalet* depicts a tent door. It implies a pathway both to and from. It can depict a door or it can mean to swing back and forth as if deciding where to stop or which path to open toward. Another key to this section is the Hebrew word *derek,* translated way. *Derek* occurs five times in this section and twice in the next one, for a concentrated seven occurrences in this season of the journey. The issue before our psalmist is this: Which way will he choose? *Dalet* reveals a believer's struggle between the flesh and the spirit—a theme that can be studied in scriptures such as Galatians 5:16-26 and Romans 7:7-8:11. Will it be the flesh or the Spirit? Will it be the natural man's ways or God's ways?

These two ways, the flesh and the spirit, connect with the two realms discussed in *gimel*. Preston Eby describes it like this: "There were two trees in the Garden of Eden, representing spirit and flesh, life and death, truth and error, heaven and earth. Every man who ever lived has had his center, his identity and his existence in one of these two realms. Adam's sin in eating of the tree of the knowledge of good and evil lay in his walking after the flesh (sense realm) instead of the Spirit. It consisted in his making the outer, physical man his center and identity rather than the inner man of the Spirit."[1]

In our journey to maturity, we learn to hear the voice of God and live by the Spirit rather than by the flesh or by our natural senses (Galatians 5:16, 25).

The flesh, in scripture, has several key applications and meanings:

1. Mankind in general: "All flesh is grass" (Isaiah 40:6). Our life on earth is short, like grass.

2. The human body–*Yeshua* came in the flesh. The Word was made flesh. This is not evil or bad. God created man in His own image as spirit, soul and body and pronounced it "very good." Though *Yeshua* came in the flesh He did not walk according to the flesh.

3. Our natural earthly life denotes mere human nature, the earthly nature of man apart from divine influence that is therefore prone to sin. We are weak in our service to God and need to train our flesh. *Yeshua* said to the sleeping disciples in Gethsemane, "The spirit is willing but the flesh is weak." Though they loved *Yeshua*, they were weak in their ability to keep watch with Him.

4. A metaphor for a physically sense-dominated life, or carnality. Sin has used our bodies (flesh) as a host for its primary expression. As believers, our job is not so much to deny the body as it is to bring the power of the body under the government (kingdom) of God. Our bodies are weapons of righteousness for advancing the kingdom of God on earth. We relate to the earth via our bodies. See Romans 6:19.

Our working definition for the flesh was coined by Alan Vincent of Outpouring Ministries and flows mostly out of point number four above: "That union of body and soul which acts independently of God."[2] The source of what we say and do—whether of human origin or from God— is more important in determining whether those words and actions are profitable than the words or actions themselves. *Yeshua* says in John

6:63, "It is the Spirit who gives life; the flesh profits nothing." Adam, in taking of the tree of the knowledge of good and evil, sought not so much to rebel against God as he sought life independent of God. That independence led to a plethora of sins.

Romans 8:6 tells us that "to be carnally (fleshly) minded is death, but to be spiritually minded is life and peace." Living according to the flesh is expressed in the following:

- Living by the passions of our bodies

- Living by the five senses

- Living in the past

- Living by human wisdom and natural thinking

- Living by human strength and resolve (even to love and serve God)

- Living by human initiative—the origin or source of a word or act determines its end

An excerpt from Addendum 4 can provide a possible explanation as to why David is suddenly grappling with his carnality and his lack of being like *Yeshua*.

A massive truth was coined by the late Virgil Johnson. I heard him speak at our local church in the late 1980's and his powerful one-liner stuck with me: "It takes the snake to expose the snake in me." Offense and injustice, which are the work of the enemy, serve to expose the sin in us. In fact, the degree to which injustice provokes our carnality is the same degree to which God is justified in allowing injustice and offense to touch us. If we will judge the sin within ourselves, God can righteously show His power on our behalf and judge sin in the world—the very sin that was employed against us. The drama is the contest between light and darkness. Our enemy wants us to get offended at a God who would allow such injustice and undeserved difficulty, and it is always our flesh that gets offended. He wants us to "Curse God and die!" God, however, wants us to recognize our carnality and judge the sin within our own members. Hence, the sin in the world is a primary key to our formation. Based on His wisdom, God allows Satan to rage against His beloved children in a fallen world!

Now, let's join David as he wrestles with his carnality and seeks assurance in his journey.

"My soul clings to the dust; Revive me according to Your word" (v. 25).

1. "Clings" (*dabaq*) means to stick, stay close, cleave, impinge upon, pursue after and adhere to.

2. "To the dust." Our psalmist discovers that something within him pursues fleshly desires and the things of this world. He has, like Paul in Romans 7:18-19, discov-

ered that "in me (that is in my flesh) nothing good dwells; for to will is present with me (a willing spirit), but how to perform what is good I do not find (in me). For the good that I will to do, I do not; but the evil I will not to do, that I practice." He has possibly fallen back into an old pattern that he thought was behind him.

- How can this be? I thought I was born from above and given a new nature.

- The next phrase is a prayer as our psalmist turns to the word of God for new life.

3.   "Revive (to live, make alive, keep alive) me according to Your word" (*dabar*). If our struggling and now contrite traveler would have had the epistle of 1 John, he could have turned there for assurance. John addresses his little children concerning two seemingly paradoxical streams of thought. One stream confronts the rebellious or licentious "believer" who uses God's grace as a license to stay in sin (see Jude 4). The other stream of thought reassures the weak-but-sincere believer who, in his weakness, stumbles in sin.

Stream 1: Do not be deceived—The righteous do not sin (truths from 1 John).

- If you claim to know Him and do not obey Him you are a liar (2:4).

- If you claim to abide in the Messiah you must walk as he walked (2:6).

- If you claim to be in the light, yet hate (an idiom for not loving from the heart) your brother, you are in darkness and a murderer (2:9-11; 3:15).

- He who practices righteousness is righteous—he who sins is of the devil (3:7-8).

Stream 2: Do not be deceived—"If You say you have no sin, the truth is not in you" (1 John 1:8).

- "But, if we confess our sins, He is faithful and just and will forgive us our sin" (1:9).

- "If anyone sins we have an Advocate with the Father" (2:1).

- "I write to you, little children, because your sins are forgiven" (2:12).

- "Beloved, now we are the children of God . . . even though we are not fully like Him until He appears" (3:2).

- "If we love one another, God abides in us" (4:12).

- God abides in anyone who confesses *Yeshua* as the Son of God (4:15).

- Whoever believes that *Yeshua* is the Son of God overcomes the world by their faith (5:4-5).

- "He who has the Son has life. . . . These things I have written to you who believe in the name of the Son of God, that you may know that you have eternal life" (5:12-13).

- James 3:2 affirms that we all stumble in many ways.

So what are we to make of all this from 1 John? Let us note a few powerful truths.

- My weak flesh does not define me. In John 13:10, *Yeshua* called Peter clean just before Peter's total and vehement denial of the Master. In Gethsemane, *Yeshua's* disciples could not watch with Him even one hour, yet *Yeshua*, rather than disparage them, said "The spirit indeed is willing, but the flesh is weak" (Matthew 26:41). He defined them by their willing spirit.

- I am not a sinner struggling to love God—I am a lover of God struggling with sin. I am not a sinner saved by grace—I am a child of God in need of grace to overcome sin.

- Immaturity is not the same as rebellion. Peter loved *Yeshua*. His heart was good but his flesh was weak. Not so with Judas—but that will be examined another time.

- Here's the deal: If I am secure in my identity as a child of God, then I can be "brutally straightforward" concerning the sin in my life. Confessing my righteousness in Messiah and my identity as a true child of God does not mean that I can't call sin what it is. Actually, it means that I can call it what it is, because it does not define me. Let's allow the word of God to judge (*mishpat*) us, both to cut away all that is sinful and of the flesh, and to define us as the beloved of God.

- On the other hand, it is not acceptable to be cavalier about sin and disobedience toward God, using grace as a license to sin. The Lord paid a terrible price to deliver us from sin and He is perpetually at war with sin.

The weaning of a child from the mother's breast onto solid food is initially a turbulent time for a child. In *gimel*, David ran into the reproach and contempt of the proud and unbelieving who hated the light emanating from him. Here, he is running into his own carnality. The struggle evident here in *dalet* is the turbulence of being weaned from one source of life to another source of life—the swinging back and forth of the door—the competition between two ways, each desiring to be our source of life, and each desiring to influence the way in which we walk.

- The Lord weans us from our sources of nourishment and comfort in the world and from the things in which we trust in order to give us something better. "Oh, taste and see that the LORD is good; Blessed is the man who trusts in

Him" (Psalm 34:8). David has already tasted this goodness in the first four verses of *gimel*.

- As carnal human beings, we are conditioned to live by our five senses. We look to the world for meeting our needs. We interpret reality by natural criteria and respond to stimuli from our surroundings. Our identity is derived from this world's criteria. The great shift that must occur in the life of every believer is to go from walking in the flesh to walking in the Spirit (see Romans 8:5-9; Galatians 5:16-17).

"I have declared my ways (*derek*), and You answered me; Teach me Your statutes" (v. 26).

1. If we do the tedious definition, verb tense and grammar work, we could arrive at this reading of verse 26: "I have in the past completely and with intensity enumerated all my (former) ways, and You heard and responded to me (with forgiveness and salvation). Now teach (intensive imperative) me Your statutes."

2. In other words, it seems that our psalmist is revisiting with the Lord the time when he first repented and turned to the Lord. He is basically saying, "Hey God, I'm yours. What are You going to do about my weaknesses and propensity to wander?" "Good and upright is the LORD; Therefore He teaches sinners in the way. The humble He guides in justice, and the humble He teaches His way" (Psalm 25:8-9). Or, it may be as simple as 1 John 1:9, "If we confess our sins, He is faithful and just and will forgive and cleanse us from all unrighteousness."

3. Whatever else is really going on here, there is clearly a contrast made between my ways and God's statutes, and David does not want to go back to his own way.

"Make me (cause me to) understand the way (*derek*) of Your precepts; So shall I meditate on Your wonderful works" (v. 27).

1. On the heels of "teach me" (v.26), our psalmist asks for an understanding of God's ways.

2. Remember Psalm 103:7, "He made known His ways to Moses, His acts (of power or wonderful works) to the children of Israel."

   - All of Israel witnessed the acts (miracles) of God but Moses knew the ways of God. He knew what God was doing and why.

   - Is our psalmist asking for the friendship with God that Moses had? In verse 17 he identified himself as "Your servant." *Yeshua* said in John 15:14-15, "You are My friends if you do whatever I command you. No longer do I call you servants, for a servant does not know what his master is doing; but I have called you friends, for all things that I heard from My Father I have made known to you."

3. "So shall I meditate on Your wonderful works" (*pala'*: wonders–see verse eighteen). Our psalmist is reaching for and praying for the capacity to walk with the LORD in full agreement as a friend and he is connecting supernatural signs and wonders with that walk.

    •   Moses, in his friendship with the Lord, performed many signs and wonders (*pala'*) in the exodus and throughout the wilderness journeys.

    •   The pattern is the Man, *Yeshua*. "God anointed Jesus of Nazareth with the Holy Spirit and power, who went about doing good and healing all who were oppressed of the devil, for God was with Him" (Acts 10:38).

    •   God's pattern is this: The Spirit's power operating through human agency. Our psalmist wants that power. But this will require walking in God's ways.

4. Ponder this question: To what extent is our involvement with God's acts of power connected to our obedience? One hundred percent? Possibly so.

"My soul melts from heaviness; Strengthen me according to Your word (*dabar*). Remove from me the way of lying, and grant me Your law graciously" (v. 28-29).

1. "My soul melts from heaviness." We seem to be back at verse twenty-five again. The battle is raging inside in the psalmist's soul for faith to run this race.

2. "Strengthen me according to Your word." Again he turns to the word of God, this time for strength (*quwm*: to rise, to stand). He is asking for strength to stand; see Ephesians 6:13.

3. "Remove from me the way of lying" (deception or falsehood). This is not just about telling a falsehood. It is about a lifestyle of deception, posturing, pretense, duplicity or hypocrisy. For example, we put on a brave face to mask the truth about our fear. We hide the truth of our nakedness behind the fig leaves of Genesis 3:7.

    •   How would my life change if I walked in truth? John writes in 3 John 4, "I have no greater joy than that my children walk in truth." This idea powerfully connects with the very first verse of the psalm, "Blessed are the undefiled (whole, complete, entire, sound) in the way."

    •   It was the happiness of those who walk in integrity and in the favor of the Lord that awakened our psalmist's longing to become this kind of person.

4. "The way." This is the third of five uses of the word "way" (*derek*) in this section. *Derek* suggests an ongoing, habitual lifestyle or pattern of living according to a certain criteria. Notice the "swinging back and forth of the door" in the following progression:

    - My ways (v. 26).
    - The way of Your precepts (v. 27).
    - The way of lying (v. 29).
    - The way of truth (v. 30).
    - The way of Your commandments (v. 32).

5. "Grant me Your law graciously." Graciously (*chanan*) here means to be gracious, show favor or pity. David is appealing to the gracious nature of the Lord to be patient as he learns to walk in the teaching (law) of the Lord. No good parent gets impatient with a child who stumbles and falls in the process of learning to walk. Neither will the Lord be impatient with His children as they learn to walk with Him.

"I have chosen the way of truth; Your judgments I have laid before me" (v. 30).

1. "I have chosen the way of truth." Our psalmist has renounced the way of lying and chosen the way of truth. Both verbs are in the perfect mood, allowing for this wording: "I had at the beginning and until now chosen the way of truth; Your judgments I had, at the beginning and until now, laid before me." The great question now concerns what David will choose for the future, especially in light of the painful encounter with the princes (v. 21-23) which the Lord allowed in *gimel*. God did not "protect" our psalmist from persecution.

2. "Your judgments (*mishpat*) I have laid before me." David, at least until now, has allowed the word of God to judge his actions. This takes courage. A powerful fleshly impulse is to justify ourselves when our carnality manifests. If the contempt of verse twenty-two provoked angry words from David, it would be natural for him to excuse himself and to blame the offender, saying "He deserved it," or "He made me angry." The truth is that the contempt of those who spoke against him in verses twenty-one to twenty-three simply provoked the anger already resident within his soul. Allowing God's word to judge his own carnality at this point, instead of pointing the finger, would be a powerful victory for the psalmist.

3. Will he make the right choice? Will he be willing to call sin what it is and own it as his own sinful choice? The very fact that he is recounting what he had done in the past is almost like saying, "I have chosen the right way. How can I turn back now?"

"I cling to Your testimonies; O LORD, do not put me to shame" (v. 31).

1.   "I cling." David has made the turn. He has made the choice to walk in God's ways. The only two occurrences of this word cling in the entire psalm are in this section.

    •   My soul clings to the dust (v. 25), but now

    •   I cling to Your testimonies!

2.   David makes his choice, and much like in verse eight, he follows up with a big, "so help me God." Instinctively he knows that he cannot overcome the sin that is operating within his own flesh alone.

3.   "Do not let me be put to shame" is like saying, "Help me. I don't want to lose this battle with my flesh and return to my old ways."

4.   David is choosing to trust in the Lord and to stay on course. He echoes the words of Psalm 25:3, "Let no one who waits on You be ashamed." This entire section is so similar to Psalm 25:1-8 that we must insert it here and read it. Every theme of this section matches these words.

    Psalm 25:1-8, "To You, O LORD, I lift up my soul. O my God, I trust in You; Let me not be ashamed; Let not my enemies triumph over me. Indeed, let no one who waits on You be ashamed; Let those be ashamed who deal treacherously without cause. Show me Your ways, O LORD; Teach me Your paths. Lead me in Your truth and teach me, For You are the God of my salvation; On You I wait all the day. Remember, O LORD, Your tender mercies and Your lovingkindnesses, for they are from of old. Do not remember the sins of my youth, nor my transgressions; According to Your mercy remember me, for Your goodness' sake, O LORD. Good and upright is the LORD; Therefore He teaches sinners in the way."

"I will run the course of Your commandments, for You shall enlarge my heart" (v. 32).

1.   "I will run the course" (*derek*). This is the fifth occurrence of the word *derek* (way). What a choice and declaration of faith—just like in verse eight, when he said, "I will keep Your statutes."

2.   "For You shall enlarge (grow wide) my heart." This is about increasing our capacity to love what God loves and hate what He hates. God specializes in changing our hearts and has promised time and again to write His law upon our hearts and minds. In Ezekiel 11:19-20 God said, "I will put a new spirit within them, and take the stony heart out of their flesh, and give them a heart of flesh, that they may walk in My statutes and keep My judgments and do them."

3.   Hence, though he makes a powerful choice in verse thirty-one, David's confidence is not so much in the power of his commitment as it is in the certainty that the Lord will fulfill His promises concerning a new heart.

Concluding Thoughts

What is God really looking for in us? Sinless perfection? No. He is looking for three things:

1.   Brokenness: God looks for humility and brokenness. Ponder these scriptures:

- Psalm 51:17, "The sacrifices of God are a broken spirit, a broken and a contrite heart. These, O God, You will not despise."

- Isaiah 57:15, "Thus says the High and Lofty One, who inhabits eternity, whose name is Holy: 'I dwell in the high and holy place, with him who has a contrite and humble spirit, to revive the spirit of the humble, and to revive the heart of the contrite ones.'"

- Isaiah 66:1-2, "'Heaven is My throne, and earth is My footstool. Where is the house that you will build Me? And where is the place of My rest? For all those things My hand has made, and all those things exist,' says YHVH. 'But on this one will I look: On him who is poor and of a contrite spirit, and who trembles at My word.'"

- Hidden and unconfessed sin may provide a show of righteousness but is ultimately rooted in pride. God resists the proud, but gives grace to the humble.

2.   Integrity: Heart and soul reunited from the great separation of Genesis 3.

- Genesis 3:7, "Then the eyes of both of them were opened, and they knew that they were naked; and they sewed fig leaves together and made themselves coverings."

- Psalm 86:11, "Teach me Your way, O LORD; I will walk in Your truth; Unite my heart."

- Recall from *aleph*, the undefiled in the way. The Hebrew word *tamiym* means entire, complete, whole, sound. *Tamiym* points in two directions:

    o   To Integrity – A life without duplicity, pretense or hypocrisy. It suggests unity of our spirit, soul and body, undefiled by impure motives.

    o   To maturity (Christ-likeness).

- Duplicity versus a single eye. "If you eye is single, your whole body will be full of light (Mathew 6:22)."

- 3 John 4, "I have no greater joy than to hear that my children walk in truth."

3. Holiness: Set apart from the world and consecrated to God—"Holy unto the LORD."

Scriptures to ponder in closing this section include Hebrews 2:11 and Hebrews 10:14, where we learn that acknowledging that I am already perfected forever, and yet that I am being sanctified at the same time, is not a contradiction (Hebrews 10:14). Hebrews 2:11 tells us that both He who sanctifies (*Yeshua*) and those who are being sanctified (believers with weak flesh) are all of one, for which reason He is not ashamed to call them brethren (*adelphos*: out of the same womb). Every person who has received Messiah has been given the right to become a child of God (John 1:12), a younger sibling of Messiah Himself, "Who is to be the Firstborn among many brethren (Romans 8:29)."

It is time for hard choices based on a bold faith that God will do what He promised—that which I cannot do in my own strength. I cannot change myself (as if by the effort of the flesh), but I can be changed through His faithful dealings. And He is faithful. We will run this course and not be ashamed, because God will write His *torah* on our hearts. Decree it. Speak it. Pray it.

Steve Sabol said to Knights of the 21st Century: "Many men are anxious to improve their circumstances, but are unwilling to improve themselves. Therefore, they remain bound to what they want to be free from. 21st Century Knights should be willing to take a long, hard look within, for therein lies the true challenge of manhood."[3]

Questions to Ponder

1. Can you identify with the flapping of the tent door—that is, the struggle to make the shift from walking in the flesh to walking in the Spirit?

2. Name some ways in which the sin that yet operates within your own flesh has been revealed when others sinned against you.

3. Memorize verse thirty-two. It is a powerful declaration in this war that rages within. Have you come to a place of faith that God will enlarge your heart, that is, increase your capacity to walk the walk of *The Blessed Life?*

Chapter 7

Praying for the Promise: An Enlarged Heart

HEY

³³Teach me, O LORD, the way of Your statutes,
And I shall keep it to the end.
³⁴Give me understanding, and I shall keep Your law;
Indeed, I shall observe it with my whole heart.
³⁵Make me walk in the path of Your commandments,
For I delight in it.
³⁶Incline my heart to Your testimonies,
And not to covetousness.
³⁷Turn away my eyes from looking at worthless things,
And revive me in Your way.
³⁸Establish Your word to Your servant,
Who is devoted to fearing You.
³⁹Turn away my reproach which I dread,
For Your judgments are good.
⁴⁰Behold, I long for Your precepts;
Revive me in Your righteousness.

Hey—Psalm 119:33-40

We now come to the fifth stage of our psalmist's journey, the fifth letter of the Hebrew alphabet, *he(y)*. The ancient pictograph depicts a man with outstretched arms as if saying, "Lo!" or "Behold!" The letter actually means, "Hey!" It is as if our psalmist is going straight to God concerning the battle with his carnality in *dalet*, and saying something like, "Hey God, look at me. What are you going to do about this mess of sinful passions and weak flesh? You said you would change my heart. Please do it!" The outstretched arms could also portray the act of receiving something. In this case, as we shall see, it is the receiving of grace from God in the form of the initiation of a transformation.

David has just won a great battle concerning his identity as a child of God in the context of the struggle with his weak flesh. As we have already learned in *dalet*, acknowledging that I am simultaneously perfected forever and also being sanctified is not a contradiction (Hebrews 10:14). Remember Hebrews 2:11, which states, "For both He who sanctifies (*Yeshua*) and those who are being sanctified (believers with weak flesh) are all of one, for which reason He is not ashamed to call them brethren" (*adelphos* literally means out of the same womb). Not only are we to confess our sins, but we are also to confess our faith (see 1 Timothy 6:12-14; Hebrews 3:1; 4:14; 10:23).

Neither my bold faith concerning my identity in Messiah as a child of God nor my confidence in the running of this course (v. 32) are aborted by an honest confession of my need and my sin. The mature apostle Paul, near the end of his life, referred to himself as "chief of sinners" (1 Timothy 1:15). That is not to say that his sin defined him. But as the revelation of who we are in Messiah grows, so does the revelation of who we are outside of Messiah. The one grows in proportion to the other. It is two sides of one coin. We cannot have one without the other. Or, we might say that our knowledge of ourselves grows in proportion to our knowledge of God. When we know God as He is, we know ourselves as we are in Him and we also see who we are apart from Him.

2 Peter 1:9 tells us that "he who lacks these things (faith, virtue, knowledge and so forth) is shortsighted, even to blindness, and has forgotten that he was cleansed from his old sins." Certainly we should never forget where we came from.

In this section, our psalmist has a prayer meeting around the growing revelation of his desperate condition outside of Messiah. This in no way contradicts his confidence that he is accepted in the Beloved (Ephesians 1:6). In fact, it is because of this confidence that he can boldly hold God to His word.

Consider these questions from 2 Corinthians 8:9, a verse that gives what I believe to be the best definition of grace in the word of God: "For you know the grace of our Lord Jesus Christ, that though He was rich, yet for your sakes He became poor, that you through His poverty might become rich."

1. How rich was the Son of God in eternity past? How high was He? Read John 1:1-2.

2. How poor did He become? How far did He descend? See Philippians 2:6-8; Ephesians 4:9; Psalm 40:1-2.

3. How rich are you? How far did he lift you up? Read Ephesians 2:1-6; Psalm 113:7-9.

God doesn't love us, respond to us or give us something good because we attained a standard, were diligent, disciplined, obedient or brought sacrifices of worship. We respond to His goodness, not vice versa. We didn't find the Lord—He found us. Or, as the Lord put it to Jeremiah in 29:14, "I will be found by you." Here then is how grace works:

1. God draws us: He initiates the relationship and gives us a desire for and a taste of His goodness.

2. After tasting His goodness, we search for Him. Effort on our part is not the same thing as legalism, and it is necessary.

3.   It is as if He peeks out from behind the sofa while we happened to be looking in His direction and we find Him—only because He wanted to be found.

4.   This principle is true for our initial salvation experience as well as for every victory in our lives and for every inch of spiritual growth in the journey of becoming like *Yeshua*. Consider again the following scriptures:

   •   "No one can come to Me unless the Father draws him" (John 6:44).

   •   Again, "Freely you have received, freely give" and "we love him because he first loved us," in that order.

In Exodus 24:12, God provided Moses with tablets of stone on which were written the Ten Commandments. Moses promptly broke them in Exodus 32:19 at the scene of the golden calf. In Exodus 34:1, he ascended the mountain again, but this time Moses cut the tablets and presented them to the Lord, as we might present our own hearts to God. God then wrote the same words on this second set. This prefigures the New Covenant in which God writes his *torah* on the human heart.

Every verse in *hey* starts with a prayer for God to do something in the psalmist's heart. These prayers spring from the great promise of verse 32: "You shall enlarge my heart." If the first great promise of the Lord is, "I will be with you," (v. 8) then the second great promise is this: "I will give you a new heart." Consider the following scriptures:

1.   Deuteronomy 30:6, "The LORD your God will circumcise your heart and the heart of your descendants, to love the LORD your God with all your heart and with all your soul, that you may live."

2.   Jeremiah 31:31-34, "The days are coming, says the LORD, when I will make a new covenant with the house of Israel. . . . I will put My law in their minds, and write it on their hearts; and I will be their God, and they shall be My people. No more shall every man teach his neighbor, and every man his brother, saying, 'Know the LORD,' for they all shall know Me."

3.   Ezekiel 36:26-27, "I will give you a new heart and put a new spirit within you; I will take the heart of stone out of your flesh and give you a heart of flesh. I will put My Spirit within you and cause you to walk in My statutes, and you will keep My judgments and do them. Then you shall dwell in the land."

4.   Ezekiel 11:19-20, "Then I will give them one heart, and I will put a new spirit within them, and take the stony heart out of their flesh, and give them a heart of flesh, that they may walk in My statutes and keep My judgments and do them; and they shall be My people."

5.   Hebrews 10:16-17, "This is the covenant that I will make with them after those days, says the LORD: I will put My laws into their hearts, and in their minds I will write them."

As we rejoin David on his journey, notice the following pattern, the pattern of grace, in almost every verse:

- Divine initiative: Prayer for God to doing something first (unmerited favor or grace).

- Human response: Only now are we empowered to respond and grow because grace works.

"Teach me, O LORD, the way of Your statutes, and I shall keep it to the end" (v. 33).

1.   "Teach (*yarah*: shoot as an arrow) me." This first Hebrew word in this section sets the tone for the entire section. David is asking the Lord to direct him just as an archer points and releases an arrow from a bow toward the desired mark. See the introduction on *yarah*.

2.   "And I shall keep it to the end" (*eqeb*: consequence). The result or consequence of the Lord teaching me is that I will keep His statutes. This shows both divine initiative (grace) and human response.

3.   "Your statutes" (*choq*: those paths that are permanent and of old). "Ask for the old paths, where the good way is, and walk in it; Then you will find rest for your souls" (Jeremiah 6:16). In six thousand-plus years of human life on earth, man has not improved on the ways of God!

"Give me understanding, and I shall keep (*natsar*) Your law; Indeed, I shall observe (*shamar*) it with my whole heart" (v. 34).

1.   "Give me understanding." Again, to ask for understanding is to ask for friendship (see John 15:15 and the notes on verse 27). God isn't looking for some kind of robotic "Yes men". He is looking for friends who know Him and walk with Him in wholehearted agreement (see 2 Corinthians 6:1).

   - It is as if David knows that if he could understand the divine wisdom (the why) behind the instructions of the *torah* (the what), he could more readily co-labor as a friend of God. He would know the heart of God!

   - He could also appreciate the value of the law (*torah*). He could then guard God's words and keep them as great treasure, loving them with his whole heart. This is the essence of friendship.

2.   Both Hebrew words, for keep (*natsar* and *shamar*) occur in this verse (see Addendum 1 for a full study). This confident commitment is amazing, but it flows from the psalmist's cry for understanding. "For all things that I heard from My Father I have made known to you" (John 15:15).

3.   Another note on friendship. Have you ever pondered the implications of God's words to Abraham at the destruction of Sodom? Genesis 18:17, "Shall I hide from Abraham what I am doing?" How about Amos 3:7? "Surely the LORD does nothing, unless He reveals His secrets to His servants the prophets." The Father desires for His sons and daughters on the earth, just like His Only Begotten Son *Yeshua*, to walk with Him in agreement in order to bring redemption to men and establish His kingdom on earth.

4.   Again, we see the pattern of divine initiative followed by human response from the heart.

"Make me walk in the path of Your commandments, for I delight in it" (v. 35).

1.   Can God make me walk rightly? If I am rebellious, He will not. But if I acknowledge my utter dependence upon Him, and the weakness of my flesh, then He will come to my aid.

   •   He leads me in the path of righteousness for His name's sake (Psalm 23:3).

   •   He is the Shepherd; we are the sheep. See Psalm 100:3 and John 10:11.

   •   He leads–we follow–He makes. In Matthew 4:19, *Yeshua* says to Peter and Andrew, "Follow Me, and I will make you fishers of men."

2.   "I delight in it." Here is the wonderful marriage of two realities: our delight and God's glory.

   •   This delight is the living of *The Blessed Life*. Remember, "The commandment (*mitzvah*) of the LORD is pure, enlightening (giving purpose to) the eyes" (Psalm 19:8). Why are the Lord's commandments pure? Because they are not self-serving. God is not a self-serving dictator extracting something from us. He is jealous for our destiny and is working all things for our good. His commands are for us!

   •   He is glorified (for His name's sake). He is glorified in and through this blessed life. We are the planting of the LORD, that He may be glorified (Isaiah 61:3).

3.   What a marriage! God has zeal, primarily for two things: the glory of His name and the fullness of His bride. In his powerful book, *Desiring God*, John Piper suggests that God's pursuit of glory and our pursuit of joy (in God) are not different pursuits but are, in fact, supposed to be one and the same. As the premise of his book he asserts that "God is most glorified in me, when I am most satisfied in him." He goes on to say that "God's pursuit of praise from us and our pursuit of pleasure in Him are the same pursuit."[1] Think about it.

4. Again, we see the pattern: divine initiative which is then followed by human response or growth.

"Incline my heart to Your testimonies, and not to covetousness. Turn away my eyes from looking at worthless things, and revive me in Your way" (v. 36-37).

1. Only here, in the entire psalm, do these two words appear:

   - "Covetousness" (*betsa*: profit, unjust gain, greed or ill-gotten gain)

   - "Worthless things" (*shav'*: emptiness, vanity, falsehood). *The Theological Workbook of the Old Testament* defines *shav'* as "anything that is unsubstantial, unreal, worthless, either materially or morally. Hence, it is a word for idols."[2]

   - *Shav'* appears in Psalm 24:4 concerning those who may ascend the hill of the LORD; "He who . . . has not lifted up his soul to an idol (*shav'*), nor sworn deceitfully."

2. These two words represent the all-time greatest competitors for the human heart. Furthermore, they represent all that is in the world, the lust of the flesh, the lust of the eyes and the pride of life (1 John 2:16). Let's compare the three descriptions of the tree in Genesis 3:6 with the three phrases of 1 John 2:15-17. In Genesis 3:6, Eve saw that the tree was:

   - Good for food = the lust of the flesh–sensuality. Pleasure without reference to the will of God.

   - Pleasant to the eyes = the lust of the eyes–greed. Possessions without reference to the will of God.

   - Desirable to make one wise = the pride of life–pride: Position without reference to the will of God.

3. It is powerful to note also that the three temptations of *Yeshua* in the wilderness run parallel to these (Matthew 4:1-11; Luke 4:1-13). Where the first Adam failed (and that in a perfect world), the last Adam (*Yeshua*) overcame (in a broken world, where He might have had an excuse for His sin). His victory is our victory. "This is the victory that overcomes the world–our faith" (1 John 5:4).

4. "Covetousness." The biblical connection between the human heart and money (or possessions) is no secret. "Where your treasure is, there will your heart be also. . . . No man can serve two masters." Read again *Yeshua's* words in Matthew 6:19-24. "The love of money is a root of all kinds of evil" (1 Timothy 6:10).

5. "Worthless (empty, vain) things." The world promises what it cannot deliver. 1 John 2:17 tells us that "the world is passing away, and the lust of it; but he who

does the will of God abides forever." If our hearts are set on anything that is in the world, it will come to nothing. See Addendum 3 for more on the human heart.

6. The great prize which both God and our adversary seek is the passion, trust, worship, love and loyalty of the human heart. The Father seeks worshippers (John 4:23). The devil seeks worship (Matthew 4:9). At the end of the age two women, representing human passion and worship, are brought to fullness—one is false and one is true.

   - The harlot of Revelation 17.
   - The bride of Revelation 19. We will love Him as He loved us.

7. "Revive me in Your way." These two verses are a cry for deliverance from all that is in the world. Let's cry out, along with David, for deliverance from these seductions.

8. Here again we see the cry for divine initiative on the heart so that we have power to overcome sin.

"Establish Your word (*imrah*) to Your servant, who is devoted to fearing You" (v. 38).

1. *The Scriptures* Bible translation renders it this way: "Establish (*quwm*: confirm, cause to stand, set) Your word to Your servant, which leads to the fear of You."

2. The fear of the Lord in scripture is a huge subject. Read Addendum 5 for a fuller discussion of this topic. We will insert a couple of excerpts here.

   - This is the first of five references to fearing God in the psalm. In our western church world, where grace and love are majored on, fearing God seems antithetical to loving God. This is a grave error. Love and fear are not opposite nor are they mutually exclusive. In fact, the one presupposes the other. To truly love God is to fear God and to truly fear God is to love Him. One cannot exist without the other. Listen to the cry of God's heart from Deuteronomy:
     - o Eleven times God says, "that you would love Me."
     - o Four times He adds, "that you would cling to Me" ("in love" is implied).
     - o Fourteen times God desires "that you would fear Me."
     - o Deuteronomy 10:12, "And now, Israel, what does the LORD your God require of you, but to fear the LORD your God, to walk in all His ways and to love Him, to serve the LORD your God with all your heart and with all your soul."
     - o Deuteronomy 13:4, "You shall walk after the LORD your God and fear

Him, and keep His commandments and obey His voice; you shall serve Him and hold fast to Him."

- The result is clear. The most powerful being in the universe, who is Himself a consuming fire of holy passion, and whose name is Jealous, has set His love upon you and bound you to Himself in covenant, and He will not share you with another. Yes, He forgives sin, but even that is so that we fear Him. Psalm 130:3-4 says, "If You, LORD, should mark iniquities, O LORD, who could stand? But there is forgiveness with You, that You may be feared." Do you know what it cost to obtain your forgiveness? The Father paid a terrible price, His Son's death on the cross. One who can casually commit sin, thinking, "God will forgive," neither loves nor fears God!

- Consider Isaiah 66:2, "But on this one will I look: On him who is poor and of a contrite spirit, and who trembles at My word."

- In this verse our psalmist identifies himself as Your servant, one who is poor and of a contrite spirit. He is ready to tremble at the word of God.

- Yes, I know about 1 John 4:17-18, "Love has been perfected among us in this: that we may have boldness in the Day of Judgment; because as He is, so are we in this world. There is no fear in love; but perfect (brought to consummation, end or full completion) love casts out fear, because fear involves torment (*kolasis*: suffering correction, punishment or penalty, hence fear the day of judgment). But he who fears (that day) has not been made perfect in love. We love Him because He first loved us."

  o This is about having confidence in the Day of Judgment, not about the having the true fear of God now.

  o Receive His discipline now: Love Him and fear Him and have nothing to fear on that Day.

- C. S. Lewis wrote of Aslan in *The Chronicles of Narnia,* "He is not a tame Lion,"[3] and again, "He is not safe, but He is good!"[4] *Yeshua* is holy and the inherent power in Him is infinite. His eyes of fire see right through me. His lovingkindness draws me—His inherent power causes me to tremble. It is conceivable that one could experience both sheer delight and sheer terror simultaneously, while burying one's face and hands in the glorious "mane" of the Lion of Judah. Consider:

  o Acts 5:11, Ananais and Sapphira: "Great fear came upon all the church and upon all who heard these things." We can only respond by realizing that we must get right with God!

- o   2 Corinthians 5:10-11, "For we must all appear before the judgment seat of Christ. . . . Knowing, therefore, the terror of the Lord, we persuade men."

- o   Work out your own salvation with fear and trembling (Philippians 2:12).

- o   In Revelation 1:17, John wrote: "When I saw Him (*Yeshua*), I fell at His feet as dead."

- o   Exodus 20:20, "Do not fear; for God has come to test you, and that His fear may be before you, so that you may not sin."

- o   Judgment is more severe in the New Testament than in the Old because the light is greater. Greater light means greater accountability. Consider Matthew 11:20-24. See Addendum 5 for more on fearing God.

3.   Again, the pattern of divine initiative on the heart and human response is seen.

"Turn away my reproach which I dread, for Your judgments are good" (v. 39).

1.   "My reproach which I dread." What is this reproach that he dreads? It seems not to be the reproach of being identified with Messiah that was explored in verse twenty-two. Rather, the reproach which David dreads is that of, having begun the race, now finding that he cannot complete it. It is the reproach that would come if he loses the war of passion in his soul and returns to serving sin and covetousness. This would bring reproach on the name of the Lord, and is precisely the shame from which he wants to be delivered in verse thirty-one.

   - •   1 Timothy 3:7 (of an overseer), "He must have a good testimony among those who are outside, lest he fall into reproach and the snare of the devil."

   - •   1 Corinthians 9:27, "I discipline my body and bring it into subjection, lest, when I have preached to others, I myself should become disqualified."

2.   "Your judgments (right rulings) are good." This is quite a confession when wrestling with the flesh. The Lord's standard for measuring and judging is good. Our psalmist has no complaints against God and His ways. Rather than lower the standard of righteousness in order to accommodate his weakness, David is welcoming God's verdict (judgments) concerning his own carnality. He is confident that God is able to conform him to that standard. He has been declared righteous through his faith, and now he wants to attain to that righteousness as a lifestyle.

"Behold, I long for Your precepts; Revive me in Your righteousness" (v. 40).

1.   "I long." Longing for God is expressed. "As a deer pants for the water brooks, so pants my soul for You, O God! (Psalm 42:1)"

2.   "Revive" occurs twice in this section: "Cause me to live! I need Your grace!"

Concluding Thoughts

Divine initiative is a huge issue. We love Him because He first loved us. If God will teach me (v. 33), give me (v. 34), make me (v. 35), incline my heart (v. 36), turn my eyes (v. 37), establish His word (v. 38), and turn away my reproach (v. 39)—only then am I able (by His grace) to respond in true worship with a pure heart.

Anything else is human religious ambition rooted in pride. Any "success" we may have in defeating our sinful passions and obeying God will only serve to strengthen that pride. Any "failure" will be carefully camouflaged with a show of piety and religious activity.

- Note: Obedience is not legalism.

- Obedience to God's word shows our love for Him. God wants obedience from the heart (see John 14:15, 23).

- Remember the lesson of *bet*: God will do in us what we cannot do on our own if we will but prepare our lives as a sanctuary for His presence. He receives the glory!

In legalism, we are more committed to God than He is to us. We try to motivate God to take an interest in us when, in fact, He takes interest in us because of who He is. Legalism presupposes that we are more passionate for God than He is for us. To think that we can offer God something greater than what He has freely given to us is heresy.

Because of its pronunciation, the sages refer to the letter *hey* as the airy letter. Hence, the letter *hey* can symbolize the Spirit (breath) of God. This is precisely what grace is about. If God moves on our hearts by His Spirit, initiating our journey into Christ-likeness, we will have power to respond, to overcome and to walk as He walked (1 John 2:6).

Questions to Ponder

1.   In what ways may I have defined myself through my sin and weakness?

2.   In what ways have I presented my heart to the Lord as a tablet for Him to write upon?

3.   Can I recall a time when I obeyed God when it was difficult—a time when grace came and somehow God did something through me that I could not have done on my own? How did God receive the glory? Was there a sense of happiness and fullness that came to me thereafter?

Chapter 8

Nothing Can Separate:
A Revelation of the Love of God

Vav

⁴¹Let Your mercies come also to me, O LORD—
Your salvation according to Your word.
⁴²So shall I have an answer for him who reproaches me,
For I trust in Your word.
⁴³And take not the word of truth utterly out of my mouth,
For I have hoped in Your ordinances.
⁴⁴So shall I keep Your law continually,
Forever and ever.
⁴⁵And I will walk at liberty,
For I seek Your precepts.
⁴⁶I will speak of Your testimonies also before kings,
And will not be ashamed.
⁴⁷And I will delight myself in Your commandments,
Which I love.
⁴⁸My hands also I will lift up to Your commandments,
Which I love,
And I will meditate on Your statutes.

Vav—Psalm 119:41-48

Our psalmist has come to faith for this journey in verse thirty-two with a bold confession based on the certainty that God will actually change the desires of his heart. "I will run the course of Your commandments, for You will enlarge my heart." In the last section (*hey*) he clearly asks the Lord to do just that: enlarge his heart.

Now in *vav*, it is apparent that God responds to David's prayer in *hey* with revelation, so that in verse forty-one, our psalmist sees something of the power of God's love (*chesed*, rendered as mercies) and the extent of His salvation. His prayer, "Let Your *chesed* come to me," shows him reaching in faith to receive the promise of God (like Mary did in Luke 1:38). What ensues are bold commitments—the exact opposite of the ambivalence we saw in *dalet*. David now makes seven powerful faith-filled commitments which are rooted in this revelation of the love of God for him.

The ancient pictograph of *vav* depicts that of a nail or peg. This speaks of adding to, as in the word "and," or of connecting, fastening and securing things together. With this revelation of divine love from heaven, the first connection is heaven and earth. The second connection is our psalmist becoming fastened to (rooted and grounded in) that love. This is what inspired his bold faith and the seven commitments. The word *vav* is used in Exodus 27:9-10 to refer to the hooks of silver fastened to posts which were used to hold the curtains of the tabernacle.

The key word in this first verse of the section is the very first occurrence of the Hebrew word *chesed*. *Chesed* is the primary Hebrew word for the love of God, and occurs 250 times in the Hebrew Scriptures. It is variously translated as mercy, kindness or lovingkindness.

This revelation of the love of God is so powerful that it anchors David forever in this love. In Ephesians 3:17-19, Paul prays "that you, being rooted and grounded in love, may be able to comprehend with all the saints what is the width and length and depth and height—to know the love of Messiah which passes knowledge." Romans 8:31-39 is utterly powerful in its assertion that nothing can separate us from the love of God.

The entire life of our shepherd/king, who I believe wrote this psalm, is rooted in the revelation of this love and kindness. See the Davidic psalms and scriptures like 2 Samuel 12:22; 24:14. The great theme song of David's tabernacle, which occurs some thirty-eight times in scripture, is "O give thanks to the LORD, for He is good. For His mercy (*chesed*) endures forever" (1 Chronicles 16:34, 41; 2 Chronicles 5:13; 7:3; Psalm 106:1; 107:1; 118:1-4, 29; 136:1-26; 138:8). God's kindness is legendary and from of old (Psalm 25:6; Ex 34:6-7). David has just been fastened to and secured in (nailed to) the love of God!

This revelation produced seven powerful commitments from David. Seven times he confesses, "I will . . ." or "I shall . . . ." It is almost as if he is saying, "God, if You are like that, bring on the devil. I can't fail." His confidence is overflowing. His confidence, however, is in the mercy of God and not in the power of his own commitment, though he is, by these confessions, making commitments.

Let's say it another way: We need to have more confidence in the power of God's commitment to us than we do in the power of our commitment to Him. "He is the One who is able to keep us from falling" (Jude 2:24). Let's join David now in his journey.

"Let Your mercies come also to me, O LORD—Your salvation according to Your word" (v. 41).

1. This is the first occurrence of the word mercies (*chesed*) in Psalm 119. When the psalmist asks that God's mercies would come to him, he is asking for the experi-

ence of God's mercy, which is salvation (deliverance and breakthrough). These are not due to the victories he is gaining in his walk, but are purely based on the Lord's mercy and kindness.

2. David's appeal to the mercy of God is legendary. Twice, when David had sinned greatly and was experiencing the consequences of that sin, he shamelessly appealed to God's mercy.

    •   In 2 Samuel 12, David's child by Bathsheba was dying. Nathan had assured him that the child would surely die (v. 14). David gave himself to fasting, weeping and praying that the child would live. Now look at verse twenty-two. "While the child was alive, I fasted and wept; for I said, 'Who can tell whether the LORD will be gracious (merciful) to me, that the child may live?'"

    •   When David was being disciplined for numbering Israel in 2 Samuel 24, he said in verse 14: "Please let us fall into the hand of the LORD, for His mercies (compassions) are great."

3. *Yeshua* said in Luke 11:8, "I say to you, though he will not rise and give to him because he is his friend, yet because of his persistence (*anaideia*: shamelessness, brazen persistence, audacity or nerve) he will rise and give him as many as he needs."

    •   David often seemed shameless, almost brazen, in his requests of the Lord, because he knew the kindness of God toward him.

    •   Joel 2:14, "Who knows if He will turn and relent (from judgment), and leave a blessing behind Him?"

4. The point is this: weak broken humans can move the heart of God with their cry. In fact, the root of the word salvation (*t\eshuwah*) is cried. Many are the men and women of scripture who moved the heart of God with their cry. It is not about our merit. It is about God hearing the cry of His people and being moved by mercy. If that is God's nature, then we have every reason to hope.

"So shall I have an answer for him who reproaches me, for I trust in Your word" (v. 42).

1. "Him who reproaches" (*charaph*: taunts). Who could this be? The Hebrew word translated reproach in verse twenty-two and again in verse thirty-nine is a derivative of the Hebrew root *charaph*. This is the only place in the psalm that *charaph* occurs. It means to taunt.

2. Is taunting not the work of the "accuser of our brethren," the adversary, who "accused them (the saints) before our God day and night" (Revelation 12:10)? God is in heaven, but He also lives in every believer, hence we get to hear every accusation.

3. **Confession # 1:** "So shall I have an answer." This is the first of the seven confessions or commitments mentioned at the beginning of this chapter. How can you confidently answer the accuser? Certainly not on the basis of your performance. You may have just failed (as we suppose David did in verses 21-23) and with all these sinful passions raging in your members, you might feel that the accuser could be right. But, no. A thousand times no. A revelation of the heavenly Father's mercy will make you confident of who you are in His sight, even in your weakness. What parent will scold a young child for falling while he is learning to walk? Rather, that parent delights in the child's efforts. How much more will the Lord, who is rich in mercy, delight in His children as they learn to walk?

4. Note the order of themes in these two verses. It is precisely what *Yeshua* experienced. First the affirmation of being loved by the Father and then the test in the wilderness by the devil, or, "him who reproaches" (Mark 1:11-12).

    *   "Your mercies"—a revelation of the love of God in verse 41.

    *   "Him who reproaches"—He is put to the test in verse 42.

5. Consider the order of things at *Yeshua's* baptism recorded in Mark 1:9-13:

    *   Heavens opened and the Spirit descended like a dove. Then, a voice from heaven saying, "You are My beloved Son, in whom I am well pleased."

        o   A revelation of the Father's love

    *   Immediately the Spirit drove Him into the wilderness.

        o   Put to the test by the devil. Three times the adversary came with this taunt, "If you are the Son of God . . . ."

6. A primary tactic of our adversary is to call into question our relationship with the Father. "If you are the Son of God" is a loaded statement. It suggests that God is not pleased with His Son and that His Son is not secure in that identity. One of the characteristics of temptation is that it makes us feel defiled before we have even sinned, because it connects with the sin which yet resides in our members. If a son or daughter is not secured to (*vav*) the Father in love, and confident of his identity as a child of God, he will more easily give in to the lust of the flesh, the lust of the eyes or the pride of life as discussed in *hey.*

7. It was ultimately this taunter whom David was up against in the battle of *dalet* (v. 25-32). The accuser comes at a time of weakness ("my soul clings to the dust"), when we are very aware of sinful passions within and shortcomings without. He came to *Yeshua* in the wilderness immediately after *Yeshua* was weakened by a forty-day fast. Do these lines sound familiar?

    • "If you are the Son of God . . . ?"

    • "Did God really say . . . ?"

    • "Who do you think you are? You will never make it. You will never change. You are a loser. God does things for others, but you are just too. . . ." The accusations continue until your "soul melts from heaviness" (v. 28).

8. It is as if David is saying, "I will be ready for him the next time. Now I know what to say."

9. "For I trust (*batach*: have confidence, feel safe, run to find refuge) in Your word." This is the only occurrence of *batach* in our psalm. What word, exactly, is he running to for refuge? It is the revelation of God's mercies (v.41) and the knowledge that God loves him. If the taunter has convinced you that God is surprised by your failure and is renegotiating the covenant He has with you, then you will relate to Him accordingly. What if you have concluded the wrong thing? Maybe God knew about your sin before you did, yet chose you anyway! Was God surprised when David sinned with Bathsheba?

10. If you have concluded that God is mostly sad (or mad) when He looks at you with all your failings and weaknesses, you will carry your heart toward Him accordingly. Again, what if you are wrong about that? What if God is wildly in love with you? Try running to these words for refuge:

    • Isaiah 62: 5, "As the bridegroom rejoices over the bride, so shall your God rejoice over you."

    • Zephaniah 3:17, "The LORD your God in your midst, the Mighty One, will save; He will rejoice over you with gladness, He will quiet you with His love, He will rejoice over you with singing."

    • Maybe it's not about whether you had a good day or a bad one. Maybe it's more about who He is in His character and personhood. God likes people and He never has a bad day. (Unlike the Lord, your boss might snap at you just because he is having a bad day, and maybe his frustration actually has nothing to do with you).

"And take not the word of truth utterly out of my mouth, for I have hoped in Your ordinances" (v. 43).

1. "The word of truth"—that which is absolutely dependable, trustworthy and is established forever. His mercy endures forever. This is your answer to the one who reproaches. You do the same thing *Yeshua* did. When taunted in the wilderness with the words "If you are the Son of God. . . ," *Yeshua*, who trusted in God's word, answered, "It is written."

    *   The Father of Lights has, of His own will, brought us forth (begotten us) by the word of truth, that we might be "a kind of first fruits of His creatures" (James 1:18). James goes on to say that the man who is not a doer of God's word has "forgotten what kind of man he was" as one begotten of God (James 1:23-24).

    *   When the enemy questions your identity in a time of weakness, boldly declare, "His mercy endures forever." You are not defined by your weak flesh, but by what your heavenly Father has revealed about Himself and about how He feels about you as a child begotten of Him. The Father of Lights, with whom there is no shadow of turning, has not changed His mind about you.

2. "Hope (*yachal*: wait expectantly, hope) in Your ordinances" (*mishpat:*) This Hebrew word is usually translated as judgments or right rulings. God waits while we battle the one who reproaches, and when the time is right, He issues a ruling which delivers us from our adversary. David knows that sooner or later God will come in power with a ruling, and he is waiting expectantly (see Job 13:15-16).

"So shall I keep Your law continually, forever and ever" (v. 44).

Confession # 2 is pronounced here. The psalmist's faith is soaring!

1. "Keep Your law." David knows he will make it to the end, no matter how long the battle.

2. "Continually" (*tamiyd*: to stretch indefinitely, perpetuity, constantly, with no lapse).

3. "Forever" (*olawm*: to the vanishing point, time out of mind, eternity, antiquity).

4. "And ever" (*'ad: terminus*, perpetual advance all the way to the finishing point, continuing future).

    This is intense. We have three different Hebrew words, capturing eternity past to eternity future, with no lapses in between.

What kind of confidence is this? Not only did our psalmist have a revelation of God's mercy, he must have been given a prophetic glimpse of where and how he would finish. Maybe he caught a glimpse of the city with foundations, whose builder and maker is God—the city John saw coming down out of heaven prepared as a bride adorned for her husband. Maybe he saw his own destiny in a dream in much the same way as Joseph did in Genesis 37. Maybe he saw himself in the heart of God from eternity past, "chosen in Him before the foundation of the world, that we (he) should be holy and without blame before Him in love" (Psalm 139:15-17; Ephesians 1:4). We don't know exactly what he saw, but his confidence is immense.

Heaven and earth seem to have connected (*vav*) for a moment at this point!

"And I will walk at liberty, for I seek Your precepts (v. 45).

1. **Confession # 3:** "And I will walk at liberty" refers to a broad place as opposed to narrow straits of affliction and pressure. What is David saying?

   - "I will walk *The Blessed Life*!"

   - "I will overcome the issues of my soul," which he has been dealing with during the last two sections.

   - "I will walk in my destiny." In Psalm 18:19, it finally happened for David.

2. "For I seek Your precepts" (*piqquwd*). Remember from the introduction that God's precepts provide the consistent presence, oversight and boundaries that allow a child to feel secure and joyful. These precepts will preside over his life and attend to his destiny and security. They will see to his ultimate triumph.

"I will speak of Your testimonies also before kings, and will not be ashamed" (v. 46).

1. **Confession # 4:** "I will speak . . . before kings."

   - Peter trembled before a servant-girl and denied the Lord. Then he boldly preached before great crowds and kings. What happened to him?

   - Elijah boldly stood before King Ahab and prophesied that it would not rain.

   - *Yeshua* promised that we would be brought before governors and kings, but said that we should not worry, because "it will be given you in that hour what you shall speak" (Matthew 10:18).

2. He is fearless and unashamed before kings, who with a word could have him killed. What is happening to our psalmist? He declares that he will not be intimidated or defeated! See Acts 6:10.

3.   Ponder for a moment the prevailing role that fear often plays in our walk with the Lord. How many times does the Lord tell those whom He calls not to fear or not to be afraid? If just being directed by the Holy Spirit to tell someone about God's love causes us to tremble with fear, what would happen if we were commanded to go to Pharaoh and demand that he release his slaves. It is no accident that we have these scriptures:

   - Mark 8:38, "For whoever is ashamed of Me and My words in this adulterous and sinful generation, of him the Son of Man also will be ashamed when He comes in the glory of His Father with the holy angels."

   - Acts 4:29, "Now, Lord, look on their threats, and grant to Your servants that with all boldness they may speak Your word."

   - Romans 1:16, "For I am not ashamed of the gospel of Messiah."

Where is our psalmist's boldness coming from? These are bold confessions, but they are not mere hype because they are rooted in the revelation of the Lord's mercy and in the certainty and truth of the word of God, rather than in human resolve.

"And I will delight myself in Your commandments (*mitsvah*), which I love" (v. 47).

1.   **Confession # 5:** "And I will delight." David is confident that he will delight in being told, by the Lord, what to do. He is committing ahead of time to delight in these *mitsvah* no matter what. It is as if he is saying, "I will do anything and go anywhere You want me to, Lord!"

2.   1 John 5:3-4, "For whatever is born of God overcomes the world. For this is the love of God, that we keep His commandments. And His commandments are not burdensome." Why are His commands not burdensome? Two reasons are given in this text:

   - We love Him and are confident of His love.

   - Obedience to God's commands is the faith that overcomes the world.

3.   *Yeshua* said, "It is My food to do the will of Him who sent Me, and to finish His work" (John 4:34). Why could *Yeshua* say this? For the same two reasons found in 1 John 5:3-4:

   - He loved the Father and lived to please Him.

   - Every time He obeyed a command of the Father, heaven's power was released and the kingdom advanced. In other words, He overcame the world.

"My hands (*kaph*) also I will lift up to Your commandments (*mitsvah*), which I love, and I will meditate on Your statutes" (v. 48).

1. **Confession # 6:** "I will lift up (*nasa'*: lift up, bear up, carry, take)." Nowhere else in Scripture is there a lifting of the hands to the commandments. This is almost certainly about accepting the burden or yoke of the commandments, which according to 1 John 5:3, is not burdensome because of love. Again, "I will do anything; I will go anywhere You want me to, Lord. I am Yours!"

   - The rabbis of old taught their disciples the *torah* as they interpreted it. This became the yoke of the *torah* that their disciples took up. Some rabbis had heavier yokes than others, depending on the austerity or lenience of their school of thought.

   - In Acts 15:10, Peter addressed those from Judea who taught that one must be circumcised in order to be saved. Acts 15:1, "Why do you test God by putting a yoke on the neck of the disciples which neither our fathers nor we were able to bear?"

   - In Matthew 11:29-30, Rabbi *Yeshua* says: "Take My yoke upon you and learn from Me, for I am gentle and lowly in heart, and you will find rest for your souls. For My yoke is easy and My burden is light."

   - 1 John 5:3 says, "For this is the love of God, that we keep His commandments. And His commandments are not burdensome."

2. **"Hands" (*kaph*):** This is the open palm of the hand lifted up as if giving something to the Lord and/or receiving something from Him. There is an exchange between heaven and earth. David's worship is going up and David's destiny (the call of God) is coming down as he accepts the call of God upon his life.

   - Paul writes in 1 Timothy 2:8, "I desire therefore that the men pray everywhere, lifting up holy hands, without wrath and doubting." Many are the references in scripture to the raising of hands in worship.

3. **"Which I love."** Twice in just two verses our psalmist expresses his love and once he expresses his delight for God's commandments. Wow. He seems to be having a visitation of some kind!

4. **Confession # 7:** "I will meditate (*siyach*: to put forth, commune, ponder, speak or sing) on Your statutes." David is committing the inner world of his soul (the words of his mouth, the meditations of his heart, his thoughts and longings) to be focused upon the Lord's statutes (*choq*—that which is permanent and unchanging versus that which is of this world and passing away). He is setting his heart to live in the light of eternity.

Concluding Thoughts

Another look at *chesed* reveals that the root word means "the faithful one" or "the loyal one." The idea then, is one of an obligation of kindness based upon and appropriate to the level of relationship. God chooses us as His sons and daughters and brings us into a covenant relationship with Himself. This obligates Him as a Father to show to us the level of kindness due His own children. Hence, a fuller meaning of *chesed* is faithful or loyal kindness. Consider 2 Timothy 2:13, "If we are faithless, He remains faithful; He cannot deny Himself."

Our psalmist is soaring. Gone is the ambivalence of *dalet*. These are bold confessions. But they are not presumptuous nor are they rooted in mere human resolve. They are rooted in the revelation of the Lord's *chesed*—His faithful kindness. Heaven and earth are connecting (*vav*) as David sees eternity and glimpses something of his destiny in the Lord. He has been anchored in (*vav*), fastened to, the love of God. His hope of victory is remarkable. Romans 5:5 links fulfilled expectations with the fact that "the love of God has been poured out in our hearts by the Holy Spirit." Can anything ever separate us from Messiah's love? We will see. *Zayin* begins a new season.

Romans 8:37-39, "Yet in all these things we are more than conquerors through Him who loved us. For I am persuaded that neither death nor life, nor angels nor principalities nor powers, nor things present nor things to come, nor height nor depth, nor any other created thing, shall be able to separate us from the love of God which is in Christ Jesus our Lord."

Questions to Ponder

1. How has a revelation of the kindness of God given you confidence in your walk with the Lord? Pray Ephesians 3:17 over your heart: "That you, being rooted and grounded in love, may be able to comprehend with all the saints what is the width and length and depth and height—to know the love of Christ which passes knowledge."

2. In Psalm 18:29, David said, "For by You I can run against a troop, by my God I can leap over a wall." On what occasions have you experienced a similar burst of confident boldness? Have you had similar experiences where it seemed that heaven came down and assured you that you will overcome all obstacles?

3. Can you identify with a fainthearted Peter as he stands before that servant girl at the trial of *Yeshua* and denies his Lord?

4. Have you also known the boldness to speak openly concerning your faith in *Yeshua*, as Peter did in Acts 2, after being filled with the Holy Spirit?

Chapter 9

Remember

Zayin

⁴⁹Remember the word to Your servant,
Upon which You have caused me to hope.
⁵⁰This is my comfort in my affliction,
For Your word has given me life.
⁵¹The proud have me in great derision,
Yet I do not turn aside from Your law.
⁵²I remembered Your judgments of old, O LORD,
And have comforted myself.
⁵³Indignation has taken hold of me
Because of the wicked, who forsake Your law.
⁵⁴Your statutes have been my songs
In the house of my pilgrimage.
⁵⁵I remember Your name in the night, O LORD,
And I keep Your law.
⁵⁶This has become mine,
Because I kept Your precepts.

Zayin: Psalm 119:49-56

The ancient pictograph of our seventh letter, *zayin*, is that of an instrument like a sword, plow or a weapon. It can speak of cutting off or of warfare. Many in scripture, David, Joseph, Moses and Messiah for starters, spent time cut off from their own people. *Zayin* is also connected with the Hebrew words, *zakar* and *zikrown*, which mean remember and remembrance respectively. It is interesting to note that the very first word of our segment is *zakar*, which appears two more times, for a total of three. Neither *zakar* nor any of its derivatives appear anywhere else in the entire psalm. This is definitely a key to understanding this section.

When Samuel the prophet came to Jesse's house in 1 Samuel 16 to anoint one of his sons as the next king of Israel, David was not even considered as a possibility. He was somehow the least of the sons. However, after God refused David's seven older brothers, David was called in and subsequently chosen. And the LORD said, "Arise, anoint him; for this is the one . . . and the Spirit of the LORD came upon David from that time forward" (1 Samuel 16:12-13). It sounds similar to the glorious encounter of the previous section, *vav*, where David discovers his chosenness , or his special status and calling as a beloved son of God (see Exodus 19:5-6; Deuteronomy 7:6; 1 Peter 2:9).

Joseph also had a glorious encounter with God via dreams in Genesis 37. He was anointed as a chosen and special son of Jacob, with his coat of many colors. In those dreams he saw the glory of God and had a glimpse of his destiny in the plan of God for redemption. For both David and Joseph, this chosenness and anointing provoked great jealousy in those around them, especially among their own brothers. Both ended up being cut off from their families. Messiah was cut off from the land of the living (Isaiah 53:8) by His brethren because of envy (Matthew 27:18). *Zayin* is all about this jealousy and subsequent betrayal when faith in God's promise is put to the test. It is about remembering (*zakar*) the word of the Lord and His promises concerning redemption and destiny.

The search for comfort in my affliction (v. 50) introduces a new and negative experience —that of betrayal by his brethren. We understand the text in this way for several reasons:

1. Betrayal is a biblical pattern.

2. The letter *zayin* hints at the idea of being cut off, and the obvious context indicates that the separation is from family. Our psalmist is living in what he calls "the house of my pilgrimage" (v. 54).

3. In 1 Samuel 17:28, David's brother Eliab became angry with David and promptly unleashed a hurtful accusation. Later, David's own king, King Saul, turned on him in jealousy.

4. Jealousy. We can't stand it when God anoints our kid brother or those we deem weak or undeserving. It ruffles our pride and threatens our ambitions. Consider the role of jealousy in the persecution and cutting off of the following:

    -   Abel by Cain (Genesis 4).
    -   Joseph by his brothers (Genesis 37).
    -   David by Eliab, his older brother, and later by Saul, his king (1 Samuel 17:28; 19).
    -   Moses by his own people whom he sought to help (Exodus 2:13-14).
    -   *Yeshua* by the His brethren, the Jews, whom He came to save (Matthew 27:18).
    -   Israel by the nations (Exodus 19:5; Deuteronomy 7:6-7).

Addendum 4 develops more fully the theme of offenses and their role in our personal formation. This explosive nitro-meets-glycerin dynamic of jealousy is a strategy of the Lord to accomplish numerous things, among which are:

- Dealing with the carnality of the one who is called and anointed, helping to forge in him *Yeshua's* character, so that he can steward authority without being corrupted. Both David and Joseph were destined for a throne. This is how God raises up a deliverer.

- Dealing with the carnality of the brethren so that they can humble themselves to receive the deliverance which God intends to accomplish through the one who is called and anointed. All of David's family and all of Israel benefited from David's leadership as king in Israel. All of Joseph's brethren benefited from Joseph's role of leadership in Egypt.

Let's join our psalmist now and see how he responds to persecution from his own brethren.

"Remember the word to Your servant, upon which You have caused me to hope" (v. 49).

1. "Remember (*zakar*: recount, recall, mention, rehearse) the word to Your servant, upon which You have caused me to hope" (*yachal*: wait expectantly, hope, expect). This is almost certainly a reference to David's encounter with the Lord in *vav*, where he had a prophetic glimpse of his destiny or received a promise of some kind.

2. David is waiting expectantly for fulfillment of the promise, but something is happening which is causing him to reach back to recall it. He is reminding the Lord of what was promised so as to answer the accuser (the one who reproaches mentioned in verse 42).

"This is my comfort in my affliction, for Your word has given me life" (v. 50).

1. "Comfort (*nechamah*: consolation) in my affliction (*oniy*: affliction, poverty, misery, depression). This is a sudden turn from the elated emotions of *vav*. The root of this word means to sigh, breathe or be sorry. This is the first and only occurrence of this word in the psalm. It introduces a whole new negative experience, season of difficulty and testing.

2. "Your word has given me life." Our psalmist is rehearsing that last encounter with the Lord and seeking comfort and hope from the promise of life that he received.

We note here the occurrence of a scriptural pattern that is repeated over and over in the lives of those who walked with God. It is one of the wise ways of God, connected with the principle of keeping the word (Addendum 1). God employs this principle in the process of forming deliverers and co-laborers out of sinful human beings who were once His enemies (Romans 5:10).

The principle is simply this—God's day begins in the evening. "So the evening and the morning was the first day" (Genesis 1:5).

In other words, the day begins at sunset with a little ray of light, such as a prophetic word. Then it is plunged into the darkness of night, with the only hope being to await the dawning of a new day. 2 Peter 1:19, "So we have the prophetic word confirmed, which you do well to heed as a light that shines in a dark place, until the day dawns and the morning star rises in your hearts."

Ponder the centrality and power of hope in the life of a believer (v. 49); the hope of a promise being fulfilled and the hope of a new day. Consider in scripture some illustrations of this principle of having a promise (hope) and then persevering in faith until the promise is fulfilled:

1. Abraham was promised descendants as numerous as the stars (a little ray of light), but Sarah was barren. Now what? Abraham waited many years to see his promise fulfilled.

2. God promised to give Israel a land flowing with milk and honey (a little ray of light) and the first place they arrived as they left Egypt was the wilderness, the precise opposite of the promise. Now what? Was it all a lie?

3. In an exciting encounter with God, Joseph received a great promise concerning his destiny. He would have a throne (a little ray of light). But the next thing he knew, he was in a pit looking up at the men who had bowed down to him in the dream (Genesis 37:5-10). Now what? Was the dream (the word of God) false? Psalm 105:19 says that "until the time that his word came to pass, the word of the LORD tested him."

4. David was anointed to become king, received the Holy Spirit, and was promised the throne in Israel (a little ray of light). But the next thing he knew, his own brothers scorned him and he was running for his life from King Saul. Now what? Would he ever rule?

This all connects to the principle of keeping the word which is discussed at length in Addendum 1. The question is this: "What will you do when the enemy comes to attack or steal the promise you have been given?" The temptation is always to conclude that God's word is not true. We are taunted with the question: "Did God really say?" In *Yeshua's* parable of the sower and the seed (Matthew 13:3-23), it was the seed (the word of the kingdom in verse nineteen) which was under constant attack. But when there is a delay, that is the time it is important to remember (recall, rehearse) that word. Do not abort the seed of God's word from your heart. The life is in the seed and it has the power to bring itself to pass if we will keep it in the womb of our spirit.

God requires us to walk by faith through the long dark night, with only a promise to hold on to. We are to be just like Abraham, who believed God, "who gives life to the dead and calls those things which do not exist as though they did; who, contrary to hope, in hope believed, so that he became the father of many nations, according to what was spoken" (Romans 4:17-18).

A related truth is this: we taste now, in this present evil age, the power of the age (day) to come. Light is light, whether it is the fading light of the evening or the brightness of a new day. That little bit of light in the evening is a down-payment or foretaste of what will come in fullness when the new day dawns or when the promise is fulfilled. The Holy Spirit is the guarantee of our inheritance until the redemption—the new day (Ephesians 1:14). This is what our psalmist experienced in the previous stage, *vav*. He tasted something of the goodness and favor of God, and he seems to have received a promise from God regarding his destiny.

"The proud have me in great derision, yet I do not turn aside from Your law" (v. 51).

1. "The proud" show up again. We met them in verse twenty-one of *gimel*, but here, they are probably our psalmist's own brethren.

    - The reproach and contempt of *gimel* was in context to the proud and those princes who spoke against him because of his testimony in a world that hates *Yeshua*. This is the reproach of Messiah noted in Hebrews 11:26.

    - "The reproach which I dread" (v. 39 of *hey*) was connected to the scandal of his own sin issues which surfaced in *dalet* (v. 25-32).

2. "Great derision" means to scorn and show contempt, disdain, or ridicule:

    - This reproach (if we may call it that), the great derision of the proud, is new.

    - David faced great derision from Eliab in 1 Samuel 17:28, "Eliab's anger was aroused against David, and he said, 'Why did you come down here? And with whom have you left those few sheep in the wilderness? I know your pride and the insolence of your heart, for you have come down to see the battle.'"

    - Joseph's proud brothers demonstrate contempt and derision with these words: "We shall see what will become of his dreams" (Genesis 37:20). After all, Joseph is just their kid brother, born to the "other wife."

- David also had a promise of becoming king in Israel. One day he finds himself playing the harp in King Saul's palace. He is getting close, inside the palace, serving the king. Could this be the fulfillment? Suddenly Saul turns on David and throws his spear in a jealousy-fueled attempt to kill him. David runs for his life.

3. "I do not turn aside from Your law" (*torah*). This is our psalmist's response.

    - In verse 49, David recalled the promise on which he had set his hope.

    - Here he is speaking about a righteous response toward those through whom this offense has come. Eliab's cutting accusation in 1 Samuel 17:28 could certainly have provoked a sinful response from David. The question is this: how will our psalmist respond to this injustice?

"I remembered Your judgments of old, O LORD, and have comforted myself" (v. 52).

- This is a strategic use of judgments. In a time when the proud seem to prevail against the righteous, will God set everything right? He did in the past (of old) and He will again as our psalmist passes the tests that offenses and injustice entail. Refresh your understanding of this powerful word in Addendum 4.

- "I remembered." First David recalled the promise of God concerning himself (v. 49), now he is recounting God's powerful deliverances in history. God is the same yesterday, today and forever. He will ultimately deliver.

- There is great comfort in the truth that He (Messiah) "will not fail nor be discouraged, till He has established justice (His judgments) in the earth" (Isaiah 42:4). The new day will dawn and wrong things will ultimately be set right. "Weeping may endure for a night, but joy comes in the morning" (Psalm 30:5). Meanwhile, God is working inside of our psalmist to expose every unrighteous impulse which has not yet been crucified.

"Indignation has taken hold of me because of the wicked, who forsake Your law" (v. 53).

1. "Indignation" (*zalaphah*: burning heat, raging heat—as consuming). The root of this word means to fret, to be vexed, sad, or enraged. This is a powerful human response to injustice: "It's just wrong."

2. "Because of the wicked, who forsake God's law." Those who forsake God's law are "getting away with murder" and our psalmist, who is not turning aside from the law (v. 51), is suffering for doing the right thing and for being chosen by God. The

wicked, those proud who hold him in great derision, are prospering while he, who did the right thing, is suffering (perhaps experiencing serious loss). Read Psalm 92 and 94.

3.   This indignation could be a righteous indignation such as zeal for God and His law. However, at this stage of the journey, it seems to be mixed with our psalmist's own flesh; a real and pure zeal for the Lord comes later. Here, the situation just exasperates him. Every carnal instinct within is coming alive. What to do? The answer is to repent of the unrighteousness that is exposed within your own soul, and allow God to be the avenger of the wicked. Seize this opportunity to be conformed into the image of Messiah.

   • Romans 12:19 (ESV), "Beloved, never avenge yourselves, but leave it to the wrath of God, for it is written, 'Vengeance is mine, I will repay, says the Lord.'"

   • Remember *Yeshua's* words while on the cross in Luke 23:34. "Father, forgive them, for they do not know what they do."

   • Remember Stephen's response to his persecutors in Acts 7:60, "Lord, do not charge them with this sin."

"Your statutes have been my songs in the house of my pilgrimage" (v. 54).

1.   "Your statutes" (*choq*) are eternal truths that never change in any age or situation. Our psalmist knows that God does not change. What was right in the past is still right. What was judged in history will again be judged.

   • The psalms are all about singing and meditating on the word of God.

   • This is a faith-fostering discipline in a season when the wicked are prospering against the righteous. It will hold you steady when nothing makes sense.

2.   "My songs." *Zamiy* means song or psalm and comes from the idea of singing or making music, especially with stringed instruments.

3.   "In the house of my pilgrimage." Our psalmist has been cut off and is estranged from his home. David lived in caves, with the Philistines and then in Ziglag. Joseph lived in Egypt in Potiphar's house and then in prison. Moses lived in Midian. These were temporary dwellings until they received the fullness of the promises of God for their lives.

   • There is also the house (sanctuary) we prepare within ourselves as discussed in *bet* (v. 9-16). It is the house we live in and prepare as a sanctuary for the Lord—a house of worship while sojourning here as strangers in a fallen world (v. 19).

- David is also part of a corporate house, the House of Israel (the congregation or the church), in which God dwells. This has become the source of his test.

- Pilgrimage: Pilgrims are sojourners who travel toward a destination. Nomads just wander around looking for provision. David is on a journey to a glorious destination.

"I remember Your name in the night, O LORD, and I keep Your law" (v. 55).

1. "Remember." This is the third and final occurrence of this word in this section.

2. "Your name," To remember the Lord's name is to recount His nature—who He is. He is all-powerful, faithful to His word, righteous in all His ways and much more. "The Name of the LORD is a strong tower: The righteous run to it and are safe" (Proverbs 18:10). "I will meditate on the glorious splendor of Your majesty and on Your wonderful works" (Psalm 145:5). Reading or reciting Psalm 91 also provides a powerful meditation on the nature of God.

3. "In the night." This is the first occurrence of the word night. Evening has given way to night. Our psalmist is going to be required to walk by faith until the dawning of a new day brings the fulfillment of his promise.

4. David's determination is to keep God's law. Though the wicked, through whom this injustice has come, forsake the *torah* (v.53), David is focused on a righteous response.

    A question to ponder: To what degree must we be sinned against before a sinful response is justified?

"This has become mine, because I kept Your precepts" (v. 56).

1. Hope, comfort, songs in the house, God's law, God's name, God's promises. . . all have become our psalmist's possession (mine) for setting the course of keeping the Lord's precepts. The psalmist has not come out from under the attending, overseeing precepts of God to do things his own way, things like vengeance, retaliation or unbelief in the promise.

2. The psalmist is counting his blessings in the night. Things may not be working in the natural realm, but our psalmist still has the Lord and "every spiritual blessing in the heavenly places in Christ" (Ephesians 1:3). God told Abram in Genesis 15:1, "Do not be afraid, Abram. I am your shield, your exceedingly great reward." They can take all your stuff and sell you into slavery, but they cannot take your primary reward—the Lord Himself.

Warfare

Zayin is a sword. Israel had to fight for the Promised Land. Paul taught Timothy to follow the prophecies previously made concerning him so that by them he would be able to wage good warfare (1 Timothy 1:18). Is God's promise sure? Did God really say. . .? There are three things to remember (*zakar*: recount, rehearse, recall) as we contend for the promise of God to be fulfilled in our lives:

- "Your word" (v. 49)—God is faithful and true.
- "Your judgments of old" (v. 52)—God is righteous and He will act.
- "Your Name" (v. 55)—God is good; He is love; He is kind.

Concluding Thoughts

In this part of the psalm, it seems as if God and Satan are picking teams. God is famous for choosing (this is election) the little guy for His team—the youngest one, seemingly with the least natural ability or gifting. He then clothes him with favor, a coat of many colors if you will, and gives promises of greatness. Ponder the following:

1. 1 Corinthians 1:26-27, "For you see your calling, brethren, that not many wise according to the flesh, not many mighty, not many noble. But God has chosen the foolish things of the world to put to shame the wise, and God has chosen the weak things of the world to put to shame the things which are mighty; and the base things of the world and the things which are despised God has chosen, and the things which are not, to bring to nothing the things that are, that no flesh should glory in His presence."

2. Deuteronomy 7:7, "The LORD did not set His love on you (Israel) nor choose you because you were greater than any other people, for you were the least of all peoples."

3. Examples of God's sovereign election include the following:

    - Isaac over Ishmael and Jacob over Esau. Isaac and Jacob got the blessing and the birthright. Jacob fled from Esau and Ishmael persecutes Isaac to this day.

    - Israel over the nations. "A special treasure to Me above all peoples . . . a kingdom of priests and a holy nation" (Exodus 19:5-6).

    - David over his brothers: "And the Spirit of the LORD came upon David from that day forward" (1 Samuel 16:13).

    - Joseph over his brothers: "Israel loved Joseph more than all his children, because he was the was the son of his old age. Also he made him a tunic of many colors" (Genesis 37:3).

- *Yeshua*, born to a peasant couple from Nazareth, was chosen over His brothers: "Can any good thing come out of Nazareth?"

This strategy of election is both good news and bad news for the chosen one. Being secure in Father's love and in His chosen destiny for us inspires great love and rejoicing toward the Lord. Being clothed with favor and possessing promises of greatness is a source of great hope and confidence.

On the other hand, it seems that it is Israel's very chosenness that precipitates her troubles. Romans 11:29 tells us that "The gifts and the calling of God (for Israel) are irrevocable." God did not cast them away when they failed—that is security. But that also ensures that the Lord will continue to discipline and deal with His people until they fulfill their calling. Israel's calling in the redemption of the world is certain, but is comes with a price:

Judgment begins at the house of God. There are consequences for breaking the covenant as God lovingly disciplines His own precious elect.

As with Daniel, this favor from the Lord serves to produce several dynamics:

- It makes a way: Daniel had favor with kings and was promoted to high offices.

- It provokes jealousy – Daniel's peers were jealous (consequently the lion's den).

This strategy of election is a test for the nations. God did not choose Israel and reject the nations. He chose Israel because He loves the nations and is making a way for the salvation of all. The nations will have to humble themselves to receive the blessings God wants to give.

- Joseph's jealous brethren ultimately were "saved" by Joseph.

- David's jealous brothers all benefited as the nation prospered under David's righteous leadership.

- Everybody's pride gets dealt with in this plan.

Questions to Ponder

1. What is my attitude when I am experiencing the opposite of what I expected?

2. How do I respond to injustice?

3. How have I doubted God's word because of not seeing the fulfillment of what I believe He has promised?

Chapter 10

My Portion: Entering the Sanctuary

CHET

[57]You are my portion, O LORD;
I have said that I would keep Your words.
[58]I entreated Your favor with my whole heart;
Be merciful to me according to Your word.
[59]I thought about my ways,
And turned my feet to Your testimonies.
[60]I made haste, and did not delay
To keep Your commandments.
[61]The cords of the wicked have bound me,
But I have not forgotten Your law.
[62]At midnight I will rise to give thanks to You,
Because of Your righteous judgments.
[63]I am a companion of all who fear You,
And of those who keep Your precepts.
[64]The earth, O LORD, is full of Your mercy;
Teach me Your statutes.

Chet—Psalm 119:57-64

In *Zayin*, David has recalled, in the face of offense and betrayal, the things that belonged to him in his covenant with the Lord. The Hebrew letter *chet* depicts a fence or a wall and can speak of an enclosed or defined area such as an inner room. Boundary lines are often marked out by a fence, separating what does and what does not belong to you. There were boundary lines to distinguish the inheritance or portion (v. 57) of one tribe from that of another in ancient Israel. This inheritance or portion of every believer is a great key to this section.

Also, *chet*, as a fence or wall, can have positive or negative nuances, such as, protection, separation, freedom (within boundaries) and restriction. Our shepherd's leadership can often be experienced as a fence that keeps us on the path of life and off of the paths that lead to death. The *torah* is often described as a fence which keeps God's people in the place of life and blessing, thus protecting them from their enemies.

The greater emphasis in this segment however, seems to be the believer's portion. That portion or inheritance, is a believer's access to the Lord in the sanctuary, or inner room, while the wicked have their portion in this life. Psalm 17:14 describes precisely what is happening here in David's life as he bears the derision of the proud (v. 51): "Deliver my life from the wicked with Your sword, with Your hand from men, O LORD, from men of the world who have their portion (*cheleq*) in this life."

In the case of our psalmist, the "bands (*chebel*) of the wicked" (v. 61) have bound him and are restricting his life (like a fence). They are prospering against him, even though he has not turned from the Lord. Rather than react from his flesh, our psalmist enters the sanctuary or inner room, where the Lord, who is his portion (inheritance, v. 57) dwells. Access to the Lord is the portion or right of every believer. David does this exact thing in Psalm 73:16-17 in order to understand the prosperity of the wicked. "When I thought how to understand this, it was too painful for me until I went into the sanctuary of God; Then I understood their end." In verses twenty-six and twenty-eight of Psalm 73, David continues with these words: "My flesh and my heart fail; But God is the strength of my heart and my portion (*cheleq*) forever. . . . But it is good for me to draw near (in the inner room) to God."

Here in *chet*, David enters that inner room with the Lord in order to seek understanding. Is the LORD "hemming him in behind and before" according to Psalm 139:5 or is it his own sin which is bringing this trouble? How can a righteous God allow this injustice? David is not having a pity-party, but is seeking understanding from the Lord. He rehearses his journey and rehearses his own right response to God in the context of God's seeming unresponsiveness to him. Will he pass this bitter test?

We could divide this segment in two sections reflecting a 4–4 pattern as follows:

Doing the math: Four history statements (v. 57-60)
What to do when things do not add up (v. 61-64)

Doing the math—Four history statements

Four verbs in the first four verses are all in the perfect mood, expressing an action completed in the past which has continued to the present. These serve as four statements that David recalled in his attempt to figure out why all these troubles had come upon him. These four verbs express something our psalmist has done in the past and has been doing up to the present, and read as follows:

1.   Verse 57: "I have promised (said) . . ."

2.   Verse 58: "I have sought (entreated) . . ."

3. Verse 59: "I have thought . . ."

4. Verse 60: "I have hurried (made haste) . . ."

Let's join David during this midnight hour (v. 62), when the proud onlookers are holding him in great derision (v. 51) concerning what appears to be the failed expectation or hope of verse forty-nine.

With the first words of this section, David continues the theme of what belongs to him in his covenant with God, but he takes it to another level—God Himself is his inheritance.

"You are my portion, O LORD; I have said that I would keep Your words" (v. 57).

1. "You are my portion (*cheleq*: portion, share, part, tract or parcel of land), O LORD." This is inheritance language. The root word means to be smooth (as smooth stones were used for lots), to apportion or to separate: deal, distribute, or divide. This Hebrew word is connected to the dividing or apportioning of the Promised Land as Israel's corporate inheritance. Each tribe and family received their portion (*cheleq*) of that inheritance.

   - In Numbers 18:20, the Lord spoke to Aaron concerning the priestly tribe (the Levites), "You shall have no inheritance in their land, nor shall you have any portion (*cheleq*) among them; I am your portion (*cheleq*) and your inheritance among the children of Israel." Is our psalmist claiming the priest's portion?

   - In Psalm 16:5-6, David speaks of his lot in life: "O LORD, You are the portion of my inheritance (*cheleq*) and my cup; You maintain my lot. The lines have fallen to me in pleasant places; Yes, I have a good inheritance (*nachalah*: possession)."

   - Deuteronomy 32:9, "For the LORD's portion (*cheleq*) is His people; Jacob is the place of His inheritance." God obtains something out of this relationship, too.

     o The hint at this stage is that our psalmist is focusing on what belongs to him versus what belongs to the Lord. This is not a selfish desire. We need to know what is ours lest we allow the thief to steal from us.

     o However, as we will see, our psalmist eventually matures and is more concerned about what the Lord is obtaining than what he is obtaining for himself.

- The great inheritance promise of scripture occurs in numerous places: "I will be your God and you shall be My people. The redeemed receive the Lord as their inheritance and the Lord receives the redeemed as His inheritance." See Exodus 6:7; Leviticus 26:12; Jeremiah 7:23; 30:22; Ezekiel 36:28; Hebrews 8:10-11; 2 Corinthians 6:16-18.

- Revelation 21:3, "Behold, the tabernacle of God is with men, and He will dwell with them, and they shall be His people. God Himself will be with them and be their God."

- The portion of every believer is access to the Lord! Hebrews 4:14-16, "Seeing then that we have a great High Priest who has passed through the heavens, Jesus the Son of God, let us hold fast our confession. For we do not have a High Priest who cannot sympathize with our weaknesses, but was in all points tempted as we are, yet without sin. Let us therefore come boldly to the throne of grace (inner room), that we may obtain mercy and find grace to help in time of need" (including revelation and understanding about what God is doing).

2. God tells Abram in Genesis 15:1, "I am your exceedingly great reward." It is as if the Lord were saying to Abram, "You will always have Me even if the fulfillment of My promises are delayed."

3. What if all I had was God? Is God enough? In the following Psalms, David expressed great satisfaction and pleasure in the Lord. God was enough for him:

   - Psalm 16:11, "In Your presence is fullness of joy; At Your right hand pleasures forevermore."

   - Psalm 63:5, "My soul shall be satisfied as with marrow and fatness."

   - Psalm 65:4, "We shall be satisfied with the goodness of Your house."

   - Psalm 36:8 "They are abundantly satisfied with the fullness of Your house, and You give them drink from the river of Your pleasures."

4. **History statement # 1:** "I have said that I would keep Your words." Correctly interpreted, David indicated, "I have said (in the past) that I would always be keeping Your word." This is the first of the four history statements our psalmist makes as he seeks understanding. The point is that David had not changed his mind and turned back so as to invite the discipline of the Lord.

"I entreated (*chalah*: to become weak) Your favor (face) with my whole heart; Be merciful (*chanan*: gracious, show favor or pity) to me according to Your word (imrah)" (v. 58).

1. **History statement # 2:** In other words, "I have (completely) intensely beseeched You and I have sought Your face with my whole heart, until I was worn out and sick."

2. The primary distinction between King Saul and King David as noted in 1 Chronicles 10:13-14 is that Saul did not enquire of the Lord. David, on the other hand, was noted for seeking direction and answers from God before he acted. See 1 Samuel 22:10-15; 23:2-4; 30:8; 2 Samuel 2:1; 5:19-23; 21:1; 1 Chronicles 14:10, 14.

3. This seeking of the face of the Lord could be a reference to the prayer meeting the psalmist had back in *hey* (v. 33-40) as he labored in prayer for faith concerning his own transformation. Or it could be a more recent seeking of the Lord in context to the recent betrayal and ensuing troubles. Either way, this lifestyle of seeking the Lord has marked David's life and continued up to this point in time.

4. Ceasing from his pattern of seeking the Lord is not the reason these troubles have come upon David.

5. "Be merciful" (gracious). David is not demanding explanation, but has come "to the throne of grace to obtain mercy and find grace in the time of need" (Hebrews 4:16).

"I thought (*chashab*: plot) about my ways, and turned my feet to Your testimonies (v. 59).

1. **History statement #3:** Again, by examining the verb mood, definition and grammar work, we could say it this way: "I have (completely in the past and up to the present) thought intensely and thoroughly about my ways, and I have been determining all along to turn my feet to walk according to Your testimonies (the witness of a better way)."

    *   "Turned my feet," refers to repentance from the psalmists old ways. Our psalmist is not making a claim of sinless perfection, but he is claiming that he did not go down the wrong path in his service to the Lord. He had repented and had not changed his mind about that repentance as he continued serving the Lord.

    *   We know that in *dalet* (v. 25-32), David contrasted God's ways with his own ways. He may be referencing that initial turning to the Lord's ways. More likely, he has examined himself to see if these troubles might be rooted in his own failure but has determined that his failings were not the reason for the trouble.

2. Job also claimed to have been walking uprightly before the Lord when disaster hit. He too tried to make sense of his troubles in light of his integrity and God's promises. When facing troubles, numerous questions arise within us:

    •   About God: Is He faithful to His promises? Is He good? Is He righteous? Are God's ways really better? Will God allow the wicked to prevail?

    •   About oneself: Have I sinned? What will I believe about God? Will I persevere or will I take offense with God and quit? Will I take my own vengeance on my persecutors or will I wait for the Lord?

"I made haste, and did not delay to keep Your commandments" (v. 60).

1. **History statement # 4:** Literally this could read, "I had from that time until now hurried, and I did not delay to keep Your commandments."

2. "I did not delay to keep Your commandments." Many believers have experienced negative consequences for doing the right thing and obeying God:

    •   David, through no fault of his own, ended up running for his life from a jealous King Saul. Furthermore, in 1 Samuel 24:6, he refused to touch the Lord's anointed by killing Saul when the opportunity afforded itself, thereby prolonging his suffering under the demonized king.

    •   Daniel's three friends were thrown into the fire for standing strong (Daniel 3).

    •   Daniel was thrown into the lions' den for praying to the Lord.

    •   Joseph was thrown into the pit and later into prison for doing right. Genesis 39:11-13, "But it happened about this time, when Joseph went into the house that she (Potiphar's wife) caught him by his garment, saying, 'Lie with me.' But he left his garment in her hand, and fled and ran outside. And so it was, when she saw that he had left his garment in her hand and fled outside."

3. "I did not delay to keep Your commandments." As already discussed, injustice provokes any unrighteous impulse within our own flesh. David may even now be applying God's word to some carnal impulse that has arisen because of this injustice. At any rate, disobedience to God's commandments is not the reason for his troubles.

What to do when it doesn't add up (v. 61-64)

In spite of David's diligence in responding to the Lord as expressed by the history statements, the cords of the wicked have bound him. David is trying to determine why this trouble has come upon him, and things do not "add up." What will our psalmist do in response?

1. He remembers the *torah* (v. 61).

2. He purposes to worship God no matter what (v. 62).

3. He renews his commitment to and his confidence in both the body of Messiah and in the Lord Himself (v. 63-64).

"The cords of the wicked have bound me, but I have not forgotten Your law" (v. 61).

1. "Cords" (*chebel*): rope (as twisted), territory (as measured by a line or cord), band, company (as if tied together), a noose (as of cords), a throe (as birth pangs), ruin.

2. Bound (*uwd*): duplicate, repeat, protest, testify (by reiteration), return, do again. This word is actually the root from which testimonies is derived and almost certainly refers to multiplying words or slanderous testimonies against David which serve to make things difficult for him by fencing him in and restricting him.

3. A paraphrase: "The wicked have banded together and have mounted a major defamation campaign against me, with slanderous testimonies designed to stop me."

   • Our psalmist is restricted in his interaction with his own family and friends, much as David was restricted when he was hiding in caves from King Saul.

   • Companies of the wicked are those bound together for evil. In Acts 23:12, "some of the Jews banded together and bound themselves under an oath, saying that they would neither eat nor drink till they had killed Paul."

4. David was no stranger to the power of the lying tongue of those who hated him:

   • Psalm 52:2-4, "Your tongue devises destruction, like a sharp razor, working deceitfully. You love evil more than good . . . You love all devouring words. . . ."

   • Psalm 55:21, "The words of his mouth were smoother than butter, but war was in his heart; His words were softer than oil, yet they were drawn swords."

   • Psalm 57:1-4, "O God, be merciful to me! For my soul trusts in You; And in the shadow of Your wings I will make my refuge, until these calamities have passed by. . . . My soul is among lions; I lie among the sons of men who are set on fire, whose teeth are spears and arrows, and their tongue a sharp sword."

   • Psalm 64:2-4, "Hide me from the secret plots of the wicked, from the rebellion of the workers of iniquity, who sharpen their tongue like a sword and bend their bows to shoot their arrows—bitter words, that they may shoot in secret at the blameless; Suddenly they shoot at him and do not fear."

- Psalm 120:2, "Deliver my soul, O LORD, from lying lips and from a deceitful tongue."

- Psalm 140:3, "They sharpen their tongues like a serpent; the poison of asps is under their lips."

5. "I have not forgotten (ignored, withered in the keeping of) Your law." Our psalmist has not compromised righteousness in his response. He is becoming like the Master.

A distinguishing mark of this segment are the four statements noted above concerning the things that our psalmist had already done and has been doing. He is retracing his steps since the beginning of his walk with the Lord. It is as if he is doing some math with the Lord, enumerating the steps he has taken by saying "Okay, Lord, I followed You with all my heart and now I am getting into all this trouble. I don't get it." He is in the fire for doing the right thing. If he is not wavering, he is at least somewhat confused. The next verse is powerful.

"At midnight I will rise to give thanks to You, because of Your righteous judgments" (v. 62).

1. "I will rise" is stated in the imperfect mood, denoting an action which is about to be accomplished, but which has not yet begun. David is making a critical decision.

- Our psalmist arises at midnight, the darkest hour of the night, to give thanks to God for His righteous judgments. We can't help but remember Paul in Silas in the Philippian jail in Acts 16:25, "But at midnight Paul and Silas were praying and singing hymns to God." They were in jail for obeying the Lord—for doing the right thing. Furthermore, Roman law was actually violated in their imprisonment, compounding the unfairness of being punished for doing right.

2. "To give thanks to you, becuse of Your righteous judgments."

- Our psalmist is set to wait on the Lord's righteous judgments rather than take things in to his own hands.

- Many are the righteous throughout history, who, for a season, suffered for righteousness sake. Consider Job, Joseph, Daniel and David. Read Hebrews 11:32-40. Consider *Yeshua's* familiar words in Matthew 5:11-12, "Blessed are you when they revile and persecute you, and say all kinds of evil against you falsely for My sake. Rejoice and be exceedingly glad, for great is your reward in heaven, for so they persecuted the prophets who were before you."

- Our psalmist is giving thanks because of a great eternal truth about the Lord: God's judgments (as sovereign Ruler of the universe) are righteous. His leadership is righteous. When He decrees a thing, it is always a righteous judgment and serves to establish justice (wrong things set right). If He waits to do so, and for a season allows injustice to prevail against the righteous, He is still righteous. Here is why:

- Remember, God is revealing any unrighteous instincts or character flaws yet within His own children so that the righteous judgments of His word can judge the lack yet within us. "Judgment must begin in the house of God" (1 Peter 4:17).

- Hence, God is also righteous if He waits to set wrong things right. The Coming One who was anointed to open prison doors (Isaiah 61:1), did so for Peter twice (Acts 5:19; 12:5-10), but not for John (Matthew 11:2-6), who was later beheaded. No wonder *Yeshua* added, "Blessed is he who is not offended because of Me."

3. If our psalmist is arising in this midnight hour, still in the house of his pilgrimage (v. 54) amidst the slanderous accusations of the proud, and is worshipping around this great truth of God's righteous judgments, he has certainly made a critical decision—a decision to crucify some aspect of his flesh and trust in the Lord. He is purposing not to take offense. He has made a turn.

4. David may have composed Psalm 16 at midnight as he gave thanks to God. Consider verses 1-4, "Preserve me, O God, for in You I put my trust. O my soul, you have said to the LORD, 'You are my Lord' (*adonay*: Master). My goodness is nothing apart from You (apart from You I have no good thing). As for the saints who are on the earth, they are the excellent ones, in whom is all my delight. Their sorrows shall be multiplied who hasten after another god (looking for something good, self-preservation, compromise); Their drink offerings of blood I will not offer, nor take up their names on my lips (I will not compromise righteousness)."

- "You are my LORD." He remains trusting and submitted.

- "Apart from You I have no good thing." The Lord is still his portion (v. 57).

- "I will not . . . take up their names on my lips." No compromise for relief.

5. Ponder our propensity to compromise righteousness or blur the truth to prevent a firestorm of criticism or keep ourselves out of a difficult situation.

"I am a companion of all who fear You, and of those who keep Your precepts" (v. 63).

1. "I am a companion (united with, associated with) those who fear You." Our psalmist is not denying the Lord, nor is he leaving the congregation of Israel from whence his troubles have come. He is fully identifying with God and His people, the saints. As noted above in Psalm 16:3, "As for the saints who are on the earth, they are the excellent ones, in whom is all my delight."

    •   David seems to be choosing who he will be knit to and identify with. This is a bold stand in an environment where believers are persecuted.

    •   Daniel also stays connected to his identity as a Jew when it would have been easier for him to assimilate into the pervading identity of being a citizen of Babylon (Daniel 1:11-14: 2:17-18).

2. This is all the more poignant if those proud men who hold our psalmist in great derision are within his own house (family of faith). Believers sin against each other and manifest carnality in many ways. That carnality gives great opportunity for offenses, which exposes even more carnality, which gives opportunity for greater offenses. At some point things reach a boiling point, and we just want to run away. Does it sound familiar? Lone-ranger faith apart from the congregation or community of faith, something which does not even exist biblically, sounds easier. But it is an illusion. Covenant community is the primary context in which our carnality is exposed and dealt with, so that we are not later seduced or offended by the world.

    •   Joseph had to overcome offenses from his own brethren before he could face the temptations of Egypt.

    •   David had to overcome offenses from his own people before he could overcome the seductions that come with being a king who could have anything he wants.

    •   In Song of Solomon 1:6 and 5:7, the Shulamite's wound came from her own family.

3. Whether the cords of the wicked that have our psalmist bound are from within the congregation or from the world, he is, by his righteous response, setting the stage for an earthquake to shake open the prison doors and set wrong things right.

"The earth, O LORD, is full of Your mercy (*chesed*); Teach me Your statutes" (v. 64).

1. This is the second mention of God's mercies in the psalm. Our psalmist returns to focus on the mercies of the Lord which were first highlighted in *vav* (v. 49).

"What then shall we say to these things? If God is for us, who can be against us?" (Romans 8:31). Read Romans 11:30-32 and Ephesians 2:7. There is something ultimate about mercy.

2. The lovingkindness of God is everywhere. What a confession of faith in the context of accusation and injustice. Maybe our psalmist is wrestling with anger and bitterness toward his persecutors and sensed his own need of mercy. Maybe he realized that God is also showing mercy to his persecutors and giving them time to repent.

3. God's righteous judgments, and His goodness and mercy, really cannot be separated. In fact, consider Psalm 33:4-5, "For the word of the LORD is right, and all His work is done in truth. He loves righteousness and justice; the earth is full of the goodness of the LORD." God's mercy and His judgment are the two sides of one coin. Think about it this way:

    *   The mercy shown Israel in the exodus was experienced as judgment for Egypt.

    *   The same flood waters that lifted Noah's ark to salvation drowned the wicked.

    *   When God delivers the oppressed, He inevitably judges the oppressor, thus turning the tables on the wicked and setting wrong things right (justice).

    *   Righteous judgments are also about rewards, which are for both the righteous and the wicked. One is experienced as positive and the other as negative.

Concluding Thoughts

David is overcoming an offended heart. When everything is wrong, he asks the question: Is God good? Read Psalm 73; 92; 94. Is God enough? As we noted above, David still has the Lord and "every spiritual blessing in the heavenly places in Christ" (Ephesians 1:3). God told Abram in Genesis 15:1, "Do not be afraid, Abram. I am your shield, your exceedingly great reward." Enemies can take all your stuff and sell you into slavery, but they cannot take your primary reward—the Lord Himself. Wrong things set right and the fulfillment of God's promises are really our secondary reward.

Questions to Ponder:

1. How have I been able to draw near to God and trust Him during a time of hurtful injustice?

2. What if God does not set things right for me in this age?

3. If all I have is Him, is that enough?

Chapter 11

Kind Injustice; Loving Discipline

TET

[65]You have dealt well with Your servant,
O LORD, according to Your word.
[66]Teach me good judgment and knowledge,
For I believe Your commandments.
[67]Before I was afflicted I went astray,
But now I keep Your word.
[68]You are good, and do good;
Teach me Your statutes.
[69]The proud have forged a lie against me,
But I will keep Your precepts with my whole heart.
[70]Their heart is as fat as grease,
But I delight in Your law.
[71]It is good for me that I have been afflicted,
That I may learn Your statutes.
[72]The law of Your mouth is better to me
Than thousands of coins of gold and silver.

Tet—Psalm 119:65-72

So far, our psalmist is passing the test of offense and bitterness. When he was betrayed, he found comfort in his affliction (v. 50) by recounting the promises of God and, by faith, laying hold of all that belonged to him in the gospel. He praised the Lord at midnight, even though he was in chains of some kind (v. 61-62). Rather than taking offense at the wicked, our psalmist focuses again on the mercies of God (v. 64).

The ancient pictograph for *tet* looks like a snake coiled inside a basket. The sages deem *tet* to be a paradoxical letter revealing both good and evil. The basket represents us as human beings with a glorious capacity for God and for good. But that basket also has a capacity for evil, which is also seeking entrance into our lives as the snake. Truth be told, sin (the snake) is already operating in our flesh and we must conquer it there first. God told Cain in Genesis 4:7, "Sin lies at the door. And its desire is for you, but you should rule over it."

Tet seems to point to the mystery of how the Lord uses evil in the universe for His own good purposes. Consider Isaiah 45:7, "I form the light, and create darkness; I make peace and create evil (or calamity). I the LORD do all these things."

We are assured that everything God created was good and that His steadfast love endures forever, but the trials of living in a fallen and broken world are certainly part of our formation into the image of Messiah. Remember Romans 8:28-29, "And we know that all things (good and evil) work together for good to those who love God, to those who are the called according to His purpose. For whom He foreknew, He also predestined to be conformed to the image of His Son."

Two key Hebrew words, one related to the good, and one related to the evil, help us unlock what is happening in this section:

1. *Towb* is translated throughout scripture more than six hundred times as pleasant, well, good, right, delightful, agreeable, beneficial, happy, goodly, beautiful, fine, precious, joyful, better, pleasing, favor, prosperous. *Towb* and *tuwb* (a derivative of *towb*) appear seven times in Psalm 119, six of those occurences being in *tet* (v. 65, 66, 68 [twice],71, 72). This word is about the goodness of God and about our glorious capacity for God and for good. *Towb* is definitely a key to understanding this section.

2. *Lamad* occurs thirteen times in the entire psalm, three of which are right here in *tet* (v. 66, 68, 71). No other section employs *lamad* more than once. *Lamad* also appears immediately before (in verse 64) and immediately after (in verse 73) this section, for a concentration of five occurrences within a span of ten verses. This makes a kind of sandwich for *tet* with a focus on this word *lamad*.

    *   *Lamad* means to goad (as with a rod) and, by implication, to keep one on the right path through prodding with a goad or rod, to teach or instruct.

    *   It hints at our need to at times be goaded by negative circumstances (evil) or painful things in order to stay on the path.

    *   Ten times throughout our psalm, our psalmist says, "Teach *(lamad)* me. . . ." It is as if he is fighting some unseen inward propensity for evil and he recognizes the need to be goaded at times in order to stay on course.

The other Hebrew word for teach is *yarah*, which occurs twice in Psalm 119, and is a gentler word meaning to flow (as water), to throw or shoot (as an arrow). It pictures a father pointing the way to his son or daughter and instructing with words rather than with the goad of *lamad*.

Hebrews 12:1-15 gives a powerful teaching on this very principal of a loving heavenly Father who employs evil for our good, because He is good. He employs the pain of a goad because of His love. Consider these words from Hebrews 12 about the suffering of His Son *Yeshua*: "Consider Him who endured such hostility from sinners against Himself, lest you become weary and discouraged in your souls . . . and you have forgotten the exhortation which speaks to you as to sons: 'My son, do not despise the chastening of the Lord, nor be discouraged when you are rebuked by Him; For whom the Lord loves He chastens'" (with unjust or undeserved hostility?).

The entire subject of Father's discipline of the Son He loves (Hebrews 12:1-15) is in context to the undeserved and unjust hostility of sinners against His Son *Yeshua*. *Yeshua's* perfect character was proven perfect (revealed) in His righteous response to His persecutors. Our own degree of Christ-likeness is also revealed by our response to our persecutors. The discipline of the Father in Hebrews 12 is not so much punishment for disobedience as it is the forging of Christ-likeness in us, and the proving of that Christ-likeness. What if injustice is God's primary instrument of formation? Nothing tests our character like injustice. Nothing provokes our carnality like injustice. Nothing reveals our Christ-likeness or the lack thereof like our response to injustice.

This is precisely what is happening in the life of the psalmist. He acknowledges his need of painful goading because of a propensity to go astray (v. 67), and he sees the goodness of God in it all. Yes, they are wrong (v. 70), and woe to those through whom offenses come, but offenses do come (see Luke 17:1-2) and they are part of God's strategy of formation. Remember, judgment must begin at the house of God. When my carnality is revealed by offense and injustice, I can acknowledge the sin within, deal with it and be conformed to the image of Messiah. This is my highest goal in life. Read again Addendum 4 on God's judgments.

"You have dealt well with Your servant, O LORD, according to Your word" (v. 65).

1. "You have dealt well." What a confession in the context of betrayal and offense. Literally, it states "You have done well."

2. This verse introduces the first occurrence of key word # 1, *towb*, which appears five more times in *tet*. In the Hebrew, *towb* is the first word of the section.

3. Our psalmist is basically confessing the truth that the Lord is good, even though God seems to have orchestrated the suffering of persecution and betrayal. Only in this age do we have the opportunity to praise Him by faith when things are wrong.

4. "According to Your word." This points to God's promises concerning our entrance into *The Blessed Life*.

"Teach me good (*towb*) judgment and knowledge, for I believe Your commandments" (v. 66).

1. Key word #2: "Teach (*lamad*) me good (*tuwb*) judgment" (*taam*: a taste, a perception). Here we have the second appearance of a word from the *towb* word family.

2. "Judgment" (*taam*) here is a seldom-used word translated as taste, judgment, behavior or discretion. It is a word describing how we are tasted, perceived, judged or experienced by others in our response to life's circumstances. In 1 Samuel 21:13, David "changed his behavior (*taam*) before them;" they perceived him as insane.

3. "Knowledge" (*daath*) is rightly translated as knowledge, knowing or to know.

4. Our psalmist is basically saying, "I want to show them what God is really like. I do not want to misrepresent my God by getting in a wrong spirit toward those who wrong me." A wrong response to the injustice would give others a taste of bitterness instead of the goodness (*towb*) of the Lord's good judgment.

5. "I believe Your commandments," the psalmist declares. This phrase could be translated as "I have trusted Your commandments (*mitzvah*) as faithful, reliable and trustworthy." Sometimes obeying God's commands comes with a price. After all, Joseph's flight from sin with Potiphar's wife landed him in jail. How then are God's commands faithful? They certainly are because, as with Joseph, obeying them will ultimately bring us into our destiny and inheritance.

"Before I was afflicted I went astray, but now I keep Your word" (v. 67).

1. "Went astray" (*shawgag*) occurs only here in Psalm 119. It is translated flesh in Genesis 6:3 and is used elsewhere in scripture for inadvertent sin. Our propensity to wander from the path was acknowledged in verse ten.

2. The injustice of betrayal has exposed fault lines within David's own soul, carnal instincts that he did not even know he had. Nothing reveals our Christ-likeness, or lack thereof, like injustice or mistreatment and our subsequent response.

3. Our psalmist seems to be living James 1:2-5, "My brethren, count it all joy when you fall into various trials, knowing that the testing of your faith produces patience. But let patience have its perfect work, that you may be perfect and complete, lacking nothing. If any of you lacks wisdom, let him ask of God."

4. The five occurrences of *lamad* (teach me or that I may learn) throughout this intense season of his life (v. 64, 66, 68, 71, 73) could easily be David's cry for wisdom in context to the testing of his faith, according to James 1:5.

5. "Now I keep Your word." Our psalmist is growing. God's word is an anchor in the storm.

"You are good (*towb*), and do good (*towb*); Teach me Your statutes" (v. 68).

1. What a confession! Our psalmist is confident that in everything God is working for his good (Romans 8:28). This is the third and fourth occurrence of *towb*.

2. "Teach *(lamad)* me Your statutes *(choq)*." Although alternating between teach and learn in English, this exact phrase in the Hebrew occurs twice in this section, thrice in this season of David's journey (v. 64, 68, 71), and eight times in the psalm. This is a major prayer of our psalmist. He is not saying, "Why me?" He is seeking the what.

3. Statutes *(choq)*. This Hebrew word emphasizes God's word as that which is engraved, established, definite or permanent. "Heaven and earth will pass away (including sin, sickness, offense and injustice), but My words will by no means pass away" (Matthew 24:35).

4. Our psalmist is asking to have God's word engraved on his heart. See Jeremiah 31:31-34; Ezekiel 11:19; 36:26-27.

"The proud have forged a lie against me, but I will keep Your precepts with my whole heart. Their heart is as fat as grease, but I delight in Your law" (v. 69-70).

1. "The proud have forged a lie." This injustice continues from verses 51, 53 and 61. Here we see the contrast between the heart of the proud and the heart of our psalmist.

2. Yes, they have scandalized our psalmist with lies and restricted his life, but he is keeping his heart for the Lord and is not allowing offense and bitterness to set in.

3. "Their heart is as fat as grease" casts these proud men as being self-centered, insensitive and dull. This phrase seems to contrast two hearts:

   - The heart of the proud is enlarged to delight in sin.

   - The heart of our psalmist delights in the law of God.

4. "But I delight in Your law." Again, our psalmist is not allowing treachery to diminish his heart for God or his delight in God's word. This is a major feat.

5. Psalm 17:8-15 is precisely what is occurring in the life of our psalmist. "Keep me as the apple of Your eye; Hide me under the shadow of Your wings, from the wicked who oppress me, from my deadly enemies who surround me. They have closed up their fat hearts; With their mouths they speak proudly . . . They have set their eyes, crouching down to the earth, as a lion is eager to tear his prey. . . . Deliver my life from the wicked . . . from men of the world who have their portion in this life, and whose belly You fill with Your hidden treasure. They are satisfied with

children, and leave the rest of their possession for their babes. As for me, I will see Your face in righteousness; I shall be satisfied when I awake in Your likeness."

6.   Paul prays in Philippians 1:10 that we would be sincere and without offense.

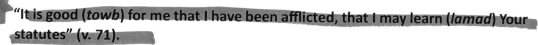

"It is good (*towb*) for me that I have been afflicted, that I may learn (*lamad*) Your statutes" (v. 71).

1.   What a confession as our psalmist accepts the Father's dealings as Messiah is being formed within him. He is acknowledging his own need for growth and is yielding to God's hand. This is the fifth occurrence of *towb*.

2.   "Went astray" in verse sixty-seven is not so much about rebellion or disobedience as it is about our carnality and weakness as immature believers. Our psalmist is yielding to the Father's rod of formation, esteeming Christ-likeness above everything. If becoming like our Master is the ultimate goal, then God is good when He exposes our lack of maturity.

"The law of Your mouth is better (*towb*) to me than thousands of coins of gold and silver" (v. 72).

1.   "The law (*torah*: instruction or teachings) of Your mouth" is the giving of instruction by the Father to the Son He loves. The hearing of those words by the Son hints at intimacy.

2.   "Better (*towb*, the sixth time) to me than thousands of coins of gold and silver" reveals that he is not coveting the wealth or prosperity of the wicked. The Father's instruction is better than riches. This is no small confession.

3.   One of David's greatest tests occurred when he saw the wicked prosper at the expense of the afflicted righteous. In Psalm 73:2-3 he writes, "But as for me, my feet had almost stumbled; My steps had nearly slipped. For I was envious of the boastful, when I saw the prosperity of the wicked." Also read Psalms 17, 92 and 94.

Concluding Thoughts

Remember—Christ-likeness is the goal. Nature is inherited but character is formed under pressure over time (see Isaiah 43:1). Consider this gripping excerpt on mistreatment from Allen Hood of International House of Prayer in Kansas City:

"Mistreatment is highly personal. It is not that mistreatment is unfair in a general kind of way. It is that it happened to me. I have the God-given right not to be mistreated. We complain: 'How dare she do that to me?' 'I cannot believe he actually said that to me.' The concern is not what made her do this or what made him say that. The concern is that they did and said it to me. I am the one challenged. I am the one resisted. I am the one in whom inconsistencies and weaknesses were pointed out. Who are they to give me instruction? What right do they have to analyze me and question me? We get angry when someone messes with our stuff—our turf—our ideas—our reputations. Thus, the defense mechanism of the fractured soul, anger, rushes to guard us from the realization that our fallenness is true. We would rather be proud and angry, clinging to our deluded solidarity than to admit to our inconsistent patterns, fractured pieces, and our humble need for grace to receive forgiveness and to forgive."[1]

Consider again this excerpt from Addendum 4, also printed out in *dalet*: "It takes the snake to expose the snake in me" (coined by the late Virgil Johnson). Offense and injustice, which are the work of the enemy, serve to expose the sin in us. In fact, to the degree that injustice provokes our carnality, to that degree God is justified in allowing injustice and offense to touch us. If we will judge the sin within ourselves, then God can righteously show His power on our behalf and judge sin in the world—the very sin that was employed against us. The drama is the contest between light and darkness. Our enemy wants us to get offended at a God who would allow such injustice and undeserved difficulty. He wants us to "curse God and die." But God wants us to recognize our carnality and judge the sin within our own members. Hence, the sin in the world is a primary key to our formation. This is the wisdom of God to allow Satan to rage against His beloved children in a fallen world.

Pressure reveals flaws and proves fixes

To help better understand the concept of pressure that reveals flaws, consider the steps required to repair a flat bicycle tire.

1. Remove the inner tube.

2. Inflate the inner tube by applying pressure (trouble or persecutions) to reveal the flaw.

3. Locate the leak exposed by the pressure.

4. Repair the leak by applying a patch.

5. Inflate the inner tube, again employing pressure, to prove your workmanship.

Remember James 1:2-3, "My brethren, count it all joy when you fall into various trials, knowing that the testing of your faith produces patience. But let patience have its perfect work, that you may be perfect and complete, lacking nothing."

James 1:12, "Blessed is the man who endures temptation; for when he has been approved (proven), he will receive the crown of life."

Questions to Ponder

1. How have unjust treatment or other trials exposed flaws in your own soul?

2. Can you say with the psalmist, "It is good for me that I have been afflicted"? What positive outcomes have you experienced as a result of suffering?

3. What are the evidences that you have grown in your love of, and delight in, God's word? Has it become better to you than thousands of coins of gold and silver?

Chapter 12

The Potter's Hand

YOOD

⁷³Your hands have made me and fashioned me;
Give me understanding, that I may learn Your commandments.
⁷⁴Those who fear You will be glad when they see me,
Because I have hoped in Your word.
⁷⁵I know, O LORD, that Your judgments are right,
And that in faithfulness You have afflicted me.
⁷⁶Let, I pray, Your merciful kindness be for my comfort,
According to Your word to Your servant.
⁷⁷Let Your tender mercies come to me, that I may live;
For Your law is my delight.
⁷⁸Let the proud be ashamed,
For they treated me wrongfully with falsehood;
But I will meditate on Your precepts.
⁷⁹Let those who fear You turn to me,
Those who know Your testimonies.
⁸⁰Let my heart be blameless regarding Your statutes,
That I may not be ashamed.

Yood—Psalm 119: 73-80

The tenth letter of the Hebrew alphabet is the letter *yood*, which means hand or arm. The first Hebrew word of the section is hand, referencing the hand of God who made me and fashioned me. The pictograph of a hand suggests a deed done or the ideas of strength, ability, dexterity, and of working. The mighty hand of God throughout scripture points to His strength, ability or power displayed in bringing salvation and deliverance (see Deuteronomy 3:24; 4:34; 5:15; 6:21; 7:8, 19; 9:26; 11:2; 26:8; 2 Chronicles 6:32).

Our psalmist is in need of a deliverance which only God's hand can provide. In fact, five consecutive verses in this section begin with "let" (or "may" depending on your translation). David cries out to the Lord for Him to arise and, by the power of His hand, show mercy. *Yood* is also often associated with the presence of the Lord. In the Hebrew, it is the first letter of the covenant Name of God, *YHVH.* The emphasis is really on the ability or power of God to save.

Several distinctive features in *yood* help unlock what is happening:

1. "Me" and "my" occur ten times as our psalmist seeks the hand of God for deliverance.

2. Verse seventy-seven has the first of two occurrences of the Hebrew word *racham* (compassion) as David appeals to the tender heart of the Father for help. Only in *yood* do the two primary Hebrew words for mercy appear in the same section:

    *   *chesed* (v. 76), usually translated as mercy or kindness

    *   *racham* (v. 77), usually translated as tender mercies

3. The phrase, "those who fear You," occurs twice, and only in this section. This hints at the idea that our psalmist's concern is also for others who are with him in the journey. He desires to strengthen others and be strengthened by others in the Body of Messiah—others who may be observing him and learning from his journey. His final prayer is that his heart be blameless so that he would not be ashamed (defeated by his own carnality or the bitterness of this test before others who are observing him).

Clearly, the afflictions (v. 67, 71, 75) and restrictions that have come from the cords of the wicked (v. 61) continue on. We need to read this section from the perspective of David, continuing to hide in the cave from King Saul, or as Joseph languishing in Egypt (maybe even in the prison). The lie forged against him by the proud (v. 69) seemingly controls his life. However, our psalmist seems not to be embittered, nor is he railing against his betrayers. In fact, he sees God's hand in everything and is submitting to God's hand as clay yields to the potter. He is appealing to God's hand of power to deliver. He even credits God's hand with his ability to remain steadfast in the test; he keeps his heart soft by seeking the merciful kindness and tender mercies of the Lord.

David does however, in verse seventy-eight, enter that rather difficult arena of "imprecatory prayers" in which one actually prays against his enemies or prays curses upon them: "Let the proud be ashamed, for they treated me wrongfully with falsehood." In verse eighty-four this approach occurs again: "When will You execute judgment on those who persecute me?" The truth is that deliverance for our psalmist means judgment for his oppressors, so that judgment and salvation are two sides of one coin. There are forty or more of these prayers throughout the psalms, mostly written by David. For example, see Psalm 139:19-24. In verses twenty-one and twenty-two we have these words: "Do I not hate them who hate You? Do I not loathe those who rise up against You? I hate them with a perfect hatred. I count them my enemies."

What is perfect hatred? What is righteous anger or indignation?

How could *Yeshua* righteously drive out the money changers from the temple with a whip? Or, how, in Acts 13:10-11, could the apostle Paul righteously speak thus to Elymas and actually curse him with blindness? "'O full of all deceit and all fraud, you son of the devil, you enemy of all righteousness, will you not cease perverting the straight ways of the Lord? And now, indeed, the hand of the Lord is upon you, and you shall be blind, not seeing the sun for a time.' Immediately a dark mist fell on him."

We cannot possibly fully develop this massive theme here, but let's take a little break from the journey and provide a foundation for understanding. What allows hatred to be perfect, and anger to be righteous, is that they **never** spring from our provoked carnality (from offense or self-interest). Nor, in the expression of such hatred and anger, can there ever be even a tinge of vindictiveness (or the enjoyment of our enemy's defeat). Righteous indignation is **always** about having zeal for God's glory, compassion for oppressed people, and a desire to see God's kingdom come in power!

Hence, to the degree that our psalmist is vindictive and desires the personal satisfaction of vengeance against his enemy, to that degree he is wrong and his prayer unrighteous. However, to the degree that he has zeal for the triumph of divine justice, for the glory of God, the freeing of the oppressed, and the coming of God's kingdom, to that degree he is righteous. By the time Joseph was on the throne in Egypt and had power over his brothers to do anything he wanted to with them, he had no desire for vengeance—only love for them. His words to them in Genesis 50:20 are powerful: "You meant evil against me; but God meant it for good, in order to bring it about as it is this day, to save many people alive." Addendum 4 will help complete this teaching.

Let's face it. To pray "Your kingdom come" is not only to pray for the coming of God's government on the earth, it is also to pray against the controlling structures of the enemy. The announcement that the kingdom of God is at hand is actually bad news for those with a vested interest in the status quo of earth's governing organizations. Human beings, whom God loves, but who have a vested interest in the corrupt governments and high places of the earth (like Pharaoh, Herod or Demetrius), may well become violent persecutors of those who are deemed to be a threat to their agenda—thus, they become our personal and mortal enemies. Our challenge is to love the person, and not develop a wrong spirit toward him or her, while still relentlessly seeking "the kingdom of God and His righteousness," albeit at the expense of those corrupt evil systems.

This leads to a perplexing paradox, the blending of two seemingly opposite attitudes or stances in prayer:

1. Intimacy: Delighting in, submitting to, trusting, and enjoying a beautiful God, our heavenly Father, who is kind and good (v. 76-77).

2.   Warfare: Partnership with the Lord of Hosts (armies), who is coming in His zeal like a man of war (Isaiah 42:13) to bring justice to the earth (Isaiah 42:1-4).

Psalm 149 powerfully brings the intimacy and warfare themes together. The first five verses are about totally enjoying a beautiful God, who takes pleasure in and beautifies His people. Suddenly in verse six, everything shifts as the high praises of God become a sword in our hand that will "execute vengeance on the nations and punishment on the peoples: to bind their kings with chains, and their nobles with fetters of iron; to execute on them the written judgment (*mishpat*). This honor is for all the saints" (Psalm 149:7-9).

In *Yeshua's* parable of the widow and the unjust judge (Luke 18:1-8) we have the prayer, "Avenge me of my adversary—Lord, give me justice and deliver me from my oppressor." In other words, setting wrong things right means that the oppressor will be judged and the oppressed set free. This is warfare. Verse seven hints at this intimacy and warfare paradox with these words: "And shall God not avenge His own elect (precious treasured people who can have intimacy) who cry out (for justice against their adversary) day and night to Him, though He bears long with them?"

We have the amazing calling and capacity in Messiah to do these two seemingly paradoxical things simultaneously:

1.   Love people who hate God and may be trafficking in hell's agenda for our communities and who are reviling us in some way as God's servants.

2.   Love God's kingdom (government) and seek to establish it, first in our lives and homes, and then in our communities. As the kingdom of God comes with power, bringing righteousness to our cities and regions, there may well be riots and violent resistance at some point. There were riots in Ephesus when the evil business of idol-making was threatened by the gospel of the kingdom (Acts 19). Those who profit from corruption in government, pornography, drugs, abortion or any other destructive and unrighteous activity may become our mortal enemies as we mobilize to see God's kingdom purposes realized in our cities. When that happens, we do not have the luxury of hating another human being whom God loves. *Yeshua*, when He was reviled, did not revile in return; when He suffered, He did not threaten, but committed Himself to Him who judges righteously. In His zeal for God's glory and kingdom (see Psalm 45:9), *Yeshua* never sinned against another person. We too are to love people and love God's kingdom.

It is important that we allow God's judgments (*mishpat*) to judge our own wrong attitudes and carnal impulses, so that we can enter this arena of warfare and not express a wrong spirit toward another human being. It is no accident that after the imprecatory prayer of Psalm 139:19-22, David prays this in verses 23-24: "Search me,

O God, and know my heart; Try me, and know my anxious thoughts; and see if there is any wicked way in me" (see Addendum 4).

Let's return to the journey to maturity, verse by verse:

"Your hands (*yad*: hand) have made (*asah*) me and fashioned (*kuwn*: established) me; Give me understanding, that I may learn (*lamad*) Your commandments" (v. 73).

1. "Your hands." This is the first mention of God's hands; it refers to God's power. The hand of God throughout scripture points to His strength and ability or His power displayed in deliverance. Consider Isaiah 50:2, "Is My hand shortened at all that it cannot redeem? Or have I no power to deliver? Indeed with My rebuke I dry up the sea."

    *   Search out the numerous references to God's "mighty hand and outstretched arm" (related to Israel's deliverance from Egypt) throughout the book of Deuteronomy. In that case, Israel is delivered and Egypt is judged.

    *   See also Numbers 11:23 and Isaiah 59:1. He is "mighty to save" (Isaiah 63:1).

    *   "Salvation belongs to the Lord" (Revelation 7:10). See also Psalm 98:1-2.

2. God knows what I can withstand: Literally this could read, "Your hands made me and established me (prepared, made firm, stable or ready)." The psalmist credits God with his ability to stand. We cannot help but remember the great assurance of 1 Corinthians 10:13, "God is faithful, who will not allow you to be tempted beyond what you are able, but with the temptation will also make the way of escape, that you may be able to bear it."

3. Submission to God: God's hand is also the Potter's hand of Jeremiah 18:6. "Look, as the clay is in the potter's hand, so are you in My hand, O house of Israel." God's hand is working a work in our psalmist. In verse seventy-five our psalmist attributes his affliction to the Lord and declares that he is submitted to His purposes.

4. "Give me understanding." Rather than asking the "why me?" of self-pity, or railing against the wicked with a bitter, offended heart, accusing God of injustice, our psalmist is yielding to God's purposes and asking to be taught God's commandments. This is significant. Many in history have asked to know God's ways so that they could enter into friendship and partnership with the Lord concerning His purposes.

5. "That I may learn Your commandments." Our psalmist is very intent on learning, and being directed by, God's commandments. According to 1 John 5:3, this demonstrates love for God. "For this is the love of God, that we keep His commandments. And His commandments are not burdensome." Consider other prayers and statements regarding God's commandments:

- In verse 10 David prayed, "Let me not wander from Your commandments!"

- In verse 35, he prayed, "Lead me in the path of Your commandments."

- In verse 49 he says, "I find my delight in Your commandments."

- In verse 66 he expressed confidence or trust in God's commandments with these words: "I believe in Your commandments."

- Looking ahead, in verse 86 we have these words: "All Your commandments are faithful."

"Those who fear You will be glad when they see me, because I have hoped (*yachal*: patient expectation) in Your word" (v. 74).

1. No man is an island. What we do and how we live affects others. 1 Corinthians 12:26 tells us that "If one member (of the body) suffers, all the members suffer with it; or if one member is honored, all the members rejoice with it." Our psalmist's victory in this test will open the way for others to gain the victory also.

2. "Those who fear You." This phrase, which occurs in verses sixty-three, seventy-four and seventy-nine, speaks of the body of Messiah:

   - In verse sixty-three it seems that David purposes to stay connected to the body.

   - Our psalmist desires that his steadfast hope in God's word will encourage others.

   - In verse seventy-nine, they will turn to me (our psalmist). Why? Because they now need help also, or have been attracted to the Lord by his testimony.

   - Many will see (God's power to save), fear and put their hope in God" (Psalm 40:2-3).

3. In the Song of Songs 6:1 the daughters of Jerusalem have just witnessed the Shulamite overcome her own betrayal and midnight hour without becoming embittered. Their incredulous question is this: "Where has your beloved turned aside, that we may seek him with you?" In other words, her victory in the test was witnessed by others and drew them to seek after the Lord also.

4. "Hoped (*yachal*) in Your word." The psalmist is expressing patient expectation in God's word, affirming that it is true and that the promises therein will come to pass. It is said of Abraham in Romans 4:18, 20, "who, contrary to hope, in hope believed, so that he became the father of many nations. . . . He did not waver at the promise of God through unbelief."

"I know, O LORD, that Your judgments (*mishpat*) are right, and that in faithfulness You have afflicted me" (v. 75).

1.   "Your judgments are right." The Lord is not issuing the decree that will set wrong things right and bring about justice. He is waiting. Meanwhile, our psalmist has to decide how to respond. Will he:

    • Retaliate or humiliate the offender by judging him and pointing out to everyone how bad or wrong he really is?

    • Justify his wrong response by pointing out the terrible injustice of what occurred?

    • Crawl into a corner in bitterness and self-pity and wait for the rapture?

    • Allow the word of God to judge (discern, separate out that which is sinful within) his own carnality and repent of his own sins?

2.   It is clear that David is making the right choice. He is judging himself according to 1 Corinthians 11:31-32. "For if we would judge ourselves, we would not be judged. But when we are judged, we are chastened by the Lord, that we may not be condemned with the world."

3.   Knowing that injustice causes our own carnality and heart issues to manifest (see Addendum 4), let's list some of the things this test could reveal. In other words, what are some of the things that Joseph or David may have had to judge themselves concerning when they were betrayed by their brothers?

    • How about these: fear, anger, bitterness, unbelief, discouragement, indignation, hatred, frustration, vengeance, despair, complaining, and so forth? The list could go on.

    • The test was for the brothers also. Think about it. Here is your hotshot kid brother, who seems to be a favorite of Dad, and who comes out with this grandiose vision from God about becoming a king. "Yeah, right," was his brother's response. "Go back to your sheep David. We know who you are."

        o   This is particularly provoking if that little brother has just been given the thing that you desire and have been grasping for. *Yeshua's* disciples fought numerous times over who would be the greatest in the kingdom. When the mother of James and John sought *Yeshua* concerning special status for her sons in the kingdom, the other ten disciples "were moved with indignation against the two brothers" (KJV).

        o   "A prophet is not without honor except in his own country and in his own house" (Matthew 13:57). Those closest to us are the first to become offended at our anointing and standing with God. See also Mark 6:2-6.

4.　"In faithfulness (fidelity, security) You have afflicted me." Our psalmist is ultimately attributing this season of testing to the Lord's work, not a capricious God who acts arbitrarily, but a faithful God who is true to His nature and bound by His word. God is being true to who He is in His essential goodness and He is true to His word. What a confession as our psalmist submits to the hand of the Potter.

- Recall again Joseph's statement to his fearful brothers in Genesis 50:19-20, "Joseph said to them, "Do not be afraid, for am I in the place of God? But as for you, you meant evil against me; but God meant it for good, in order to bring it about as it is this day, to save many people alive.'"

- Psalm 105:17 agrees with this assessment, "He (the LORD) sent a man (Joseph) before them (Joseph's father and brothers), Joseph who was sold as a slave." God Himself orchestrated this entire drama.

- Joseph's problem was God. He was chosen.

"Let, I pray, Your merciful kindness (*chesed*: goodness, kindness) be for my comfort, according to Your word to Your servant" (v. 76).

1.　David again appeals to and seeks comfort in the unending love of God. An offended, embittered heart will not be able to draw near to God in intimacy and receive His love.

2.　He seems willing to wait for deliverance and settle for receiving comfort (consolation) now. He is finding the place of rest until God sets everything right.

3.　Psalm 94:12-15 speaks precisely and powerfully about where David is in his journey. Notice the familiar Hebrew words in parenthesis: "Blessed (*esher*: happy) is the man whom You instruct (discipline), O LORD, and teach (*lamad*) out of Your law, that You may give him rest from the days of adversity, until the pit is dug for the wicked. For the LORD will not cast off His people, nor will He forsake His inheritance. But judgment (*mishpat*) will return to righteousness." God will ultimately set things right.

"Let Your tender mercies come to me, that I may live; For Your law is my delight" (v. 77).

1.　Tender mercies (*racham*) occurs only here and in verse 156. This is a word for deep gut-felt compassion. Our psalmist knows the heart of God concerning him in his affliction. It is as if he knows about Hebrews 4:15-16, which says, "For we do not have a High Priest who cannot sympathize with our weaknesses, but was in all points tempted as we are, yet without sin. Let us therefore come boldly to the throne of grace that we may obtain mercy and find grace to help in time of need."

2. Delight (*shashua*) is enjoyment or pleasure in the law (*torah*: instruction). The law of God is our psalmist's source of instruction and pleasure. An offended heart cannot delight in the Lord or in His word. Later in his journey (v. 92) David speaks these words: "Unless Your law had been my delight, I would then have perished in my affliction."

"Let the proud be ashamed, for they treated me wrongfully with falsehood; But I will meditate on Your precepts" (v. 78).

1. Psalm 25:1-2 employs some of this same kind of language: "To You, O LORD, I lift up my soul. O my God, I trust in You; Let me not be ashamed; Let not my enemies triumph over me. Indeed, let no one who waits on You be ashamed; Let those be ashamed who deal treacherously without cause." The issue here concerns who will triumph, the righteous or the wicked.

    *   Psalm 125:3 relates powerfully: "For the scepter of wickedness shall not rest (forever) on the land (inheritance) allotted to the righteous, lest the righteous reach out their hands to iniquity."

    *   In other words, if the righteous have no hope of justice, why remain righteous?

2. "I meditate on Your precepts" (*piqqud*). In the Introduction we highlighted Psalm 19:8: "The statutes (precepts; *piqqud*) of the LORD are right, rejoicing the heart." God's precepts provide the consistent presence, oversight and boundaries that allow our psalmist to feel safe. Our psalmist prays for justice, but gives himself to meditate on the word of God, hoping and trusting in that word to keep him (v. 74). Will our psalmist concentrate on the lie and the liar who is hurting him or will he meditate on God and on His word?

3. As discussed above, the degree to which our psalmist longs for the triumph of divine justice and for God's kingdom to come, to that degree this is a righteous prayer. Up to this point, he has been diligent to deal with his own heart and has been submitted to the Potter, so we will take this to be mostly righteous, not personal and vindictive in nature.

4. We will give our psalmist the benefit of any doubt concerning the purity of his heart in praying this prayer: "Let the proud be ashamed, for they treated me wrongfully." However there may yet be a mixture of two desires (he does, after all, say, "me" and "my" ten times in this section):

    *   Zeal for his own comfort and an easier life—God is not against these or against us having riches, honor and long life in this age. However, these things are not God's number one priority. God's zeal is for the greater purposes of His own glory and kingdom in the earth.

- Zeal for the triumph of divine justice and for God's kingdom and glory on earth.

"Let those who fear You turn to me, those who know Your testimonies" (v. 79).

1. Our psalmist seems to be appealing to the body of Messiah for help. This is an act of great humility. In the Song of Songs 3:3, the Shulamite, who is likewise enduring affliction, asks the watchmen for help with these words: "Have you seen the One I love?"

2. In Psalm 94:16-17, the psalmist prays: "Who will rise up for me against the evildoers? Who will stand up for me against the workers of iniquity? Unless the LORD had been my help, my soul would soon have settled in silence." We need each other in the body of Messiah.

3. The other side of this coin is that the psalmist, having gone through these deep waters, can also help others who turn to him in their time of trouble. *Yeshua* tells Peter in Luke 22:31-32, "When you have returned, (from your test) strengthen your brethren."

"Let my heart be blameless regarding Your statutes, that I may not be ashamed" (v. 80).

1. "Let my heart be blameless." This is not so much about sinless perfection as it is about integrity. Blameless is the Hebrew word *tamiym* discussed at length in *aleph* and it means entire, complete, whole, sound. *Tamiym* points primarily to two ideas:

   - To integrity—A life without duplicity, pretense or hypocrisy. It suggests unity of our spirit, soul and body undefiled by impure motives.
   - To maturity—Christ-likeness.

2. "Ashamed." Remember our psalmist's early cry in verses five and six, "Oh, that my ways were directed to keep Your statutes! Then I would not be ashamed, when I look into all Your commandments." David is still seeking the Lord concerning the issues of his heart.

3. Consider from 1 John 3:18-22 the power of a heart that does not condemn us: "My little children, let us not love in word or in tongue, but in deed and in truth. And by this we know that we are of the truth, and shall assure our hearts before Him. For if our heart condemns us, God is greater than our heart, and knows all things. Beloved, if our heart does not condemn us, we have confidence toward God. And whatever we ask we receive from Him, because we keep His commandments and do those things that are pleasing in His sight."

4.   This is a critical prayer when praying for the defeat of your enemies as our psalmist did here in verse seventy-eight. This pattern of praying for your own heart is also shown in Psalm 139:19-24 as noted above. The passions that rule in the hearts of our enemies as they persecute us have also had their day of power within our own hearts. We are in desperate need of humility.

5.   A believer's shame or defeat is to lose the battle in his soul by succumbing to bitterness and then stumbling in his faith. The real question is this: Will he get bitter or better?

Concluding Thoughts

Read Psalm 73, 92, and 94. What is God doing "when the wicked spring up like grass, and when all the workers of iniquity flourish . . . while the righteous suffer"? Here are a few ideas:

1.   As we discussed, God is judging sin in His people. The Judge exposes that sin through the injustices that abound so that we can allow the judgments of His word to purify us to become just like His Son. Read 1 Corinthians 11:31-32 and 1 Peter 4:17.

2.   God is seeking to promote you. He wants to increase your anointing and spiritual authority just as He did for Job (his influence was doubled after the test). This is Psalm 92:10, in context to the wicked prospering (Psalm 92:7). "But my horn (authority) You have exalted like a wild ox; I have been anointed with fresh oil (increased anointing)."

3.   God is allowing time for your persecutor to repent. He is working on behalf of those who are persecuting the righteous. He wants them to witness the Messiah-like responses of His children and repent. He is not willing that any perish. This scenario of injustice and offense sets the table for a display of Christ-likeness that will draw sinners to repentance. This is Romans 12:19-21, "Beloved, do not avenge yourselves, but rather give place to wrath; for it is written, 'Vengeance is Mine, I will repay.' If your enemy is hungry, feed him; If he is thirsty, give him a drink; For in so doing you will heap coals of fire on his head. Do not be overcome by evil, but overcome evil with good." This is how Saul of Tarsus became the Apostle Paul—by witnessing the stoning of Stephen. *Yeshua* instructs us this way: "Love your enemies, bless those who curse you, do good to those who hate you, and pray for those who spitefully use you and persecute you" (Matthew 5:44).

4.   God is allowing iniquity to become complete or full. When Israel finally entered the Land of Canaan to destroy the inhabitants, two things had come to fullness:

   •   Israel had come to full glory and power as the righteous army of the Lord.

- The iniquity of the Amorites was complete (Genesis 15:16). They had fully made their choice to not repent, and it was right for God to judge the nations in Canaan.

There could be a thousand reasons for taking up offense. This strategy is the bait of Satan to put us on the wrong path. Don't take the bait. You can afford to be slandered, persecuted and robbed. You are infinitely wealthy, a child of the King. Freely you have received, freely give. You have been forgiven much—therefore love much.

1. "You are my portion O LORD" (v. 57). A poverty spirit can be easily offended. How rich are you? 2 Corinthians 8:9 gives us a powerful definition of grace: "For you know the grace of our Lord Jesus Christ, that though He was rich, yet for your sakes He became poor, that you through His poverty might become rich." See also Hebrews 10:34; James 1:2; Acts 5:41; Matthew 5:11-12.

2. We, who have experienced the generosity of the kingdom, do not have the luxury of bitterness and vengeance. We too have hurt others and have been forgiven. "The whole earth is full of Your mercy" (v. 64).

3. Consider how a rich and powerful King David responded to Shimei's cursing in 2 Samuel 16:5-11, "Shimei the son of Gera . . . came out, cursing continuously as he came. And he threw stones at David and at all the servants of King David . . . he cursed: 'Come out! Come out! You bloodthirsty man, you rogue! The LORD has brought upon you all the blood of the house of Saul, in whose place you have reigned; and the LORD has delivered the kingdom into the hand of Absalom your son. So now you are caught in your own evil, because you are a bloodthirsty man!' Then Abishai the son of Zeruiah said to the king, 'Why should this dead dog curse my lord the king? Please, let me go over and take off his head!' But the king said, 'What have I to do with you, you sons of Zeruiah?' So let him curse, because the LORD has said to him, "Curse David." Who then shall say, "Why have you done so?"' And David said to Abishai and all his servants, 'See how my son who came from my own body seeks my life. How much more now may this Benjamite? Let him alone, and let him curse; for so the LORD has ordered him.'"

Questions to Ponder

1. When have I been able to trust the Lord in painful circumstances and yield to His hand as clay yields to the potter?

2. When have I doubted the goodness and kind intentions of the Lord? What specific promises have helped me in times of painful trials and offenses?

3. When have I been able to effectively help or comfort someone else because of the similar difficulties I have gone through?

Chapter 13

Help Me—How Long, O Lord?

KAPH

⁸¹My soul faints for Your salvation,
But I hope in Your word.
⁸²My eyes fail from searching Your word,
Saying, "When will You comfort me?"
⁸³For I have become like a wineskin in smoke,
Yet I do not forget Your statutes.
⁸⁴How many are the days of Your servant?
When will You execute judgment on those who persecute me?
⁸⁵The proud have dug pits for me,
Which is not according to Your law.
⁸⁶All Your commandments are faithful;
They persecute me wrongfully;
Help me!
⁸⁷They almost made an end of me on earth,
But I did not forsake Your precepts.
⁸⁸Revive me according to Your lovingkindness,
So that I may keep the testimony of Your mouth.

Kaph—Psalm 119:81-88

The Hebrew letter *kaph* depicts an open hand, or the palm of the hand. It is actually translated as spoon twenty-four times in certain translations (Numbers 4:7 for example), as the palm of an open hand forms a kind of spoon or hollow in the context of offering something up to God or receiving something from Him. Captives in Babylon are told in Lamentations 3:41, to "lift up our hearts with our hands (*kaph*) to God in heaven." *Kaph*, the open hand, can also mean to cover or to open.

A key to this section is the word faint occurring three times in *kaph* (out of four times in the entire psalm). Our psalmist is almost at the breaking point. His soul is fainting as he languishes in prison (or a cave) enduring great injustice and awaiting the fulfillment of his promise. If *yood* was about the power and ability of God's hand to work, sustain and deliver, *kaph* is about the desperate weakness of our psalmist's hand to save himself. Hence, he opens his hand to God for help, as if he knows 2 Corinthians 12:9, where God said to the apostle Paul, "My grace is sufficient for you, for My strength is made perfect in weakness."

Proverbs 31:20 speaks of the mighty or valiant woman, "She extends her hand (*kaph*) to the poor; yes, she reaches out her hands (*kaph*) to the needy." Likewise the poor who would receive from her must open their hand and form a spoon in order to receive the provision. In Isaiah 49:16, the Lord poignantly declares that He has engraved Jerusalem upon the palms (*kaph*) of His hands, thus illustrating His abiding concern for Zion. This section is about the cry of the oppressed who come to God with an open hand, in need of divine help. There is a certain humility or brokenness, as well as faith, associated with this posture. It acknowledges our lack—but God's sufficiency.

The cry of the oppressed throughout history seems to echo in every verse of this section. "How long, O LORD, until You act?" Job asks the question in Job 7:19. David in Psalm 6:3-4 cries out, "My soul also is greatly troubled; But You, O LORD—how long? Return, O LORD, deliver me! Oh, save me for Your mercies' sake!" Again in Psalm 13:1-2, David says, "How long, O LORD? Will You forget me forever? How long will You hide Your face from me? How long shall I take counsel in my soul, having sorrow in my heart daily? How long will my enemy be exalted over me?" Yet again in 35:17 he cries, "LORD, how long will You look on? Rescue me. . ." and again in 74:10, "How long will the adversary reproach me? Will the enemy blaspheme Your Name forever?" See also Psalm 79:5; 82:2; 89:46; 90:13; 94:3; Habukkah 1:2; Zechariah 1:12. This echoes the cry of the martyrs in Revelation 6:10, "How long, O Lord, holy and true, until You judge and avenge our blood?"

This could easily be Ziglag (1 Samuel 30) in David's life. After seven or eight years of running for his life from his own king, King Saul, he returns to his home in Philistine country only to find the city "burned with fire; and their wives, their sons, and their daughters had been taken captive. Then David, and the people who were with him, lifted up their voices and wept, until they had no more power to weep" (1 Samuel 30:3-4). His own men were ready to stone him because of the grief for their sons and daughters. But David strengthened himself in the Lord his God (1 Samuel 30:6). David then seeks the Lord (with open hands) and obtains the promise that they will be able to pursue and overtake the raiding band of Amalekites. Everything would eventually be restored, but the pressure and difficulty of the moment was a supreme test.

This could also be Joseph, being thrown into prison in Egypt for doing the right thing in Genesis 39, or any number of afflicted saints throughout the ages. How much can a man endure? Lord, where are You? How long until You set it right? Psalm 125 assures us that to trust in the Lord means certain protection. That protection comes, however, in context to the "scepter of wickedness" that is working injustice toward us. Verse three assures us that "the scepter of wickedness shall not rest (forever) upon the land allotted to the righteous, lest the righteous reach out their hands to iniquity." Can you see the "how long" question there? If we believe that the wicked will prevail and never be judged, and that the righteous will never be rewarded, then even the righteous might give up and reach out their hands to iniquity. Where is the breaking point?

Let's join our psalmist as he clings to the promises of the Lord while crying out for deliverance.

"My soul faints (*kalah*) for Your salvation, but I hope in Your word" (v. 81).

1. "My soul faints (*kalah*)." Literally, this means to end, to accomplish, cease, consume, determine, fail, find complete. *Kalah* is used three times in this section (v. 81, 82, 87) and then once more in verse 123.

2. "For Your salvation (*t\eshuah*)." God has not yet acted to deliver David from his oppressors and set wrong things right. In his need, he is coming to God with an open hand to receive the provision of God's hand.

3. "But I hope (*yachal*)." The meaning of *yachal* is to wait with expectation (as if for something that is promised and sure, but not yet here; to hope).

4. "In Your word (*dabar*)." God's word assures us that in the end, He will set it right. Both the wicked and the righteous will be rewarded according to their works. Citing Psalm 125:3 again, David knows that "the scepter of wickedness shall not rest (forever) upon the land allotted to the righteous." He is stirring up his confidence in the word of God which promises that, ultimately, the tables will be turned and the meek shall inherit the earth (see Matthew 5:5; Daniel 7:21-22; Psalm 35:9-11; 125:1-5).

"My eyes fail from searching Your word, saying, 'When will You comfort me?' For I have become like a wineskin in smoke, yet I do not forget Your statutes" (v. 82-83).

1. "My eyes fail (*kalah*) from searching Your word (*imrah*)."

   - *Kalah* is the same Hebrew word that is translated faint in verse eighty-one. This is the second occurrence of that word.

   - Our psalmist is desperately looking for some assurance that everything will be okay. The palm of his hand is open and ready to receive the answer.

2. Comfort (*nacham*) means to be sorry, be comforted, console oneself, repent, regret, or comfort. This word appears only three times in the psalm, in verses fifty-two, seventy-six and eighty-two. Like someone near the breaking point, our psalmist pleads for comfort, as it were, with an open hand.

3. "Like a wineskin in smoke." This resembles Job 30:30, where Job says, "My skin grows black and falls from me." Dried out and ready to crack seems to be the meaning here.

    •   Again, this could be David's Ziglag or Joseph's Egyptian prison.

    •   Our psalmist is truly being put to an ultimate test. How much can he take? This pressure certainly reveals what we are made of.

4. "I do not forget (*shakach*: forget, ignore, or wither) Your statutes (*choq*)." Although he is withering under the power of this test, our psalmist is not withering in his meditation on the statutes (*choq*) of the Lord.

5. Statutes (*choq*) are the engraved and eternally unchanging truths of the word of God. David is not withering in his confidence that ultimately there will be justice.

6. That engraved and unchanging statute that David is meditating upon may well be the truth already discussed, that ultimately, wrong things will be set right and the meek shall inherit the earth. God has a reputation for hearing the cry of the oppressed and, at the right time, acting in power to save and vindicate the righteous.

"How many are the days of Your servant? When will You execute judgment (*mishpat*) on those who persecute me? The proud have dug pits for me, which is not according to Your law" (v. 84-85).

1. "How many are the days of Your sevant?" Can you hear the great "how long" question of God's afflicted throughout history? The clear hint concerns the frailty of man, whose life is but a vapor and who is like the grass of the field which is here today and gone tomorrow (Psalm 144:4; 90; 103:15-16; Isaiah 40:6-7). This would be a great place to read Psalm 90.

2. "When will You execute judgment (*mishpat*)?" Judgment on David's persecutors is also his salvation. Remember that mercy and judgment are two sides of one coin. God's judgments in this age are always redemptive in their intent. This prayer is not a vindictive desire to see his persecutors get what they deserve.

3. This is a great place to review the subject of God's judgments in Addendum 4. What occurs when God's judgments are manifest in the earth?

    •   The oppressed are delivered and vindicated.

    •   The oppressor is judged, but also has a renewed opportunity to turn from sin to the living God. Remember that many Egyptians turned to the Lord during the plague judgments upon Egypt.

    •   "The inhabitants of the world will learn righteousness" (Isaiah 26:9).

- Many scriptures in the Psalms deal with this subject (Psalm 5:10; 7:15-16; 9:15; 10:9-18; 28:4; 31:23; 35:8; 37:14-15; 64:8; 92:7; 94:13, 23; 119:85-86; 140).

4. "Persecute" (*radaph*) is described as running after with hostile intent, to follow after, pursue, persecute.

   - The word occurs five times throughout the psalm, two of those being here in *kaph*. This provides another key regarding what this section is about.

5. "The proud have dug pits for me." The wicked falling into their own pit is a huge theme of David in his writings.

   - We know that in the end, Haman will hang on his own gallows and the wicked will fall into their own pit, but meanwhile, the saints of God are being put to the test and purified (see Esther 5:14; 7:9; Psalm 92:7; 94:23).

6. "Which are not according to Your law (*torah*)." David's persecutors are not acting righteously. Can we perceive in this statement a growing desire for truth and righteousness overtaking our psalmist's desire for his own comfort and deliverance?

"All Your commandments (*mitzvah*) are faithful (fidelity, steadfastness, faithfulness); They persecute me wrongfully; Help me" (v. 86).

1. "All your commandments are faithful." What a declaration! In verse sixty-five the psalmist said, "You have dealt well with Your servant." God is not capricious in His nature or arbitrary in what He requires of us. He is not self-serving when He gives us commands and orders our lives. He is absolutely true to who He is in His essential goodness, even when obedience to His commands precipitates persecution. He is for us, not against us. His commandments are designed to help us enter into our destiny and *The Blessed Life*.

2. "They persecute (*radaph*) me wrongfully (*sheqer*)." *Sheqer* is the primary Hebrew word for lies, deception, or falsehood. Review the scriptures concerning the power of a lying and slanderous tongue in *chet* (v.61).

   - This is the second occurrence of persecute (*radaph*) in *kaph*, which means a perversion of justice!

   - Our psalmist is being maliciously lied about and slandered. There may well have been a great loss of stature within his community, loss of friendship or loss of income which was threatening his very survival (physically).

3. "Help (*azar*) me." This is a cry for God's provision. God is our help in times of need. See scriptures like Psalm 121:3 and 46:1. If we are honest about our lives, we could probably perceive an unrelenting tendency to resort to our own strength, gifting,

resource and knowledge to solve the problems of life. This propensity to lean upon one's own understanding needs to be dealt a death blow. This is happening to our psalmist right here as he, in total weakness and brokenness, turns to the Lord for help. "For without Me you can do nothing" (John 15:5). Self-reliance is not a kingdom value!

"They almost made an end of me on earth, but I did not forsake Your precepts. Revive me according to Your lovingkindness, so that I may keep the testimony of Your mouth" (v. 87-88).

1. "They almost made an end of me" sounds like David's Ziglag discussed above.

2. "I did not forsake Your precepts." God's word is still dictating David's responses.

3. "Revive me according to Your lovingkindness (*chesed*)." This is a prayer for renewed strength through encountering the lovingkindness of God. The psalmist is strengthening himself in the Lord (1 Samuel 30:6)! Although he is hurting, he is clearly not offended at the Lord or embittered by the test he is going through, but is drawing near to God.

4. "So that I may keep (as great treasure) the testimony of Your mouth." At any point our psalmist could take up offense, curse God and die, abort the seed of His word, and throw God's purposes and promises for his life in the trash. Psalm 105:19 says of Joseph, until "the time that his word came to pass, the word of the LORD tested him." Instead, he keeps the word!

Concluding Thoughts

Two questions concern the wicked versus the righteous:

1. What motivates the proud to dig pits for David? Why do they desire to see him fall? We might also ask why they killed *Yeshua*, or why Joseph's brothers betrayed Joseph.

    *   The short answer is envy (Matthew 27:18). "And his (Joseph's) brothers envied him" (Genesis 37:11). The same is true of King Saul toward David. Saul was jealous because of the anointing of the Spirit upon David for kingship, which was a threat to Saul.

    *   Another perspective involves what occurs within our own hearts when the light of someone more righteous than ourselves exposes our own lack, thus precipitating the conviction of sin within. John 3:19 states that "men love darkness rather than light because their deeds are evil." A response to that light would be to attempt to snuff it out, hence the persecution of our psalmist.

2.   If God does not deliver our psalmist, what will happen? *Yeshua* did not rescue John the Baptist from Herod. What are God's purposes in deliverance and what are his purposes in loss and even martyrdom? Shadrach, Meshach, and Abednego, facing the fiery furnace in Daniel 3, said this to King Nebuchadnezzar: "Our God whom we serve is able to deliver us from the burning fiery furnace, and He will deliver us from your hand, O king. But if not, let it be known to you, O king, that we do not serve your gods." They did not know for sure what God would do. They only knew that either way, in deliverance or in martyrdom, they would not bow to the image.

- In Revelation 12:11 the saints overcome Satan and in Revelation 13:7, "It was granted to him (the beast) to make war on the saints and overcome them (in martyrdom)." See also Daniel 7:21.

- In Acts 5, Peter and the apostles are delivered, but in Acts 7, Stephen is killed.

- In Acts 12 James is killed and Peter is set free within the same chapter.

- In Revelation 7, one group has a seal of protection and refuge throughout the great tribulation while another group is martyred and is singing before the throne.

- In Hebrews 11:35-38, after a long list of supernatural deliverances by faith, we have these words: "Others were tortured, not accepting deliverance, that they might obtain a better resurrection. Still others had trial of mockings and scourgings . . . chains and imprisonment, stoned, sawn in two . . . tempted, slain with the sword. They wandered about . . . destitute, afflicted and tormented—of whom the world was not worthy."

Consider these two possible answers to the question stated above regarding what will happen if God does not deliver our psalmist.

- In deliverance God manifests His power to save. He showcases the superiority of His power and His kingdom over all the kingdoms of men as in the days of Daniel and his three friends in Babylon (the fiery furnace, the lion's den, and others). In witnessing God's power to deliver, many will come to believe in Him and kings will be reminded that they answer to a throne that is higher than their own.

- In martyrdom, God displays His power to transform humans. Martyrdom showcases the nobility of a heart that will go to the death for love. Many will believe in *Yeshua* as they witness the death of martyrs. Accepting martyrdom is the exact opposite of self-worship and self-preservation, which is the foundation of Satan's kingdom. Martyrdom displays the power of redemption to change a human heart. In martyrdom, Satan's boast concerning Job is proven wrong. "Does Job fear God for nothing? Have You not made a hedge around him, around his household, and around all that he has on every side? You have blessed the work of his hands, and his possessions have increased in the land. But now, stretch out Your hand and touch all that he has, and he will surely curse You to Your face" (Job 1:9-11).

Kaph is about brokenness and humility

1. Recall from *dalet* the three character traits that God is looking for in us:

   • Brokenness: God looks for humility and brokenness. Ponder Psalm 51:17.

   • Integrity: Heart and soul reunited from the great separation of Genesis 3.

   • Holiness: Set apart from the world and consecrated to God for a purpose.

2. Self-reliance must give way to trusting in the Lord: "Trust in the LORD with all your heart and lean not on your own understanding" (Proverbs 3:5). Our unrelenting tendency to resort to our own strength, gifting, resources, wisdom, initiative and knowledge, in order to solve the problems of life and vindicate ourselves, must be dealt a death blow. Self-reliance must be broken as we turn to God in faith and love. Turning inward in unbelief, self-pity, bitterness, defeat and fatalism is the opposite of faith.

   • "The flesh (human initiative) wars against the Spirit (divine initiative) and these are contrary to one another" (Galatians 5:17).

   • "The LORD will have war with Amalek (the flesh) from generation to generation" (Exodus 17:16).

   • *Yeshua*, in His death, would not move to save Himself from the cross, but committed Himself to Him who judges righteously (1 Peter 2:23; Matthew 27:40).

   • In His life and ministry, *Yeshua* never took the initiative, but always did what He saw the Father doing (John 5:19-20).

3. A life of serving self must give way to zeal for God's kingdom and His righteousness. David's doctrine of judgment (v. 84) is not some vindictive call for vengeance upon his enemies. It is zeal to see the triumph of divine justice and zeal for God's kingdom prevail. To this end he prays and labors, laying down his own life.

   • Righteousness and justice are the foundation of His throne (kingdom).

   • "Your kingdom come. Your will be done on earth as in heaven" (Matthew 6:10).

4. Brokenness is acutely necessary when the Lord finally does answer the prayer of verse eighty-four, "When will You execute judgment on those who persecute me?" Our attitude toward our enemies is critical. To gloat over their downfall is a huge mistake and proves that we are not yet broken of our own pride. Our prayers for rescue from our persecutors must be purged of any vindictiveness or desire for personal vengeance. God's temporal judgments are redemptive in their intent. He takes no pleasure in the death of the wicked and is not willing that any perish. This is their chance to repent and join the family of God. If we have pride, we will gloat at the demise of our enemy when God finally does bring them to judgment, and will not be able to receive them into the family. Consider the following:

    - The injustice of Israel's enslavement in Egypt is legendary (Exodus 1-14). God used Egypt to be an iron furnace whose fire would produce a broken people for Himself. "The LORD has taken you and brought you out of the iron furnace, out of Egypt, to be His people" (Deuteronomy 4:20). When Israel finally left Egypt in freedom, many Egyptians joined them. Quite probably, there were converted slave drivers and oppressors in their very midst who became part of the family of God. No time for gloating.

    - The early body of Messiah had to receive a former persecutor in Saul of Tarsus. In great power, the Lord confronted Saul, showed him his error and vindicated as right the very people he zealously persecuted. This would have been an opportunity for many to gloat.

    - In his death, the demonized King Saul, who pursued righteous David, got what he deserved. But David lamented over his downfall; there was no gloating or rejoicing. Why? Because zeal for God's glory trumped any zeal for his own relief, vengeance or vindication. Read 2 Samuel 1:17.

    - Joseph, having become second in command in Egypt, said to his brothers: "Do not be afraid, for am I in the place of God?" What an opportunity this would have been to gloat and take vengeance. But Joseph is a broken and humble man, now entrusted with great authority.

    - Romans 12:19-21, "Beloved, do not avenge yourselves, but rather give place to wrath; for it is written, 'Vengeance is Mine, I will repay' says the Lord. Therefore, 'if your enemy is hungry, feed him. If he is thirsty, give him a drink; For in so doing you will heap coals of fire on his head.' Do not be overcome by evil, but overcome evil with good."

    - "Father forgive them for they do not know what they do" (Luke 23:34).

    - "Lord, do not charge them with this sin" (Acts 7:60).

- Obadiah 1:12-13, "You should not have gazed on the day of your brother in the day of his captivity . . . or rejoiced . . . in the day of their destruction; Nor should you have spoken proudly in the day of distress . . . you should not have gazed on their affliction in the day of their calamity."

Questions to Ponder

1. Have you ever felt that you would faint under the pressure, or that somehow the test was more than you could bear? How did God work out that season of your life for good?

2. How have God's dealings in your life produced brokenness and faith?

3. Have you ever wanted to take vengeance into your own hands?

Chapter 14

Eternity and Majesty:
Seeing Eternity Established the Heart

LAMED

[89]Forever, O LORD,
Your word is settled in heaven.
[90]Your faithfulness endures to all generations;
You established the earth, and it abides.
[91]They continue this day according to Your ordinances,
For all are Your servants.
[92]Unless Your law had been my delight,
I would then have perished in my affliction.
[93]I will never forget Your precepts,
For by them You have given me life.
[94]I am Yours, save me;
For I have sought Your precepts.
[95]The wicked wait for me to destroy me,
But I will consider Your testimonies.
[96]I have seen the consummation of all perfection,
But Your commandment is exceedingly broad.

Lamed—Psalm 119:89-96

Will our fainting psalmist make it? What will it take to sustain him in the test? In this section of the psalm, we can say that David is no longer a victim, held captive by his enemies. A sense of eternity is established in his heart.

The ancient Hebrew pictograph for *lamed* is a cattle goad or shepherd's staff. The name of the letter itself, *lamed*, comes from the root *lamad*, meaning to learn or teach, a word which we studied back in *tet* (v. 65-72). In *tet*, we saw the role of negative and painful circumstances functioning as a kind of goad in the hand of a loving heavenly Father to instruct or discipline us. Here in *lamed*, the emphasis is clearly not on the role of negative, painful experiences (of injustice) in our formation, but on the positive experiences of encountering the presence of God and then of seeing, learning, being taught and gaining understanding by revelation.

According to the Hebrew sages, the goal of learning and teaching (*lamed*) is heart knowledge that spurs us unto love for God and the performing of righteous acts. This section is really about the true knowledge of God in our hearts, and its power to propel or goad us toward *The Blessed Life* of whole-hearted worship and service to God.

Interestingly enough, the previous section (*kaph*) brought us to the exact center of the psalm. We now begin the second half with verse eighty-nine, and we notice a dramatic shift in the tone of our psalmist. According to verses ninety-four and ninety-five, his earthly circumstances may not have changed, but there has obviously been a great breakthrough within his own fainting soul. Much like Isaiah in Isaiah 6, John in Revelation 1 and 4 to 5, Daniel in Daniel 10, Ezekiel in Ezekiel 1, or Micaiah in 2 Chronicles 18, our psalmist has seen the Lord, high and lifted up. The Apostle Paul also was "caught up to the third heaven . . . up into Paradise and heard inexpressible words, which it is not lawful for a man to utter" (2 Corinthians 12:1-4).

Our psalmist has joined the ranks of those who have tasted eternity and have seen the throne of God and something of the splendor and majesty of the Lord Himself. Every one of these servants of the Lord became unquenchable in their zeal for the Lord and His kingdom. No measure of trouble, persecution or threats from their enemies could move them. In Acts 20:24, after commenting on his tears and trials and knowing that chains and tribulations awaited him in Jerusalem, Paul resolves to go to Jerusalem anyway. He states, "But none of these things move me; nor do I count my life dear to myself, so that I may finish my race with joy." He became compelled (goaded) by the love of Messiah (2 Corinthians 5:14). David's perspective too has changed dramatically and the revelation he received becomes the goad or motivation which keeps him steady under pressure and establishes his heart to boldly follow the Lord.

2 Corinthians 3:16-18 may help us understand what has just happened to our psalmist. "Nevertheless, when one turns to the Lord, the veil is taken away. Now the Lord is the Spirit; and where the Spirit of the Lord is, there is liberty. But we all, with unveiled face, beholding as in a mirror the glory of the Lord, are being transformed into the same image from glory to glory, just as by the Spirit of the Lord."

Let us note three truths from these verses which also apply to David:

1. First, it is evident that our psalmist turned to the Lord in his time of affliction. Hence, the veil is taken away and he encounters the Lord in a supernatural way, seeing more fully who God really is. The first and only occurrence of the word heaven in Psalm 119 is here at the beginning of the second half of the psalm. A huge eternity theme emerges in this section as David sees something beyond this world with its injustices and difficulties—or its blessings and pleasures, for that matter.

2. Second, we can clearly see a new buoyancy, confidence and liberty in our traveler, because where the Spirit of the Lord is, there is liberty.

3. Third, we see the transforming power of beholding the glory of the Lord "as in a mirror." The mirrors of the ancient world were made of polished metal and thus gave only a dim reflection. However, even a dim view of the Lord which comes by the Holy Spirit and the word of God through faith has the power to transform us into that same image. Growing in the knowledge of God is presented in the New Testament as the number one calling and premier privilege of every believer. This unveiling of God to the human heart becomes our psalmist's positive motivation, or goad, for whole-hearted love, obedience and service to God. Consider a few scriptures:

    -   John 17:3, "And this is eternal life, that they may know You, the only true God."

    -   Philippians 3:8, "I count all things loss for the excellence of the knowledge of Christ."

    -   2 Peter 3:18, "But grow in the grace and knowledge of our Lord and Savior, Jesus Christ."

    -   2 Corinthians 10:4-5, "For the weapons of our warfare are not carnal but mighty in God for pulling down strongholds, casting down arguments and every high thing that exalts itself against the knowledge of God, bringing every thought into captivity."

    -   In Proverbs 2:1-5, the knowledge of God is described as the greatest treasure.

    -   The revelation of *Yeshua*, the Messiah, to the human heart is the Bread of Life that sustains us. Holy Spirit loves to "break our bread" on the revelation of who He is (see John 6:35; 16:15). Bread has been called the staff of life because it represents basic sustenance. This brings us back to *lamed* as a shepherd's staff.

The highest spiritual warfare we can wage is the battle in our minds for the true knowledge of God. Our accuser, the "accuser of the brethren" (Revelation 12:10) is busy sowing lies about God in our mind. That is his job. He taunts: "Did God really say. . .?" He calls into question the integrity of God's character, the righteousness of His ways, His faithfulness to His promises and the kindness of His intentions toward us. In painful circumstances, these questions can seem reasonable, and thus, doubts about God's goodness can easily take root in our spirit.

Our job is to fight the good fight of faith, to walk in truth, to believe the truth, to be true, and to wait in faith for the promise. Our psalmist's declaration of God's goodness and faithfulness in the face of great injustice and affliction is, in essence, the waging of warfare against the river of lies that flows night and day from the "accuser of the brethren" (see Revelation 12:10-12).

The paradox of *kaph* and *lamed* is this: God wants brokenness concerning our confidence in the flesh, so that we walk with a limp, leaning fully upon Him. Without Him we can do nothing. On the other hand, God wants bold, faith-filled obedience based on confidence in Him. "I can do all things through Messiah who strengthens me." David's revelation in *lamed* ignites bold faith.

Features of *lamed* that set it apart from other sections and help to unlock its truths include:

1. As noted above, the one and only mention of heaven (*shamayim* in v. 89) occurs here. An eternity theme is revealed in words like forever, all generations, abides, and continuing.

2. Related to eternity is that which is established and cannot be moved, or settled, faithful, established, abiding, and continuing.

3. One notable distinction between the first half of the psalm (v. 1-88) and the second half (v. 89-176) is the frequency with which our psalmist refers to himself.

    "I", "me", and "my" occur 309 times, 201 times in the first half and only 108 times in the second. Is John 3:30, when John the Baptist declared "He must increase but I must decrease," being demonstrated by our psalmist?

We will outline these eight verses in a 3-3-2 pattern:

*   God's word: Eternally faithful and established forever (v. 89-91).

*   David: Alive because of the word of God (v. 92-94).

*   Unmoved by threats: Moved by revelation (v. 95-96).

Let's join David in his journey:

God's word: Eternally faithful and established forever

"Forever, O LORD, Your word is settled in heaven. Your faithfulness endures to all generations; You established the earth, and it abides. They continue this day according to Your ordinances, for all are Your servants" (v. 89-91).

1. God's word (*dabar*) is:

    *   "Forever" (*owlam*), literally to the vanishing point, past or future, eternity, perpetuity.

    *   "Settled (*natsab*) in heaven to stand" (be stationed, establish).

2. "Your faithfulness endures to all generations." In the long view of history, the consistent testimony of all generations is that God is faithful. Read Psalm 145:4, "One generation shall praise Your works to another, and shall declare Your mighty acts."

    - Psalm 36:5 says, "Your faithfulness reaches to the clouds." What is the faithfulness of God? It means that God is absolutely faithful or true to who He is as God. He is absolutely true to who He is in His essential goodness. His word is utterly true and trustworthy. He is not capricious, but is in fact, bound by His nature in everything He does. There is always absolute integrity. This reminds us of our discussion of the Hebrew word, *tamiym*, used in verse one.

        o He never violates His righteousness when allowing the righteous to suffer and the wicked to prevail. He is faithful when He delivers us and He is faithful when He does not deliver us in this age but allows us to be martyred.

        o He never violates mercy when displaying wrath, discipline or judgment.

        o He never violates His holiness when showing mercy and forgiving sin.

        o His word is true even when we get the opposite of the promise for a time.

3. God's word is eternal. His revealed purposes and promises remain intact. Just because justice is perverted for a season and things on earth are shaking does not mean that heaven is shaking. God is looking for those who stand firm, settled and unmoved by circumstances on earth or by the threats of the enemy. God is looking for those who are moved, not by circumstances, but by His voice and revealed will.

    - 1 Peter 5:10 is powerful: "But may the God of all grace . . . after you have suffered a while, perfect, establish, strengthen, and settle you."

    - In Acts 20:24, Paul responded thus to the threat of chains and tribulations which awaited him in Jerusalem: "But none of these things move me; nor do I count my life dear to myself, so that I may finish my race with joy."

4. Eternity is a major theme here. Living in the light of eternity changes everything!

    - We cannot make sense of the afflictions in this life if there is no eternity. In fact, if there is no eternity, then God is cruel, because our troubles have no purpose. However, if the difficulties of the journey in this age prepare us for an eternity to come, then our troubles have a purpose and God is love, no matter what.

- Neither can we steward our success, prosperity and blessings unless we live in light of eternity; otherwise, we will squander it all on ourselves (James 4:3).

- Consider Paul's words in 2 Corinthians 4:16-18, "Therefore we do not lose heart. Even though our outward man is perishing, yet the inward man is being renewed day by day. For our light affliction, which is but for a moment, is working for us a far more exceeding and eternal weight of glory, while we do not look at the things which are seen, but at the things which are not seen. For the things which are seen are temporary, but the things which are not seen are eternal."

5. "For all are your servants." The heavens and earth are "your servants." The entire created order serves God's purposes and testifies to His faithfulness. "For since the creation of the world His invisible attributes are clearly seen, being understood by the things that are made, even His eternal power and divine nature" (Romans 1:20). See also Psalm 89:2, 5, 36-37.

    - The constancy of the natural order illustrates, and is a picture of, the sureness of His word and His faithfulness.

    - Even the wicked ultimately serve His purposes, as we learned in *tet* (Exodus 9:16). History could be described as a study of the interplay between the sovereignty of God, the free-will and sin of man, God's love for man, Satan's rage against man, and the word of God operating in and through believers. Ultimately, everything and everyone serves His purposes, even our adversary, the devil.

6. His word and plans remain. Psalm 33:11 tells us that the counsel of the LORD stands forever. In these first three verses we encounter four occurrences of three different Hebrew synonyms, all which could be translated to stand or remain.

    - Settled (*natsab*): to stand (v. 89)

    - Established (*kuwn*): to be firm, stable or established (v. 90)

    - Abides (*amad*): to stand, remain, endure (v. 90, 91)

David: Alive because of the word of God

"Unless Your law had been my delight, I would then have perished in my affliction. I will never forget Your precepts, for by them You have given me life. I am Yours, save me; For I have sought Your precepts" (v. 92-94).

1. "Unless Your law (*torah*) had been my delight." David's love of God's word is legendary (see Psalm 119:97). This love of God's word held him steady through persecution and great affliction.

2. "I would then have perished in my affliction." Psalm 94:17 has a similar theme: "Unless the LORD had been my help (in time of great persecution and injustice from evildoers), my soul would soon have settled in silence." We cannot endure without the Lord. His promise has always been, "I will be with you!"

3. Delighting in the Lord and His word is the great antidote to encountering the evil in the world. Psalm 37 also connects this antidote with evil. It begins with the words, "Do not fret because of evildoers" and continues in verses three to four with these words: "Trust in the LORD, and do good; Dwell in the land, and feed on His faithfulness. Delight yourself also in the LORD, and He shall give you the desires of your heart."

    *   The believer who can cultivate intimacy and grow in love for God during the storm, before the circumstances change for the better, gets the victory.

    *   Our human tendency is to think that when things are better, we will be able enjoy God and enter into intimacy. But the truth is actually the opposite: when peace and prosperity prevail, our propensity to drift away from intimacy with the Lord increases.

4. "I will never (*owlam.*)" To the vanishing point future, the psalmist promises, "I will not forget Your precepts, for by them you have given me life." He has learned that the word of God is the very food which gives him life.

    *   "Man shall not live by bread alone, but by every word that proceeds from the mouth of God" (Matthew 4:4).

    *   "I am the Bread of Life. . . . If anyone eats this bread, he will live forever. . . . Unless you eat My flesh and drink My blood you have no life in you. . . . The words that I speak to you are spirit, and they are life. Lord, You have the words of eternal life" (excerpts from John 6:48-68).

5. God is establishing the heart of David to overcome anything that can possibly come against him in this world. Consider these scriptures concerning an established heart:

    *   1 Thessalonians 3:13, "So that He may establish your hearts blameless in holiness before our God and Father at the coming of our Lord Jesus Christ."

    *   2 Thessalonians 2:16-17, "Now may our Lord Jesus Christ Himself . . . comfort your hearts and establish you in every good word and work."

- James 5:8, "Be patient. Establish your hearts, for the coming of the Lord is at hand."

- Hebrews 13:9, "Do not be carried about with various and strange doctrines. For it is good that the heart be established by grace."

6. "I am Yours, save me." The pressure is probably still on. David is appealing to the Lord for help or deliverance on the basis of God's ownership of his life and his own submission to God's purposes in his life.

    - We were created for God and for His will (Revelation 4:11).

    - We were purchased for God by the blood of His Son.

        o 1 Corinthians 6:19-20, "Do you not know . . . you are not your own? For you were bought at a price; therefore glorify God."

        o 1 Peter 1:18-19, "You were not redeemed with corruptible things like silver and gold . . . but with the precious blood of Jesus." See Revelation 5:9 and Acts 20:28.

7. "I have sought." The word *daresh*, Hebrew for sought, means to tread, beat a path to, or frequent. In other words, our psalmist has consistently followed after, beat a path to, and submitted to God's precepts (*piqquwd*), allowing them to preside over his life and set righteous boundaries.

Unmoved by threats: Moved by revelation

"The wicked wait for me to destroy me, but I will consider Your testimonies. I have seen the consummation of all perfection, but Your commandment is exceedingly broad" (v. 95-96).

1. An amplified reading on the next phrase might go like this: The wicked wait (*qavah*: look for, expect) for me intensely intent on destroying me, so as to see me perish.

    - Wait also occurs in Isaiah 40:31, "Those who wait on the LORD shall renew their strength. . . ."

    - We have encountered the wicked in verses fifty-three and sixty-one, but here they become aggressive. In verse 110 they will lay a snare.

2. "But I will consider (*biyn*: to separate, discern, distinguish) Your testimonies." David does not even seem to be listening to the roaring lion that seeks to devour him (1 Peter 5:8). His focus is on the Lord's voice. He is hearing and seeing something from another realm.

3. "I have seen the consummation (*qets*: end or extremity) of all perfection (*tiklah*: complete accomplishment, completeness)." In other words, "It is finished." Could it be that David saw the coming of Messiah? All the prophets saw and spoke of a day in the future: The "day of the Lord" or "that day" or "the great and terrible day of the Lord" or "the great day of God Almighty." There are probably several hundred references in scripture to the future day when Messiah comes. They saw a day in which the Messiah would come in power and establish justice in the earth. It would be a terrible day for the wicked and a glorious day for the righteous. His coming would be in two stages and totally overthrow Satan's dominion, establish the kingdom of God on earth and initiate an era of unprecedented peace and prosperity.

    *   The first coming of Messiah was with the accompanying announcement of "on earth peace, goodwill toward men" (Luke 2:14).

    *   In John 19:30, as *Yeshua* was on the cross, it was all paid for with these words: "It is finished" (*teleo*: bring to a close, finish).

    *   At the second coming of Messiah, the days of the sounding of the seventh angel, "the mystery of God would be finished (*teleo*), as He declared to His servants the prophets" (Revelation 10:7).

    *   Also, in Revelation 16:17; 21:6, we have these words related to the completion of God's purposes, concerning both the wicked and the righteous: It is done!

4. Another distinct possibility is that the consummation of all perfection could be the bride of Messiah. When the angel in Revelation 21:9 showed John the bride, the Lamb's wife, John was so overcome that he fell down and worshipped the angel (Revelation 22:8). He saw a city, New Jerusalem, as a glorious bride, shining with the glory of God.

    *   This may well be what the Apostle Paul saw when he was caught up to paradise (paradise has bridal connotations). What he saw was unlawful to utter.

    *   Abraham looked for a city, the glorious corporate bride of Messiah (Hebrews 11:10).

    *   Our psalmist may well have seen the masses of redeemed humanity from all nations, tribes, peoples and tongues brought to perfection as a glorious bride of Messiah. When he saw this culmination of redemption, suddenly, his troubles not only had meaning, but by comparison were simply the light and momentary afflictions, which Paul referenced in 2 Corinthians 4:17. It is worth it all.

5. "But Your commandment (*mitzvah*) is exceedingly broad." Having seen the throne of God, glimpsed eternity and the coming of Messiah, our psalmist perceives God's commands, not as bonds and cords, as do the nations in Psalm 2:1-3, or as something that restricts and limits his life, but as being broad beyond measure. This is an important concept. God's commandments are liberating and meant for our good. They lead to great blessing.

    *   The first words of the psalm agree: "Blessed are the undefiled in the way, Who walk in the law (*torah*) of the LORD."

    *   John said it this way in 1 John 5:3-4, "For this is the love of God, that we keep His commandments. And His commandments are not burdensome. For whatever is born of God overcomes the world. And this is the victory that has overcome the world—our faith."

Concluding Thoughts

Suffering saints throughout history often processed their unjust and difficult persecutions by beholding the majesty of the throne of God and catching a glimpse of eternity and the certainty that divine justice would prevail. Some of them saw the glory of the bride of Messiah. What they beheld set them on fire and made them shining lights in their day.

1. In Job 26, Job is on the ash heap scraping his sores with broken pottery when he turns his gaze toward eternity and beholds the Lord. This keeps him steady.

2. Job again had this kind of encounter in Job 38 to 41, when God Himself began to speak. In Job 42:5, we have these words in response: "I have heard of You by the hearing of the ear, but now my eye sees You."

3. Ezekiel was in exile when he saw the throne of God in Ezekiel 1.

4. John was in exile in Patmos when he encountered the resurrected *Yeshua* and saw the throne of God and the bride of Messiah.

5. In Psalm 73, David was tormented by the perversion of justice, as the wicked prospered and the righteous suffered "Until I went into the sanctuary of God; Then I understood their end" (v. 17).

6. Israel was in political crisis at the death of King Uzziah in Isaiah 6:1, when Isaiah "saw the Lord sitting on a throne, high and lifted up."

7. Micaiah, the one true prophet of the Lord in King Ahab's day, was under enormous pressure from the political correctness of his day. Under the threat of imprisonment, Micaiah gave the true word of the Lord. In 2 Chronicles 18:18, "he saw the LORD sitting on His throne, and all the host of heaven standing on His right hand and His left."

8. Furthermore, *Yeshua* Himself could be described as the Consummation of all things:

   • Romans 10:4, "For Messiah is the goal (*telos*: aim, end purpose) of the *torah* for righteousness for everyone who believes" (*The Scriptures*).

   • Romans 11:36, "For of Him and through Him and to Him are all things, to whom be glory forever."

   • Revelation 1:8, "I am the Alpha (*Aleph*) and the Omega (*Tav*), the beginning and the end . . . who is and who was and who is to come."

   • Colossians 2:9, "For in Him dwells all the fullness of the Godhead bodily."

   • John 1:1; Revelation 19:13, "His Name is called The Word of God."

   • Ephesians 1:22, "He put all things under His feet, and gave Him to be head over all things to the church, which is His body, the fullness of Him who fills all in all."

Questions to Ponder

1. How has a glimpse of eternity changed your outlook in life's trials? How has it ignited boldness and faith within your heart?

2. How does living in the light of eternity change the way you live now?

3. How have the commands of God been liberating for you? Have those same commands ever seemed too difficult and restrictive?

Chapter 15

Wisdom: Passion and Discipline

MEM

⁹⁷Oh, how I love Your law!
It is my meditation all the day.
⁹⁸You, through Your commandments,
make me wiser than my enemies;
For they are ever with me.
⁹⁹I have more understanding than all my teachers,
For Your testimonies are my meditation.
¹⁰⁰I understand more than the ancients,
Because I keep Your precepts.
¹⁰¹I have restrained my feet from every evil way,
That I may keep Your word.
¹⁰²I have not departed from Your judgments,
For You Yourself have taught me.
¹⁰³How sweet are Your words to my taste,
Sweeter than honey to my mouth!
¹⁰⁴Through Your precepts I get understanding;
Therefore I hate every false way.

Mem—Psalm 119:97-104

The ancient Hebrew pictograph for the letter *mem* portrays waves of water. Words like much, exceedingly, mighty, many or massive are indicative of its meaning—much like the mighty oceans and rivers of the earth. *Mem* can be a metaphor for either blessing or chaos, life or death, as water can be both life sustaining and life threatening. *Mem* can symbolize the spring or fountain of the *torah* (water of the word), which leads to life. There are many places in scripture where the word of God is likened to water. For example, Deuteronomy 32:1-2, "Hear, O earth, the words of My mouth. Let My teaching drop as the rain, My speech (words) distill as the dew, as raindrops on the tender herb, and as showers on the grass."

David's encounter with God in *lamed* overflows into *mem*. Consider his opening words: "Oh, how I love Your law (*torah*). It is my meditation all the day." In Psalm 45:1 David says, "My heart is overflowing with a good theme." It is as if David is in the river of God described in Psalm 36:8-9, "They are abundantly satisfied with the fullness of Your house, and You give them drink from the river of Your pleasures. For with You is the fountain of life; In Your light we see light." Our psalmist is experiencing the superior pleasures of knowing God. He is seeing the ways of God revealed in Messiah, whose life is the light of men (John 1:4). The water of the *torah* is flowing with revelation.

In Psalm 63, while fleeing from King Saul in the wilderness of a dry and thirsty land where there is no water, David enters the sanctuary of God to behold God's power and glory. The ensuing revelation of God and His ways is like water to his thirsty soul. It is better than life itself (Psalm 63:1-3). Here in *mem*, with its emphasis on wisdom and understanding, it is as if God is answering the cry of Moses in Exodus 33:13 when he prayed, "Show me now Your way that I may know You," or the cry of David in Psalm 25:4-5 when he prayed, "Show me Your ways, O LORD; Teach me Your paths. Lead me in Your truth and teach me." Our psalmist is drinking deeply from the waters of the *torah*, growing in the knowledge of God, gaining understanding, and seeing the wisdom of God's ways.

It is unlikely that natural circumstances have changed much in the life of our psalmist, but a new reality is being experienced—one which trumps all natural circumstances and equips him with strength to live in light of eternity and with wisdom from above.

Several distinct features set this section apart from the others and help unlock what is happening. These include the following:

1. Five words related to this key theme of wisdom, teaching (or learning) and understanding reach far beyond what has been noted in earlier segments:

    *   Verse 98: Wiser (*chakam*) means to be wise (in mind, word or act). This is the only use of chakam in the entire psalm.

    *   Verse 99: Understanding (*sakal*) means to be prudent, to be circumspect, intelligent or skillful with wisdom applied so as to prosper. This is the only use of *sakal* in Psalm 119.

    *   Verse 99: Teachers (*lamad*) means to learn, teach, instruct, goad toward the goal.

    *   Verses 100 and 104: Understand (*biyn*) means to separate, distinguish, discern, understand, consider. *Biyn* occurs ten times throughout the psalm as understanding, twice here in *mem*.

    *   Verse 102: Taught (*yarah*) is used only here and in verse thirty-three. *Yarah* is discussed in the introduction as the root word behind *torah* (law). It is often translated teach, but can mean to shoot (as an arrow) cast or throw. *Yarah* is actually translated archer five times in scripture. Contrasted in *tet* with *lamad* (goad), this is the gentler Hebrew word for teach. It pictures a father

pointing the son or daughter he loves, like an arrow, toward the target, which they are to hit, the goal, or the way in which they are to go in order to live *The Blessed Life*.

2. The first and only occurrence in the entire psalm of the Hebrew word *kala'* (restrict, restrain, withhold, shut up), translated restrained in verse 101, connects the subject of self-control or self-discipline with experiencing this river of God's pleasures in which our psalmist is presently swimming. We will discuss this at verse 101.

3. Opposite passions. Note the "passion sandwich" of *mem*:

   - The first phrase in verse 97: "Oh, how I love Your law."

   - The last phrase in verse 104: "Therefore I hate every false way."

   We will outline our reflections on the verses of *mem* in a 4–4 pattern as follows:

   - Verses 97-100: The excellence and superiority of God's ways revealed (Deuteronomy 4:6; Isaiah 55:9). Or we could title the verses, "Passion for *Yeshua*: Loving what God loves."

   - Verses 101-104: The life-transforming power of God and His word (see Romans 8:6; John 6:63). Or we could title it "Purity in our walk: Hating what God hates."

The excellence and superiority of God's ways revealed (v. 97-100).

Let's ponder scriptures which speak of the superiority of God's wisdom and ways:

Deuteronomy 4:6-8, "Therefore be careful to observe them (God's statutes and judgments); for this is your wisdom (*chokmah*: from *chakam*) and your understanding (*biynah*: from *biyn*) in the sight of the peoples who will hear all these statutes, and say, 'Surely this great nation is a wise (*chakam*) and understanding (*biyn*) people. For what great nation is there that has God so near to it, as the LORD our God is to us, for whatever reason we may call upon Him? And what great nation is there that has such statutes and righteous judgments as are in all this law (*torah*) which I set before you this day?'" Consider also Isaiah 55:7-9 and 1 Corinthians 1:20-25.

Let's join David now in the river of God:

"Oh, how I love Your law! It is my meditation all the day" (v. 97).

1. "Oh, how I love Your law (*torah*)." What an outburst. It comes on the heels of the preceding statement that God's commandments are actually liberating (exceedingly broad) and not restricting. When David saw the consummation of all

perfection (v. 96), maybe that revelation included powerful correlations with and explanations of things in the scriptures he had known about for years.

- Twelve times throughout this psalm, David confesses his love for the word of God in some fashion, and all but two of them are in the second half of the psalm. Both of the early confessions are in *vav* (v. 47, 48) during his encounter with the presence of God in which God's love was so powerfully revealed.

- "Let him kiss me with the kisses of his mouth—For your love is better than wine" (Song of Songs 1:2). Rabbis throughout history have taught the kisses of His mouth in the Song of Songs to be the kiss of the *torah* on the human heart. Our psalmist is certainly experiencing the kiss of God's word upon his heart in this season.

- Meditation: Revisit plank # 6 in *bet* (v. 15) for a refresher on meditation.

"You, through Your commandments (*mitzvah*), make me wiser than my enemies; For they are with me" (v. 98).

1. "You, through Your commandments, make me wiser (*chakam*) than my enemies."

   - *Chakam* is the root of the Hebrew words for both wise (man) and wisdom (*chochmah*). Together they appear about three hundred times in scripture, especially in the wisdom books, Proverbs and Ecclesiastes.

   - Those who walk in God's ways are deemed wise because of the ultimately good outcome (Deuteronomy 4:6-8 and Isaiah 55:7-9).

   - Although a believer may be put to the test in his stand for righteousness and pay a price to remain true, in the long run those who "walk undefiled in the way . . . in the law of the LORD, will be blessed (*esher*)." It becomes manifest that walking in heaven's ways is to walk wisely and with understanding (see Psalm 16:3).

2. "My enemies" (*'oyeb*: hating, an adversary, enemy, hostile). This is the first and only occurrence of this Hebrew word in Psalm 119.

   - The wicked: We met them in verses fifty-three and sixty-one. In verse ninety-five they get more aggressive as they lay in wait to destroy our psalmist. We will meet them again in verse 110, where they will lay a snare.

   - The proud: We met them five times in the first half of the psalm and we will meet them once more in verse 122. These could refer to our psalmist's own brethren who betrayed him.

   - Evildoers: We have yet to meet them in verse 115.

- My enemies: We meet them only here, but they may include all of the above who are hostile to the kingdom of God. David has accepted the fact that life in this world will be lived in context to enemies; enemies within (such as sin in its many forms) and enemies without (those who hate followers of God).

3. "For they are ever (*owlam*) with me." Is it God's commandments or is it his enemies that are ever with the psalmist? Although it is difficult to tell from the Hebrew text, the answer is both: The commandments of the Lord are hidden in David's heart and his enemies (within and without) are present. Sin is yet within us, operating in our members (Romans 7). Galatians 5:17 says, "The flesh wars against the Spirit and the Spirit against the flesh and these two are contrary to one another." We also need to recall:

   - The great promise of our faithful God: "I will be with you."

   - The Word made flesh said, "And surely I am with you always, to the very end of the age" (Matthew 28:20).

   - David's words in Psalm 16:8, "Because He (the LORD) is at my right hand (near) I shall not be moved" (by enemies, temptation or pressure).

   - Psalm 23:5 says, "You prepare a table before me in the presence of my enemies."

4. We have an adversary and we need one. "Your adversary, the devil walks about like a roaring lion" (1 Peter 5:8). How will one become strong without the resistance of the weights that he is lifting? How will one become a good soldier or fighter without an opponent on whom to practice? Runners often carry weights as they run in preparation for a big race. How can we be overcomers if there is nothing to overcome?

   - Paul spoke of his Jewish brethren in Romans 11:28, "Concerning the gospel they are enemies for your sake."

   - *Yeshua*, in John 15:18-20, tells us that as the world hated and persecuted Him, so they will do to you.

Our Enemies Without

As believers in *Yeshua* as the Messiah, and seekers of His kingdom, we have only one ultimate enemy, noted above in verse ninety-eight and in 1 Peter 5:8. We also are to love our enemies and hate no man (Matthew 5:44). However, like it or not, there are those who hate believers because of what they represent. Paul prays to be delivered from "unreasonable and wicked men; for not all have faith" (2 Thessalonians 3:2). The martyrdom of believers for their faith is escalating in the earth. A war is raging against the biblical world view in unprecedented ways and with great fury. Believers are the target.

Recall this excerpt from *yood*. The announcement of the kingdom of God is actually bad news for those with a vested interest in the (corrupt) status quo. Human beings, whom God loves but who have a vested interest in the corrupt governments and high places of the earth (such as Pharaoh, Herod or Demetrius), may well become violent persecutors of those who are deemed a threat to their agenda. Thus, they become our personal and mortal enemies. Our challenge is to love the person, and never foster a wrong spirit toward him or her, while still relentlessly seeking "the kingdom of God and His righteousness," albeit at the expense of those corrupt evil systems.

"I have more understanding than all my teachers, for Your testimonies are my meditation. I understand more than the ancients (the aged), because I keep Your precepts" (v. 99-100).

1. "I have more understanding (*sakal*)." *Sakal* and its derivatives appear eighty-five times in scripture. This word is all about applying godly wisdom so as to prosper and showcase *The Blessed Life*. Walking according to God's wise ways is the emphasis of the last four verses of *mem*.

2. "Than all my teachers (*lamad*)." Who are these teachers?

    •   The educators and intellectuals of the day?

    •   David's persecutors and betrayers (those wicked and proud who are serving as "goads" in the Father's hand, for his formation)? We discussed this in *tet*.

    •   His carnal brethren? Job's friends thought they knew the answer to Job's woes.

3. "I understand (*biyn*: to separate, distinguish, discern, understand, consider) more "

    •   *Biyn* occurs ten times throughout the psalm and means understanding. The psalmist has already asked for *biyn* three times (v. 27, 34, 73) and will yet ask for understanding three more times (v. 125, 144, 169).

    •   We have equated this prayer for understanding to a longing to be counted a friend of God (John 15:15). Ultimately, to separate is to distinguish between the flesh and the Spirit (see more in *dalet*). This is our journey to maturity.

    •   Scripture makes it clear that the distinguishing mark of maturity is to walk in the Spirit. The mark of immaturity is to walk in the flesh (1 Corinthians 3:1-3; Romans 8:3-10).

4. "The ancients" (the aged). Consider *Yeshua*'s words in Matthew 11:25, "You have hidden these things from the wise and prudent and have revealed them to babes."

    •   Those who walk by spiritual truth have the mind of Messiah (1 Corinthians 2:16).

- Read 1 Corinthians 2:9-16, where those who with childlike faith believe and obey the word of God, and who cultivate an intimate relationship with the Lord through His Spirit, will receive amazing revelations from God. "Though the things of the Spirit are foolishness to the natural man," these will have become truly wise compared to the wise and prudent intellectuals and educators of the day, who walk only in natural truth.

The life-transforming power of God and His word (v. 101-104)

"I have restrained my feet from every evil way, that I may keep Your word. I have not departed from Your judgments, for You Yourself have taught me" (v. 101-102).

1. "I have restrained" (*kala'*) means to restrict, withhold, forbid my feet. This is the only occurrence of *kala'* in the psalm. It introduces the character qualities of self-control, self-discipline and self-denial. It opens the subject of the disciplines of the believer's life, such as prayer and fasting. In 1 Corinthians 9:27 Paul said, "I discipline my body and bring it into subjection, lest, when I have preached to others, I myself should become disqualified."

2. "From every evil (*ra*) way." *Ra* also occurs only once in Psalm 119 but almost 350 times in scripture. It has a broader meaning than something wicked or sinful. It includes the concepts of bad, inferior, ugly, disagreeable, unwholesome, injury, of bad quality and bad-tempered. Our psalmist has not only restrained his feet from illegitimate and sinful pleasures but also has restrained his flesh in the areas of legitimate pleasures. He has not inordinately used even the good gifts of God for wrong purposes. These include food, sexuality and a thousand earthly pleasures. This theme is dealt with in a fuller way in Addendum 6.

3. "I have not departed from (turned aside from or put aside) Your judgments" (*mishpat*). Our psalmist has consistently allowed the word of God to judge his own carnality, while waiting on and trusting God for the judgment of his enemies (see Addendum 4). It is evident that when sinned against, David restrained himself from carnal responses.

4. "You Yourself have taught (*yarah*) me." Here is what I have called the gentler word for teach. David has been taught, not only by the painful goad of the *lamad* but also by the intimate instruction of the Father showing him the way.

    - Psalm 25:8-9, "Good and upright is the LORD; Therefore He teaches sinners in the way. The humble He guides in justice, and the humble He teaches His way."

    - John 6:45, "It is written in the prophets, and they shall all be taught by God."

- This is the promise of the new covenant (see Deuteronomy 30:6; Jeremiah 31:34; Hebrews 8:10-11).

- In the kingdom yet to fully come, all the nations will be taught by the Lord. "Many nations shall come and say, 'Come, and let us go up to the mountain of the LORD, to the house of the God of Jacob; He will teach us His ways, and we shall walk in His paths.' For out of Zion the law shall go forth, and the word of the LORD from Jerusalem" (Micah 4:2).

"How sweet are Your words (*imrah*) to my taste, sweeter than honey to my mouth" (v. 103).

1. "How sweet are Your words (*imrah*)." Remember from the introduction that *imrah* seems to be to the Hebrew what *rhema* is to the Greek: a word spoken in the context of intimacy. The sweetness of honey is a pleasure which symbolizes and points to the transcendent pleasure of intimacy with the Lord.

   - This echoes Psalm 19:10, "More to be desired are they than gold, yea, than much fine gold; Sweeter also than honey and the honeycomb."

   - Proverbs 8:11, "For wisdom is better than rubies, and all the things one may desire cannot be compared with her."

2. God is desirable. His presence and word can become a holy addiction. In Haggai 2:7, the pronoun He refers to "the Desire of all nations." Any self-denial of temporal pleasures for the purpose of the transcendent pleasures of knowing God more displays our esteem of and hunger for that which is ultimately fulfilling. This is something that temporal pleasures cannot do.

"Through Your precepts I get understanding; Therefore I hate every false way" (v. 104).

1. "Understanding" (*biyn*): See notes on verses ninety-eight to one hundred.

2. "I hate every false (*sheqer*)" or lying and deceptive way or path. In verse 128, David again says, "I hate every false way," and again in verse 163, "I hate and abhor lying." What is it exactly that he hates? Hating the false way in others is one thing, but hating it in yourself is something completely different. What is happening to our psalmist?

   - In verses sixty-nine, seventy-eight and eighty-six, our psalmist becomes the victim of the lies and false accusations of the proud and the wicked who schemed against him. This was part of a great betrayal and wound in his life. Is this why he hates every false way?

- In *dalet*, however, our psalmist asked God to remove "the way of lying" from his own life. As noted there, the way of lying goes beyond telling a falsehood. It is about a lifestyle of deception, posturing, pretense, and hypocrisy for the sake of self-promotion or self-protection. In 3 John 4, John says, "I have no greater joy than that my children walk in truth." See *aleph* and *dalet* again for a refresher on integrity and walking in truth.

- There is no doubt that David has passed the tests ensuing from injustice. He is not embittered or remorseful in any way, but sees the hand of God in his loss and turns to the Lord for strength. He allowed the word of God to judge his own carnality along the way. This first confession of hating every false way is in context to the glorious revelation of divine wisdom and the ways of God. Our psalmist literally hates the way he used to be and the entire world system, which is predicated upon deception and self-promotion. Instead, he is gripped by the compelling beauty and power that a life of integrity and truth showcases.

- The "passion sandwich" can be found in the framework of the first and last phrases of *mem*: "Oh, how I love Your law" vis-a-vis "I hate every false way." Love and hate are really two sides of one coin. To love God's true ways is to hate every false way. The second passion will grow in proportion to the first passion. One presupposes the other.

3. A diet of meditation on God's word along with a pattern of submission to God is literally changing the desires of our psalmist. He is actually beginning to love what God loves and hate what God hates. Recall the cry of David in verses five and six, "Oh, that my ways were directed to keep Your statutes! Then I would not be ashamed, when I look into all Your commandments." At that point, he could hardly imagine hating the world's ways.

   - In Psalm 45:7, it is said of Messiah, "You love righteousness and hate wickedness."

   - Psalm 97:10, "You who love the LORD, hate evil!"

   - The warning cry of John to his "little children" in 1 John 2:15-17 is "Do not love the world or the things in the world."

   - Consider *Yeshua's* words in Luke 16:15, "God knows your hearts. For what is highly esteemed among men is an abomination in the sight of God."

Additional Thoughts on Verse 101: "I have restrained my feet"

Biblical holiness is happy holiness. God gives us all things to enjoy, but not to worship. We must learn to trace the pleasure and joy of such things back to the Giver. We are to be lovers of God and enjoyers of the pleasures He gives, not lovers of pleasure rather than lovers of God as in 2 Timothy 3:1-5. See more on self-denial in Addendum 6.

Our dignity as humans is to be seekers of the true and lasting transcendent pleasure of being lovers of God. When we inordinately seek after temporal pleasures, we betray the fact that we are worshipping and serving the creature and the creation rather than the Creator. When we temporarily deny ourselves temporal pleasures (such as fasting) for the sake of knowing God more, we display our esteem of and hunger for knowing God. Without this hunger for God, which must drive our self-denial, we will never obtain all that is available.

David's restraint and self-control are not some kind of legalistic effort to move God on his behalf, nor a morbid show of religious self-denial or strict adherence to a law. His restraint flows from love for God and longing for the transcendent pleasures of knowing God and His ways even more. Self-denial is always encouraged in the context of a greater personal advantage such as the pleasures of following *Yeshua*, the ultimate saving of our life, and our welcome into God's eternal kingdom. It is not an end in itself, which simply makes it some kind of religious show. See Addendum 6 for a fuller discussion of this huge subject.

Concluding Thoughts

Wisdom adopts the long view of eternity, seen in *lamed*:

- Wisdom (*chochmah*) is the capacity for reason and the ability to foresee import or outcome of actions. Biblical wisdom is directed by a moral and ethical standard. It tells us what to do in light of the future. An investor is said to be wise if he invests now in light of the future.

- Understanding (*binah* and *sakal*) gives insight into the complex and instructs us how to apply wisdom. It is the ability to think in abstract terms, to conceptualize beyond the obvious surface of a problem and propose a solution. If wisdom is the 'what', then understanding is the 'why' and 'how.'

Consider Proverbs 4:7, "Wisdom (*chochmah*) is the principal thing; Therefore get wisdom. And in all your getting, get understanding (binah)." The power of wisdom is that by applying it, one will prosper and become truly great in the kingdom of God. Consider the following:

1.   Solomon: Kings came from the ends of the earth to hear Solomon's wisdom. Solomon's prayer is recorded in 2 Chronicles 1:10, "Now give me wisdom (*chokmah*) and knowledge . . . for who can judge this great people of Yours?"

2.   Colossians 2:3 speaks of Messiah, "In whom are hidden all the treasures of wisdom and knowledge."

The essence of wisdom is that it takes a long view. It sacrifices the temporal for the eternal, whereas a fool sacrifices the eternal for temporal pleasures and desires. If, for example, true greatness comes as a result of humbling oneself to serve others, then it is wise to humble oneself now in this age and serve others rather than grasp for greatness in the wrong way (Mark 9:33-37; Matthew 20:20-28) and lose out in the age to come. Proverbs 1 and 2 are about wisdom in context to future crisis—that day of transition—the Great and Terrible Day of the Lord. See also Proverbs 1:20-33.

The question is this: What will you do with your life now, before the crisis? Prepare for eternity, or squander your life on temporal pursuits?

Who receives wisdom? Only those who value it and ask for it (James 1:5). Daniel 2:21 says, "He gives wisdom to the wise and knowledge to those who have understanding." The wise are those who, like Daniel, prepare ahead of time. Wisdom is the divine divider in that day. In the hour of crisis it is too late to prepare. Consider:

1.   Matthew 25:1-13: The wise virgins had extra oil. They paid the price to get extra oil in order to be prepared for the Bridegroom's delayed coming.

2.   Esau foolishly sold his birthright for a bowl of soup. Hebrews 12:17 says, "Afterward, when he desired to inherit the blessing, he was rejected, for he found no chance to repent, though he sought it with tears." His temporal values cost him his future.

3.   While the people mocked, Noah wisely spent his life preparing for a coming flood. When the rains came, it became evident who was wise and who was foolish.

The Overcomers

Overcomers obtain crowns by living wisely, and in the light of eternity. This is revealed in *lamed*.

Initially, Adam and Eve were perfect, but they were not yet tested or proven. God is putting us to the test in order to develop our love for Him, our stamina in the race and our ability to rule the created order with *Yeshua* in the kingdom. We must grow to love what He loves and hate what He hates (Psalm 45:7) if we are to be entrusted with true authority in His kingdom. We need to overcome the world, just as He overcame, if we are to rule with Him. Consider *Yeshua*'s words in Revelation 3:21, "To him who overcomes I will grant to sit with Me on My throne, as I also overcame and sat down with My Father on His throne." Suffering precedes glory (Luke 24:26; Acts 14:22). If we want that future throne, we need to choose wisely now and live accordingly.

The twenty-four elders sitting on twenty-four thrones in Revelation 4:4 have "crowns (*stephanos*) of gold" on their heads. *Stephanos* is the wreath of a victor in an Olympic contest. It is not the crown (*diadema*) that is a badge of political royalty. Every crown associated with *Yeshua* or the saints in the New Testament is a *stephanos* until Revelation 19:12 where we see *Yeshua* with many crowns (*diadema*) on His head. This appearance was announced in Revelation 11:15 with the words, "The kingdoms of this world have become the kingdoms of our Lord and of His Messiah, and He shall reign forever." The only other occurrence of *diadema* is in Revelation 12:3 and 13:1, where a usurper sought to pre-empt this event. Consider the following appearances of the Greek word, *stephanos* in the New Testament:

1.   The crown of thorns *Yeshua* wore at His crucifixion (Matthew 27:29).

2.   The incorruptible crown of 1 Corinthians 9:25.

3.   The crown of righteousness in 2 Timothy 4:8.

4.   The crown of life in James 1:12 and Revelation 2:10, which comes to those who endure.

5.   The crown of glory that does not fade away in 1 Peter 5:4.

6.   The crowns of gold on the twenty-four elders in Revelation 4:4.

7.   "One like the Son of Man, having on His head a golden crown" (Revelation 14:14).

Questions to Ponder

1.   When was a time that you wisely sacrificed a temporal benefit or immediate pleasure for a longer term goal? Were you glad you paid the price?

2.   How has hunger for more of the Lord affected your walk?

3.   How have you restrained your feet from inferior things for the sake of the superior pleasures of knowing God?

4.   Are you resistant to sacrificing any temporal benefits that God may be asking of you?

Chapter 16

Life Is Light: Establish Your Heart

NUN

¹⁰⁵Your word is a lamp to my feet
And a light to my path.
¹⁰⁶I have sworn and confirmed
That I will keep Your righteous judgments.
¹⁰⁷I am afflicted very much;
Revive me, O LORD, according to Your word.
¹⁰⁸Accept, I pray, the freewill offerings of my mouth, O LORD,
And teach me Your judgments.
¹⁰⁹My life is continually in my hand,
Yet I do not forget Your law.
¹¹⁰The wicked have laid a snare for me,
Yet I have not strayed from Your precepts.
¹¹¹Your testimonies I have taken as a heritage forever,
For they are the rejoicing of my heart.
¹¹²I have inclined my heart to perform Your statutes
Forever, to the very end.

Nun—Psalm 119:105-112

Coming from a powerful place of encounter with God, our psalmist begins to demonstrate a new level of maturity in his walk. The first line talks about his feet, which speaks of his walk, actions, or life. The ancient pictograph of the letter *nun* portrays a fish swimming, conveying the idea of life or activity. *Nun* is also seen as a seed, sperm, or new sprout of vegetation, all which point to life and the idea of sprouting, reproducing, growing, or spreading. All of these are actions of something that is alive and doing what it was designed to do.

We can see our "keeping the Word" teaching with its listen–keep–do progression working in the life of our psalmist. The first half of his journey, described in verses one through eighty-eight, has primarily been about applying the word of God to his own heart and soul. The emphasis is on what God is doing in him. He has been diligently meditating on the word, hiding it in his heart, submitting to God's dealings and learning the ways of God. When his carnality and weakness got exposed by the injustices of life and offenses within the body of Messiah, he was careful to judge himself according to

1 Corinthians 11:31, rather than justify himself and accuse the evildoer. He learned to "receive with meekness the implanted word which is able of save (heal) your souls" (James 1:21) in order to be like *Yeshua* and subsequently maintain his testimony to others. This section ends with our psalmists heart inclined to actually perform or do the Lord's statutes (v. 112). In other words, the psalmist is setting his heart to do God's will.

Relating to David, the word perform does not appear even one time in the first half of this psalm. This is not because the psalmist was disobedient or that there was nothing God was asking him to do. It is because in the second half of the journey, the emphasis was clearly shifts to what God is doing through David. It is about the impact of a son of God in a fallen world. Three times our psalmist declares that he has performed or fulfilled the word, the first being in verse 112.

What does God really want from us? The obedience of a compliant slave? Obviously, we will always be His servants, since He is God and we are not. But there is more. Human beings are to the Lord what canvas and oils are to an artist. God desires to be glorified in His saints (2 Thessalonians 1:10). Paul spoke in Colossians 1:27 of "Christ in you, the hope of glory." This does not refer to going to heaven, but about the dignity of being human with a capacity to showcase the glory of God on earth. Redeemed humans have the capacity through the power of the Holy Spirit to put the beauty and character of *Yeshua* on display. This is the prize of the upward call of God in Messiah *Yeshua*. The same prize was the goal toward which the Apostle Paul pressed in Philippians 3:14. This is *The Blessed (esher) Life* of verses 1-2 of our psalm. "Blessed (*esher*) are the undefiled in the way. . . . Blessed (*esher*)are those who keep His testimonies."

Just as *Yeshua*'s life did, the psalmist's life showcases the value system, resources, atmosphere, power, character and beauty of God's kingdom. *Yeshua*'s life showed us the Father. "He who has seen Me, has seen the Father" (John 14:9). "I have declared to them Your Name" (John 17:26). *Yeshua*'s prayers were answered. He had authority over the natural order. He had authority over disease. He overcame the tempter. He walked intimately with the Father and fully obeyed Him. His walk showcased heaven on earth. "In Him was life and the life was the light of men" (John 1:4). *Yeshua*'s life IS the light of men. *Yeshua* is the Pattern Son into whose likeness God desires to conform every believer (Romans 8:29).

Yeshua's life also provoked division and controversy everywhere He went. Likewise as pattern sons, our lives are offensive and confrontational to the system of this world. The light of our life exposes the corruption and bankruptcy that is in the world. Those with a vested interest in what is being confronted may react in anger and become our persecutors. But others will come to the light. Whenever one government confronts another, things can get turbulent. That happens whenever the kingdom of God is advanced.

Aspects of *nun* that distinguish it from other sections and help to unlock its truths include the following:

1. Both lamp (*niyr*) and light ('owr) occur only in verse 105. The unmistakable message of *nun* is that our walk (life) is the light that others see.

2. Sworn (v. 106) occurs only here as our psalmist commits his life to the mission of the kingdom of God. The connotation is that of a soldier vowing to lay down his life for a cause, or of a king taking an oath of office (Psalm 101), or of a subject's pledge of allegiance to his King.

3. "Freewill offerings" (*n\edabah*) convey the action of tabernacle offerings that were given voluntarily and from the heart (see Exodus 35:5).

4. Perform (*asah*: do, fashion, accomplish, make) is the primary Hebrew word for actively doing or acting. God's familiar statement in Jeremiah 1:12 is classic, "I am ready to perform (*asah*) My word." It is one thing to say it and another to do it. Until *nun*, it was the Lord who was working and doing things in our psalmist (v. 65, 73, 84). But in verse 112, our psalmist sets his heart to do or perform the will of God.

We will outline these eight verses according to a 2–4–2 pattern as follows:

- The vow: Part 1 (v. 105-106). "I commit my life to be a light" (I am Yours, Lord).

- The context and mission (v. 107-110). A fallen world, hostile to God's kingdom. The rigors of war begin (or are reviewed).

- The vow: Part 2 (v. 111-112). "I will go to the death for this cause." David perseveres. He endures hardness as a good soldier (2 Timothy 2:3).

Let's again join our psalmist on his journey.

The vow: Part 1. "I commit my life to be a light. Here am I, send me" (v. 105-106).

"Your word is a lamp to my feet and a light to my path" (v. 105).

1. David's revelatory encounters with the Lord in *lamed* and *mem* are producing zeal to see God's kingdom come on earth. This statement is really a commitment to apply God's word to his feet, his walk or life. Like Isaiah said, "Here am I! Send me" (Isaiah 6:8), *Yeshua's* life is our light. Here is the progression:

- From our life in darkness, we see the light in someone else.

- We respond to the light. Hopefully we say "yes" to that light.

- Our life becomes a light to others who are living in darkness.

2. Our walk in the New Testament is a huge subject. It is about our conduct and our lifestyle (actions) as believers before the eyes of unbelievers. Recall *Yeshua's* words in Matthew 5:14, 16, "You are the light of the world. . . . Let your light so shine before men, that they may see your good works and glorify your Father in heaven." His life shone and so must ours.

3. The twin themes of light and our walk before men come together in many places.

    •   Proverbs 6:23, "For the commandment is a lamp, and the law a light; Reproofs of instruction are the way of life."

    •   Ephesians 5:8, "For you were once darkness, but now you are light in the Lord. Walk as children of light."

    •   1 John 2:6, "He who says he abides in Him ought himself also to walk just as He walked."

    •   See Ephesians 4:1, 17; 5:1-17; Philippians 3:17-19; Colossians 1:10; 2:6; 3:7; 4:5; 1 Thessalonians 2:12; 4:1, 12; 2 Thessalonians 3:6-11; 1 Peter 4:3; 2 Peter 2:10; 3:3; 1 John 1:6-7; 2 John 4-6; 3 John 3-4.

"I have sworn and confirmed that I will keep Your righteous judgments" (v. 106).

1. "Sworn" (*shaba*: to be complete, to swear [as if by repeating a declaration seven times], to adjure). This powerful word occurs only here in our psalm. To walk as *Yeshua* walked, as a light to the world, requires a kind of "pledge of allegiance" or "oath of office" so that our hearts are set beforehand to do the right thing when we are tempted or pressured to do otherwise.

2. "Confirmed" (*quwm*: literally, to rise, to abide, accomplish, confirm). This word is translated strengthen in verse twenty-eight, establish in verse thirty-eight and rise in verse sixty-two.

3. These strong words reveal a major shift that was made at the half-way mark of this journey. It is no longer so much about "I, me and my" as in the earlier part of the journey. It is now more about *Yeshua* and His kingdom. It is as if our psalmist is being sworn in as a soldier in the army and is entering the war to see God's government established in his city or region. It requires a love for God's kingdom and an established heart to endure the rigors of warfare.

    •   Matthew 6:33, "But seek first the kingdom of God and His righteousness. . . ."

    •   2 Timothy 2:3-4, "You therefore must endure hardship as a good soldier of *Yeshua* Messiah. No one engaged in warfare entangles himself with the affairs of this life, that he may please him who enlisted him as a soldier."

    •   James 5:8 says, "Establish your hearts, for the coming of the Lord is at hand."

4. It is interesting to note that the Shulamite, in the Song of Songs, makes the same shift in the exact center of the Song. In 4:16, in context to saying "yes" to the warfare of partnership with *Yeshua* in the world, she sets her heart to endure the rigors of war with these words: "Awake, O north wind, and come, O south! Blow upon my garden, that its spices may flow out. Let my beloved come to his garden and eat its pleasant fruits."

    •   Note the shift from "my garden" (her heart and life) to "his garden."

    •   North wind: In other words, let the rigors of the north wind touch me, so that I may please Him. This too hints at a willingness to endure hardship as a soldier.

5. "Your righteous judgments" relays the fact that our psalmist has applied these judgments to his own heart and life and will continue to do so. However, now it seems as if he also wants them applied in the culture in which he lives. He is taking a stand for righteousness in his city--and that means war. He is setting his heart to endure.

6. Our psalmist is exercising his free will and setting his heart for endurance. Obviously, one cannot follow the Lord in one's own strength, but that does not minimize or negate the power and dignity of freely saying "yes" to the call of God. God's grace can be compared to power steering on a vehicle. We are the ones who turn the steering wheel, but the power is there to back up that action. The power of the human will in the setting of the heart to endure difficulty or do the right thing is a major theme in scripture. Consider these verses:

    •   Rehoboam, in 2 Chronicles 12:14, "did evil, because he did not prepare his heart to seek the LORD."

    •   Jehoshaphat, in 2 Chronicles 19:3, was told "You have removed the wooden images from the land, and have prepared your heart to seek God."

    •   2 Chronicles 30:18-19, "May the good LORD provide atonement for everyone who prepares his heart to seek God, the LORD God of his fathers."

    •   Ezra endures the rigors and dangers of the journey from Babylon to Jerusalem as recorded in Ezra 7:10, "For Ezra had prepared his heart to seek the Law of the LORD, and to do it, and to teach statutes and ordinances in Israel."

7. The vow of Psalm 101 seems to be a kind of "oath of office" for David as he became king. Here, David is establishing his heart to seek first God's kingdom. Consider 1 Peter 4:1-2, "Therefore, since Christ suffered for us in the flesh, arm yourselves also with the same mind, for he who has suffered in the flesh has ceased from sin, that he no longer should live the rest of his time in the flesh for the lusts of men, but for the will of God."

8. Nothing will help us establish our hearts to live righteously while enduring difficulty more than a revelation of eternity and of the throne of God, as our psalmist has just experienced in *lamed* and *mem* (see especially verse ninety-six). Consider this biblical pattern: Before God reveals future judgments to His prophets, He first shows them the heavenly throne room and gives them a glimpse of eternity. Examples include:

    •   The Apostle John: Before John saw the troubles of Revelation 6 to 16, he saw the throne that was set in heaven in chapters 4 and 5.

    •   Ezekiel: Before Ezekiel saw the terrible things that were coming to Israel, he saw the throne of God and "One like the Son of Man" on the throne (Ezekiel 1).

    •   Isaiah: Isaiah saw the Lord high and lifted up (Isaiah 6).

9. Consider again these verses on an "established heart:"

    •   Hebrews 13:9, "For it is good that the heart be established by grace."

    •   James 5:8, "You also be patient. Establish your hearts, for the coming of the Lord is at hand."

    •   1 Thessalonians 3:13, ". . . so that He may establish your hearts blameless in holiness."

    •   2 Thessalonians 2:16-17, "Now may our Lord *Yeshua* Messiah Himself . . . comfort your hearts and establish you in every good word and work."

Context and mission: A fallen world, hostile to God's kingdom (v. 107-110).

"I am afflicted very much; Revive me, O LORD, according to Your word. Accept, I pray, the freewill offerings of my mouth, O LORD, and teach me Your judgments. My life is continually in my hand, yet I do not forget Your law. The wicked have laid a snare for me, yet I have not strayed from Your precepts" (v. 107-110).

1. The rigors of war begin (v. 107). This affliction could simply be or at least include the weight of the burden of the Lord related to his calling. Maybe our psalmist is called to a certain people group to preach the gospel of the kingdom. There is a weight to the call, a price to pay, resistance from the adversary and warfare in which to engage.

2. "Revive me" occurs sixteen times throughout the psalm. This is a staple prayer that taps us into the very resurrection life of our Master *Yeshua*!

3. "Accept" (*ratsah*: be pleased or satisfied, take pleasure in, delight in), I pray, the freewill offerings (v. 108).

    •   Freewill offerings are freely given out of an overflowing heart because one desires to please the Lord. The highest motivation for answering the call of

God in mission is not compassion for the people to whom you are sent, but the desire to please the Lord—zeal to see *Yeshua* obtain what is His.

- "That he may please him who enlisted him as a soldier" (2 Timothy 2:4). This is abandonment to our Commander-in-Chief out of our own free will.

- "Everyone came whose heart was stirred, and everyone whose spirit was willing, and they brought the Lord's offering for the work of the tabernacle of meeting" (Exodus 35:21). "They spoke to Moses, saying, 'The people bring much more than enough'" (Exodus 36:5).

4. "Of my mouth" refers to the "sacrifice of praise" which is the fruit of our lips (Hebrews 13:15). Praise itself is a form of warfare (see Psalm 149:6). Psalm 138:1 is almost certainly a declaration of war on the idolatry of a city-state in David's day. "Before the gods I will sing praises to You." If not a declaration of war on regional idolatry, praise at the least is a major part of our own stamina and victory during the rigors of war.

5. "Teach (*lamad*) me Your judgments." God is waging perpetual war with sin, first within our own members, and then in the earth. David has submitted to God's dealings within his own life, and now it seems that he is desiring to partner with God in the warfare in the world. In Psalm 144:1, David blesses *YHVH*, "Who trains my hands for war, and my fingers for the battle."

6. "My life is continually in my hand" (v. 109) is a phase about the risking of his life or the sense of total vulnerability. "Do you not know that . . . you are not your own? You are bought with a price; therefore glorify God in your body" (1 Corinthians 6:19-20). We are on call to our Commander and Chief. He can give us any order He deems necessary!

- In 1 Samuel 19:5, Jonathan is defending David before his father with these words: "For he (David) took his life in his hands and killed the Philistine."

- The woman, a medium at En Dor, risked her life when she called up Samuel for the tormented King Saul. In 1 Samuel 28:21 she said, "I have put my life in my hands and heeded the words which you spoke."

- How natural is it for self-preservation instincts to kick in when the Lord has told us to do something? Radical obedience to every whisper of the Holy Spirit is rare. What would it look like to be totally at His disposal?

7. "The wicked have laid a snare for me" (v. 110). As was observed in verse ninety-five, the wicked are getting more aggressive. *Yeshua* is both the most loved and the most hated Man on earth. We will encounter the same kind of love and hatred as we become like Him.

- Recall *Yeshua's* words in John 15:20, "A servant is not greater than his master.

'If they persecuted Me, they will also persecute you. If they kept My word, they will keep yours also.'"

- Look at David's words in Psalm 140:4-5, "Keep me, O LORD, from the hands of the wicked; Preserve me from violent men, who have purposed to make my steps stumble. The proud have hidden a snare for me, and cords; They have spread a net by the wayside; They have set traps for me."

The Vow: Part Two. "I will go to the death for this cause" (v. 111-112).

"Your testimonies I have taken as a heritage forever, for they are the rejoicing of my heart. I have inclined my heart to perform Your statutes forever, to the very end" (v. 111-112).

1. "Your testimonies I have taken as a heritage (*nachal*: inheritance, possession) forever" communicates that our psalmist has already received his primary reward. The Lord told Abram in Genesis 15:1, "Do not be afraid, Abram. I am your shield, your exceedingly great reward." We already have Him and His word, and no one can take that away.

2. "The rejoicing of my heart" is a notice to all intercessors; to all who are contending for the kingdom of God to come; to all who cry out for righteousness in the schools and businesses of their regions; to all who long for abortion, poverty and injustice to cease; to all who cry out for corruption in government to be exposed and the righteous to rule; to all who long for that prophesied "last days outpouring" of the Spirit and cry out night and day for revival; to all who cry out day and night for Jerusalem to become a praise in the earth; to all who, like our psalmist, have entered the battle. Remember this: you already have your primary reward. You have HIM. While you contend for the kingdom to come and long for the God who is to come, don't forget to rejoice in the God who already is.

3. "I have inclined my heart to perform Your statutes forever, to the very end." This is intense. David will go to the death if necessary, and do whatever is required for however long it takes. What a pledge of allegiance to the kingdom of God. Many believers lose hope and quit because life is more difficult than they expected or the answers take longer than hoped. The only way to sustain our love for Him and our zeal for His kingdom is to enjoy Him now.

4. Acts 3:19-21 gives us a key to waiting for the Lord's return, at which time He will set all wrong things right, "that times of refreshing may come from the presence of the Lord, and that He may send *Yeshua* Messiah, who was preached to you before, whom heaven must receive (hold) until the times of restoration of all things."

5. Our psalmist is sustaining his zeal for the cause of the kingdom while enjoying intimacy with the Lord in this age. Remember, God said of the Levites in Numbers

18:20, "You shall have no inheritance in their land, nor shall you have any portion among them; I am your portion and your inheritance among the children of Israel." God Himself is our portion, even if the kingdom tarries and it is more difficult than we thought.

Concluding Thoughts

There is a great boundary line in God's plan of redemption. It is the free moral agency of human beings. He will not violate our free will in the process of redeeming us from sin. We (in Adam) chose Satan in a perfect world (Eden). Subsequent history shows that when times are good, cultures tend toward decadence and rebellion. But God is obtaining a people for Himself who choose Him when times are hard. God wanted two trees in the garden because He is love and He wants us to choose Him of our own free will. The war for the passions, loyalty and affection of the human heart is on. Who will we love, worship and obey? To whom will we be loyal? Under what conditions will we choose the Lord?

Consider God's boast to Satan in Job 1:8-11, "Have you considered My servant Job, that there is none like him on the earth, a blameless and upright man, one who fears God and shuns evil?" So Satan answered the LORD and said, "Does Job fear God for nothing? Have You not made a hedge around him, around his household, and around all that he has on every side? You have blessed the work of his hands, and his possessions have increased in the land. But now, stretch out Your hand and touch all that he has, and he will surely curse You to Your face!"

It is a powerful thing to choose the Lord in the context of a world that is under the government of our enemy. Choosing *Yeshua* means we will be at war—we will need to swim upstream in a downstream world. Although we might have a thousand reasons to be offended at God for all the injustices and difficulties, yet we still choose Him. We choose Him for love.

The accounts of David's mighty men in 2 Samuel 23 powerfully showcase this love and allegiance to the king and his kingdom. These men risked everything to please the king and to advance the kingdom. These are the mighty acts of soldiers who would not be intimidated or back down from what was right.

Questions to Ponder

1. Have you counted the cost of whole-hearted discipleship?
2. How have you endured hardness as a good soldier in order to please your Commander-in-Chief?
3. How have you prepared you heart for enduring the rigors of warfare?
4. Have you inclined your heart to fulfill everything the Lord has requested of you?

Chapter 17

Commitment: The Vow is Tested

SAMECH

¹¹³I hate the double-minded,
But I love Your law.
¹¹⁴You are my hiding place and my shield;
I hope in Your word.
¹¹⁵Depart from me, you evildoers,
For I will keep the commandments of my God!
¹¹⁶Uphold me according to Your word, that I may live;
And do not let me be ashamed of my hope.
¹¹⁷Hold me up, and I shall be safe,
And I shall observe Your statutes continually.
¹¹⁸You reject all those who stray from Your statutes,
For their deceit is falsehood.
¹¹⁹You put away all the wicked of the earth like dross;
Therefore I love Your testimonies.
¹²⁰My flesh trembles for fear of You,
And I am afraid of Your judgments.

Samech—Psalm 119:113-120

We come to the fifteenth letter of our Hebrew alphabet, *samech*. The ancient pictograph of the letter *samech* is a hand on a staff, essentially, a prop. The meaning is to support, to assist, to lean upon, to uphold. The word *samech* actually means to lean, lay, rest or support. It also represents a *sukkah*, a tabernacle, pavilion, or covering. Psalm 27:5-6 says, "For in the time of trouble He shall hide me in His pavilion; In the secret place of His tabernacle He shall hide me; He shall set me high upon a rock. And now my head shall be lifted up above my enemies."

This is precisely what our psalmist is doing here in *samech*—making the Lord his hiding place, support and protection as he sets to follow through on the commitment he made in *nun*.

Our psalmist has just made a powerful commitment in *nun* to answer the call of God on his life. He seems to be making moves to follow through, only to encounter a negative response from some "evildoer," who seems set on turning him from his mission.

Someone seems to be attempting to turn David away from his calling via intimidation, threats or seduction.

Nehemiah faced this exact thing in Nehemiah 2:10. As soon as Nehemiah prepared to follow through on his calling to rebuild a devastated Jerusalem, we have these words, "When Sanballat the Horonite and Tobiah the Ammonite official heard of it, they were deeply disturbed that a man had come to seek the well-being of the children of Israel."

Nevertheless, Nehemiah shared the vision with the people and, as reported in Nehemiah 2:18, he gained a commitment from them to build. So they said, "Let us rise up and build." Then they set their hands to the work. This is precisely where our psalmist is in his journey. He has made the commitment and is poised to follow through.

In response, Nehemiah receives this scornful and veiled threat in Nehemiah 2:19, "But when Sanballat the Horonite, Tobiah the Ammonite official, and Geshem the Arab heard of it, they laughed at us and despised us, and said, 'What is this thing that you are doing? Will you rebel against the king?'" More than a veiled threat that was intended to intimidate, the element of scorn suggests an attack on Nehemiah's worth as a person—as if to say, "Who do you think you are?"

Nehemiah's answer in verse twenty is what *samech* is all about. It is David's answer to his enemies: "So I answered them. . . 'The God of heaven Himself will prosper (rush to help) us; therefore we His servants will arise and build, but you have no heritage, right or memorial in Jerusalem.'"

So, they arose and actually begin building the walls of the city. The intimidation and resistance continued and actually escalated with their adversary's response in Nehemiah 4:1, "But it so happened, when Sanballat heard that we were rebuilding the wall, that he was furious and very indignant, and mocked the Jews." Sanballat went on to conspire to stop the work any way he could. Nehemiah had to rebuild Jerusalem in the midst of his enemies (see Psalm 23:5). The drama plays out in Nehemiah 2 to 6. So, with David and with each of us, there is an adversary resisting us in the fulfillment of our assignment in the kingdom. Here in *samech*, we have David's answer to their scornful threats and intimidation, and his decision to obey God.

Distinct features of *samech*, which set it apart from other sections and aid in unlocking its truths, include the following:

1. In keeping with *samech* as a pavilion or hiding place, two new words unique to *samech* appear, both in verse 114: hiding place (*cether*: shelter, covering) and shield (*magen*: to defend, cover or surround).

2. Also, in keeping with the meaning of *samech* as a prop, two new words appear in verse 117, also unique to *samech*: uphold (*camak*: to prop, to lean, lay, rest, sup-

port, sustain me) and hold me up (*caad*: to support, sustain, establish, strengthen, comfort, refresh, and I shall be safe).

3.   The great and terrible day of the Lord is alluded to in verses 118-120 as four new words appear here and only here in our psalm. They point to the wrath to come which John the Baptist warned of in Matthew 3:7, the judgment of the wicked, and the fear (dread, terror) of the Lord as a righteous Judge:

   •   "You reject (*calah*—v. 118) those who stray:" to make light of, toss aside, to weigh in the balance, tread under foot or trodden down in KJV).

   •   "You put away (*shabath*—v. 119) all the wicked:" cease, desist, rest. *Shabath* is the root word behind sabbath, when we are to cease from our labors and rest.

   •   "My flesh trembles" (*camar*—v. 120): bristle up, shiver.

   •   "For fear (*pachad*—v. 120) of You:" terror, dread.

We will outline our thoughts on these verses in a 3–2–3 pattern as follows:

   •   Verses 113-115: God is my hiding place—I will trust and obey.

   •   Verses 116-117: Prayer upholds, supports and sustains me.

   •   Verses 118-120: Judgment on the wicked is sure. They cannot prevail.

Let's join our psalmist as he enters the battle for the kingdom.

God is my hiding place; I will trust and obey (v. 113-115).

"I hate the double-minded, but I love Your law. You are my hiding place and my shield; I hope in Your word" (v. 113-114).

1.   "I hate the double-minded" (*ceeph*: divided in heart or mind, a skeptic, vain thoughts). *The Scriptures* translation reads, "I have hated doubting thoughts, but I have loved Your *torah*." Both verbs (hate and love) are in the perfect mood, which express an action completed in the past which has continued to the present. This is not just about others who are double-minded. Our own psalmist has in the past and is again fighting doubts about something—and he hates it!

   •   Doubts about what? Almost certainly the vow of *nun* and the implications of following through on his commitment.

   •   The bold faith which precipitated the bold vow in *nun* is under assault. Whether internally or externally, like Nehemiah, he is being intimidated.

   •   Do you suppose that, when Moses finally agreed to go to Pharaoh as God instructed, he had to fight doubts and fears along the way? He probably thought something like, "This is crazy. Why did I ever say 'yes?' Pharaoh will kill me." Moses, too, had to remember the promise of the Lord, "I will be with you."

2. We can't help but recall some familiar scriptures at this point:

   - James 1:6-8, "For he who doubts is like a wave of the sea driven and tossed by the wind. For let not that man suppose that he will receive anything from the Lord; he is a double-minded man, unstable in all his ways."

   - 2 Timothy 1:7, "God has not given us a spirit of fear (timidity, cowardice, fearfulness), but of power and of love and of a sound mind."

3. We also note Elijah's words to the prophets of Baal on Mount Carmel in 1 Kings 18:21, "How long will you falter between two opinions (*caiph*: divided opinion)? If the LORD is God, follow Him; but if Baal, follow him."

   - The prophets of Baal seemed whole-hearted enough as they called on their god for fire. Their ambivalence, skepticism and vain thoughts regarded the Lord, the God of Elijah, whom they were about to encounter, not their god, Baal.

   - Elijah's mission was to turn the tables and cause Israel to begin to doubt Baal's legitimacy and potency, and then return in faith to the God of Israel.

4. "You are my hiding place (*cether*: shelter, covering) and my shield" (*magen*: to defend). This is the first and only occurrence of both *cether* and *magen*. Our psalmist is making a powerful confession. He is stirring up his confidence in God and recalling the great promise of God has given to every emissary He has ever sent on a mission: "I will be with you!"

   - The hiding place refers to that place of intimacy and immunity near to the heart of God. This mirrors John 15; it is all about abiding in the Vine.

   - The shield defends and protects during warfare. The root word means to defend, to cover, to surround. The Lord will cover him. This word also appears in Psalm 91:4 and 144:1-2. Note the words of Psalm 144:1-2, "Blessed be the LORD my Rock, who trains my hands for war, and my fingers for battle—My lovingkindness and my fortress, my high tower and my deliverer, my shield and the One in whom I take refuge, who subdues my people under me."

"Depart (turn aside or turn away) from me, you evildoers, for I will keep the commandments (*mitzvah*) of my God" (v. 115).

1. Our psalmist has made his decision and is giving his answer, as did Nehemiah in Nehemiah 2:20. "The God of heaven Himself will prosper (rush to help) us."

- We have found the source of the doubts, "you evildoers," and our psalmist is turning them away and making his decision.

- In Psalm 6:8-10, David prays the same thing: "Depart from me, all you workers of iniquity. . . . The LORD has heard my supplication; The LORD will receive my prayer. Let all my enemies be ashamed."

2. "I will keep the commandment (*mitzvah*: a command) of my God." What a response to doubts and fears within (or threats and intimidation without). As noted in the introduction, *mitzvah* could refer to the specific mandate to a given sent one (like Moses or Noah) regarding their specific calling, or it could be about keeping the commandments of God revealed in scripture which are for everyone. Either way, there is plenty of pressure to compromise either one or both for the sake of self-preservation.

Uphold, Support, Sustain Me (v. 116-117).

"Uphold me according to Your word, that I may live; And do not let me be ashamed of my hope. Hold me up, and I shall be safe, and I shall observe Your statutes continually" (v. 116-117).

1. "Uphold (*camak*: to prop, to lean, lay, rest, support, sustain) me." This is the only occurrence of this word in the psalm.

- This word is employed in Psalm 37:17, "For the arms of the wicked shall be broken, but the LORD upholds the righteous." The message here is that the Lord upholds the righteous in the season when the evildoers are prospering. This psalm begins with the words, "So do not fret because of evildoers. . . ."

- Also see Isaiah 26:3, "You will keep him in perfect peace, whose mind is stayed (*camak*) on You, because he trusts in You."

2. "Hold me up (*caad*: to support, sustain, establish, strengthen, comfort, refresh), and I shall be safe." This is also the only time this word occurs in Psalm 119.

- This word also occurs in Psalm 94:18 in context to the wicked prospering. "If I say, 'My foot slips,' Your mercy, O LORD, will hold me up."

3. This is the core of *samech* which, as already stated, means to lean upon, to uphold or to support. David is running into the hiding place of verse 114, and he is praying and leaning into that support.

4. "And do not let me be ashamed of my hope" (*seber*: wait, hope)." *The Scriptures* translation says, "Do not put me to shame because of my expectation." In other words, "I will do what I said and You do what You said. Don't let me down!" This word also appears in the following verses:

- Psalm 146:5, "Happy is he who has the God of Jacob for his help, whose hope (*seber*) is in the LORD his God."

- Psalm 145:15, "The eyes of all look expectantly (*sabar*: the root of *seber*) to You, and You give them their food in due season."

Certain judgment on the wicked by the righteous Judge (v. 118-120).

"You reject all thse who stray from Your statutes, for their deceit is falsehood. You put away all the wicked of the earth like dross; Therefore I love Your testimonies. My flesh trembles for fear of You, and I am afraid of Your judgments" (v. 118-120).

1. These last three verses touch the theme of judgment of the wicked and the powerful truth that the wicked cannot ultimately prevail—a necessary point of faith when doubts assail our minds. Ponder again these words:

   - "You reject (*calah*) those who stray:" to make light of, toss aside, to weigh in the balance, tread under foot (trodden down in KJV).

   - "You put away (*shabath*) all the wicked:" cease, desist, rest, the root word behind Sabbath, when we are to cease from our labors and rest.

   - "My flesh trembles (*camar*) for fear of You:" bristle up, shiver, for fear (*pachad*) of You: terror, dread.

2. Ultimately, these verses allude to the great and terrible day of the Lord (Joel 2). In Psalm 2:10-12, King David warns the kings of the earth, after he prophetically saw the Messiah "dash them to pieces like a potter's vessel: Now therefore, be wise, O kings; Be instructed, you judges of the earth. Serve the LORD with fear, and rejoice with trembling. Kiss the Son, lest He be angry, and you perish in the way, when His wrath is kindled but a little. Blessed are all those who put their trust in Him."

3. Read Job 40:6-14. The greatest expression of God's power is His ability look on everyone who is proud, and humble him and bring him low, and tread down the wicked in their place. God basically tells Job, "If you can humble the proud, then I will also confess to you that your own right hand can save you."

4. This is an enormous theme in scripture with hundreds of references. Here are just a few. Ultimately, the wicked will be removed and the meek will inherit the earth (Matthew 5:5).

   - Proverbs 10:30, "The righteous will never be removed, but the wicked will not inhabit the earth." This is what happened in Noah's day.

- Proverbs 2:21-22, "For the upright will dwell in the land, and the blameless will remain in it; But the wicked will be cut off from the earth, and the unfaithful will be uprooted from it."

- 1 Peter 4:17, "And if it (judgment) begins with us first, what will be the end of those who do not obey the gospel of God?"

- In Psalm 73:17, David was troubled by the prosperity of the wicked until he "went into the sanctuary of God; Then I understood their end."

- Matthew 13:40-43, "Therefore as the tares (sons of the wicked one) are gathered and burned in the fire, so it will be at the end of this age. The Son of Man will send out His angels, and they will gather out of His kingdom all things that offend, and those who practice lawlessness. . . . Then the righteous will shine forth as the sun in the kingdom of their Father."

5. Can we see why this is an important truth to note? The ultimate victory is fully assured, but on any given battlefront it may appear like the enemy is winning and the righteous are losing. In Revelation 13:7, it was granted to the beast to make war on the saints and overcome them (physically in martyrdom). No matter whether we see the victory manifest as we envisioned or not, it is assured in the end.

6. One of the surprising truths in the New Testament is this: Judgments are more severe under the New Covenant than under the Old. In the New Covenant, when the kingdom of God is "at hand," there is greater access, greater light (via demonstration) and greater privilege than there was under the old. Think about these scriptures:

- Read Matthew 11:20-24. Verse twenty-four says, "I say to you (Capernaum, Chorazin) that it shall be more tolerable for the land of Sodom in the Day of Judgment than for you." How can this be? Because in the face of the increased light of *Yeshua's* mighty works and the corresponding greater privilege and access, they refused to repent.

- Consider Hebrews 10:28-29, "Anyone who has rejected Moses' law dies without mercy on the testimony of two or three witnesses. Of how much worse punishment, do you suppose, will he be thought worthy who has trampled the Son of God underfoot, counted the blood of the covenant by which he was sanctified a common thing, and insulted the Spirit of grace?"

- The greater the light the greater the responsibility to respond appropriately. This is why *Yeshua* could say in John 15:24, "If I had not done among them the works which no one else did, they would have no sin; but now they have seen and also hated both Me and My Father."

- It is so important that we grow up into Christ-likeness and bring light into our world. It will provide opportunity for many to come to the light and be saved. But, also, many will hate that light because their deeds are evil. *Yeshua* said, "A servant is not greater than his master. If they persecuted Me, they will also persecute you. If they kept My word, they will keep yours also." Whether accepted or rejected, the purity of the light shed provides for both salvation and judgment.

7. "My flesh trembles for fear (*pachad*: terror, dread) of You."

- In Revelation 1:17, John fell like a dead man before his best Friend, *Yeshua*. Our flesh cannot withstand the raw power of His person—the utter intensity of His glory unveiled.

- 1 Corinthians 15:50-52, "Flesh and blood cannot inherit the kingdom of God; nor does corruption inherit incorruption. That is why we shall all be changed—in a moment, in the twinkling of an eye, at the last trumpet. For the trumpet will sound, and the dead will be raised incorruptible, and we shall be changed."

- Although it is true that no man can see God and live, it is equally true that no man can see God and die. Men do not die in God's presence, but neither do they live as they used to live. Rather, they are changed. Consider 1 John 3:2-3, "Beloved, now we are children of God; and it has not yet been revealed what we shall be, but we know that when He is revealed, we shall be like Him, for we shall see Him as He is. And everyone who has this hope in Him purifies himself, just as He is pure."

- Deuteronomy 10:12, "And now, Israel, what does the LORD your God require of you, but to fear the LORD your God, to walk in all His ways and to love Him, to serve the LORD your God with all your heart and with all your soul."

- Deuteronomy 13:4, "You shall walk after the LORD your God and fear Him, and keep His commandments and obey His voice; you shall serve Him and hold fast to Him."

- The fear of God is a massive truth in scripture that many of us do not know what to do with. This is a good place to go to Addendum 5, and ponder the fear of the Lord.

Concluding Thoughts

Love and wrath: Two sides of one coin

As salvation and judgment are two sides of one coin, so love and wrath are two sides of one coin. God is a consuming fire, a jealous God (Deuteronomy 4:24). In fact His very name is Jealous (Exodus 34:14).

Jealousy implies hot emotion, both fiery love and hot anger. Proverbs 6:34, "For jealousy is a husband's fury; Therefore he will not spare in the day of vengeance." If there was no love there could be no wrath. This jealousy can be provoked if the affection due the Lord is stolen by another lover (such as the "image of jealousy" in Ezekiel 8:3), or if someone touches, in a wrong way, the apple of His eye.

God's wrath on the wicked at the end of the age will be in proportion to His love for His bride, and it will be directed toward those who persecuted the bride. There cannot be love without wrath. They are one and the same passion. If a burglar were to hurt one of my beloved children, my wrath toward the burglar would be in proportion to my love for my son or daughter. If my heart remained unmoved, there would be something wrong with my love. So it is with the Lord. This theme was introduced with the passion sandwich of *mem* and will develop more as we progress on this journey.

The first verse of this section, verse 113, emphasizes our psalmist's love for God's law and the last one identifies his fear and trembling before the judgments of God. Love and fear come together in the same heart. In one of C.S. Lewis' *Chronicles of Narnia* series, when the children heard about Aslan the Lion, they asked the question, "Is he safe?" The answer quickly came, "Oh no! He is not safe, but He is good!"[1] In the story, the children go on to love and trust this Lion, though His raw power and utter fierceness were terrible to behold.

Questions to Ponder

1. How have you run to the Lord for refuge during a time of doubts and fears?

2. How has God supported you in times of wavering (double-mindedness)?

3. Read Job 40:6-14. How does the assured removal of the wicked from the earth serve to help you remain faithful to the call of God upon your life?

Chapter 18

It is Your Move, Lord

AYIN

¹²¹I have done justice and righteousness;
Do not leave me to my oppressors.
¹²²Be surety for Your servant for good;
Do not let the proud oppress me.
¹²³My eyes fail from seeking Your salvation
And Your righteous word.
¹²⁴Deal with Your servant according to Your mercy,
And teach me Your statutes.
¹²⁵I am Your servant;
Give me understanding,
That I may know Your testimonies.
¹²⁶It is time for You to act, O LORD,
For they have regarded Your law as void.
¹²⁷Therefore I love Your commandments
More than gold, yes, than fine gold!
¹²⁸Therefore all Your precepts concerning all things
I consider to be right;
I hate every false way.

Ayin—Psalm 119:121-128

David's opening statement here in *ayin*, "I have done (*asah*) justice and righteousness," shows us that he had victory. He actually overcame his fears (noted in *samech*) and obeyed the call of God. Having followed through on the commitment made back in *nun* to obey the Lord, the psalmist now turns his eyes toward the expected and promised outcome of his obedience—God's response.

The perplexing thing is that it seems as if the Lord is nowhere around. There has been a full-blown backlash from oppressors in response to our psalmist's obedience—possibly not unlike the riot in Ephesus against Paul in Acts 19 or the backlash of Pharaoh against Moses and the children of Israel in Exodus 5. Basically, David is saying, "Okay Lord, I did what you said and it only stirred up a hornet's nest of trouble. Things are worse than ever and You have not fulfilled Your promise to deliver at all. It's Your move. Help me!"

Several themes clearly come together in *ayin* that distinguish this eight-verse segment from the others and help unlock its truths:

1. Key phrases: "Your servant" and "have done" (*asah*). Three times David identities himself as "Your (the Lord's) servant" (v. 122, 124, 125)—a servant who did (*asah*) what the master asked. These two ideas distinguish this section.

    *   In verse 112 of *nun*, our psalmist said, "I have inclined my heart to perform (*asah*) Your statutes."

    *   He claims in verse 121, as God's servant, to "have done" (*asah*: performed, done, acted) according to the Lord's will in full obedience.

    *   Then, in verse 126, he says, "It is time for You to act (*asah*) O LORD."

2. The ancient Hebrew pictograph of *ayin* portrays an eye, and means to see, look for, experience or understand. In verse 123, David's eyes are wearily straining to see God fulfill His part of the equation and bring the promised salvation. But all he is seeing is the enemy's fierce backlash. The eyes of this servant are looking to the Lord for deliverance. Psalm 123:2, "Behold, as the eyes of servants look to the hand of their masters . . . so our eyes look to the LORD our God, until He has mercy on us." Where we focus our eyes determines what we see. Am I seeing:

    *   Naturally or spiritually through fear or by faith, defeat or victory?

    *   The rage of my enemy or the armies of the Lord? See 2 Kings 6:13-18.

3. Key word: Surety (*arab*: pledge, exchange, mortgage, guarantee) appears only in verse 122 in our psalm. In the repercussion, there is great danger of losing everything to his oppressors and David desperately needs assurance now: a sign, a pledge or guarantee that salvation is certain.

Patterns of spiritual warfare

Matthew 11:12, "The kingdom of heaven suffers violence, and the violent take it by force." In seeking His kingdom, inevitably, there will be resistance and counterattack. After all, two governments are clashing and our obedience is threatening the rule of darkness. This is exactly what is happening to the psalmist, and what happened to Moses in Exodus 5.

After convincing the children of Israel that God was about to deliver them from Pharaoh's hand in Exodus 4, Moses finally steps up to face Pharaoh with these words: "Thus says the LORD God of Israel: 'Let My people go.'" Moses obeys the call of God on his life, probably with some fear and trembling. All he has is God, Aaron, his rod and God's promise to deliver Israel.

Pharaoh is immediately angered, and makes it more difficult than ever for the slaves of Israel. And even more troubling is that Moses' own people turn on him with these words from Exodus 5:21, "Let the LORD look on you and judge, because you have made us abhorrent in the sight of Pharaoh and in the sight of his servants, to put a sword in their hand to kill us."

Moses' prayer in Exodus 5:22-23 is essentially the prayer of our psalmist here in *ayin*—"Lord, why have You brought trouble on this people? Why is it You have sent me? For since I came to Pharaoh to speak in Your name, he has done evil to this people; neither have You delivered Your people at all."

One of the patterns of spiritual warfare is that often before things get better, they get worse.

This is a test. In Exodus 5, the kingdom of heaven has just suffered violence as Pharaoh pushed back. Here is where, as believers, we need to guard against two things:

1.   Doubting or second-guessing the call of God upon our lives.

2.   Taking offense toward the Lord for not seeming to keep His promises.

In Acts 4, Peter and John also suffer persecution after an initial advance of the kingdom. They were arrested, held for questioning, threatened and ordered to speak to no man in this name. What do they do? Quit? Certainly not. They join a prayer meeting, pray for boldness and ask the Lord to stretch out His hand in power (Acts 4:29-30). They come back stronger than ever. They actually used the force of the resistance to increase the manifestation of the kingdom of heaven. Acts 5 is the result. Read it.

The greater the manifestation of the enemy against you, the more spectacular is his fall. This is precisely why God raised up Pharaoh. "But indeed for this purpose I have raised you up, that I may show My power in you, and that My name may be declared in all the earth" (Exodus 9:16). Here's the question: when the push-back comes, will I press in or shrink back? When the kingdom of heaven suffers violence, will I doubt God and quit, or will I, with spiritual violence, stay the course and take it by force? Pharaoh put up a lot of resistance in Moses' day, but it only served to showcase God's power. The harder a fast ball comes at you, the further it flies when you hit it.

In verse 161 we learn that it is often the princes, rulers or leaders in high places who do the persecuting—those who have the most to lose when their corrupt structures begin to shake because of the harvest of souls into the kingdom of God. It was Pharaoh in Moses' day, the Sadducees in Peter's day, Demetrius in Paul's day (at Ephesus) and Herod at the birth of *Yeshua* (Matthew 2:1-18).

Another great principle, shown in *Yeshua's* end-time parables and teachings, has to do with His delayed-but-promised coming. This delay can refer to His ultimate second coming, or it can apply to His delay in coming in power to keep His promises now, in this age. The question is, how will we live during the delay? Did Moses quit and go back to shepherding?

The ruler of the house in Matthew 24:48 said, "My master is delaying his coming," and he ceased watching. The ten virgins of Matthew 25:1-13 were characterized as either wise or foolish based upon what they did during the delay of the bridegroom in his coming. Verse five says "While the bridegroom was delayed, they all slumbered and slept" (see also Luke 12:41-46). See Addendum 4 for thoughts on why God waits.

Let's join David in his journey and see how he responds to backlash. Will he pass the test? We will outline this set in two four-verse segments and match them to the two phrases in Matthew 11:12 noted above.

- The kingdom of heaven suffers violence in verses 121-124: "I did what You said and it did not work. Help!"

- The violent take it by force in verses 125-128: "LORD, please do something," David entreats. "You should act now. They are defying Your word which I love!"

The kingdom of heaven suffers violence (v. 121-124).

"I have done justice and righteousness; Do not leave me to my oppressors. Be surety for Your servant for good; Do not let the proud oppress me" (v. 121-122).

1. "I have done" (*asah*: to do, fashion, accomplish, make) occurs more than 2,600 times in scripture as the primary word for doing or making or acting. It occurs eight times in our psalm, three of which are in this section. This is a key to the section.

2. "Justice (*mishpat*: judgments) and righteousness" (tsedeq: justice, rightness, equity). The psalmist is questioning why, even though he did the right thing, it did not work. Why does God, who loves righteousness, wait to vindicate our psalmist? This is exactly what happened to Moses in Exodus 5.

   - The Lord backed up Elijah's obedience in 1 Kings 18:38 with fire from heaven. Why does He delay to act now?

   - Our psalmist is basically saying, "I have done what You, My King, have decreed."

   - "Righteousness and justice are the foundation of Your throne" (Psalm 89:14). Although translated and combined in various ways, these two Hebrew words occur together more than fifty times in scripture, twenty times in the context of ruling from a throne. We have developed the theme of God's judgments *(mishpat)* at some length in Addendum 4.

3.	"Oppressors" (*ashaq*: to press upon, oppress, violate, defraud, get deceitfully, do violence, wrong). Our psalmist wants to be delivered from his oppressors.

	•	Throughout scripture, this word is solidly linked with injustice and the oppression of the poor.

	•	The interests and self-serving agendas of those who persecute believers who seek to advance the kingdom of God can always be deemed to be unjust causes. There is an absolute moral standard revealed in scripture by which we can judge oppression, morality, corruption, and other evils. Pharaoh was wrong. Herod was wrong. The Sadducees in Acts 4 were wrong.

4.	"Be surety (*arab*: to braid or intermix, to traffic as if by barter, to pledge, give as security, guarantee, exchange) for Your servant for good." In other words, "You and I, Lord, are braided together as partners in this mission. I fight for Your interests on earth; You back me up with the power and resources of heaven—both of our reputations are on the line (not to mention the danger I am in). Where are You, God?"

5.	"The proud" (*zed*: arrogant, insolent, presumptuous, proud). The proud sounds exactly like Pharaoh in Exodus 5.

"My eyes fail from seeking Your salvation and Your righteous word" (v. 123).

1.	"My eyes fail" (*kalah*: to end, cease, be finished or perish).

2.	Our psalmist's eyes are tiring from looking for God's promised deliverance (salvation). This phrase also occurs in verse eighty-two. There seems to be a sense of desperation to see and experience the deliverance of the Lord. Moses is really in a tough situation in Exodus 5.

3.	Our Hebrew letter, *ayin*, depicts an eye, meaning to see or experience, and by extension to understand.

	•	Psalm 130:6 may well capture something of what is happening here. "My soul waits for the Lord more than those who watch for the morning."

4.	The question again is this: When Pharaoh is breathing out fire and seeming to prevail, what will our psalmist do? Will he turn his eyes to the Master and remain His servant or will he turn his eyes to the circumstances, become anxious and react in his own strength? This was precisely the failure which cost King Saul the kingdom. This inability (or unwillingness) to wait for the Lord, while the enemy is mustering his forces, marked his life in several specific occasions (see 1 Samuel 13:8-9; 14:18-20; 1 Chronicles 10:13-14).

5.   This is actually a huge issue. How often will we back off from believing and pray-
     ing for kingdom breakthroughs because it does not seem to be working? Besides,
     the backlash and the unfulfilled assurances make us look bad. Moses was neither
     impressed nor impressive when he prayed in Exodus 5:22-23, "Lord, why have You
     brought trouble on this people? Why is it You have sent me? For since I came to
     Pharaoh to speak in Your name, he has done evil to this people; neither have You
     delivered Your people at all."

"Deal (*asah*) with Your servant according to Your mercy, and teach me Your statutes" (v. 124).

1.   "Deal with (*asah*) according to Your mercy" (*chesed*). This is the cry from our
     psalmist for God to show mercy and arise, to act, and save. Under the pressure,
     when his very life seems to be in the balance, our psalmist is casting himself upon
     the great love and mercy of God.

     •   Psalm 25:6 is powerful, "Remember, O LORD, Your tender mercies and Your
          lovingkindnesses, for they are from of old."

     •   God has a reputation of kindness and David is appealing to that impulse deep
          in the heart of God.

2.   "Your servant." In the master-servant relationship, it was the master's responsibility
     to protect and provide for every need of the servant. The pressure of Pharaoh's
     counterattack and its implications concerning the promises of God and the life of
     His servants are the Master's problem, not the servant's.

3.   "Teach (*lamad*: goad) me Your statutes" (*choq*). When the psalmist says statutes,
     he turns the focus away from the perplexing circumstances, which have shifted
     in the wrong direction, back to that which is permanent and unchanging. "For I
     am the LORD, I do not change" (Malachi 3:6).

Lord, act! (v. 125-128).

"I am Your servant; Give me understanding, that I may know Your testimonies" (v. 125).

1.   "I am Your servant." David remains submitted to God as his Master. He is not quitting.

     •   Three times in this section our psalmist identifies himself as "Your servant."

     •   We must note Psalm 116:16-17, "O LORD, truly I am Your servant; I am Your
          servant, the son of Your maidservant; You have loosed my bonds. I will offer
          to You the sacrifice of thanksgiving, and will call upon the name of the LORD."

2.   "Give me understanding" (*biyn*). There is a subtle shift in focus and tone, a shift from focusing on the danger of the circumstances to that of a desire to gain understanding: "Help me" is becoming "What is it that You are doing?" Again, David asks for the friendship of John 15:15, "No longer do I call you servants, for a servant does not know what his master is doing; but I have called you friends, for all things that I heard from My Father I have made known to you."

"It is time for You to act (*asah*), O LORD, for they have regarded Your law as void" (v. 126).

1.   Verse 123 basically says, "LORD, save," with an eye on our psalmist's plight and need for salvation (deliverance from the oppressor).

2.   Verse 126 essentially says, "LORD, act" (in power), with an eye toward God's reputation. "For they (proud oppressors) have regarded Your law (*torah*: instruction) as void" (*parar*: to break up, violate, frustrate, disannul, defeat, cast off, defy, brought to nothing).

   •   Consider Pharaoh's words to Moses in Exodus 5:2, "Who is the LORD, that I should obey His voice to let Israel go? I do not know the LORD, nor will I let Israel go."

   •   The proud are defiant against biblical righteousness. "Let us break their bonds in pieces and cast away their cords from us" (Psalm 2:3). They do not want their agenda to be restricted in any way by the bonds and cords of the word of God.

3.   Here in verse 126, our psalmist cries for vindication for the sake of God's own name or reputation. Zeal for God's glory, reputation and interests on the earth is growing within him.

   •   This was the cry of Moses' heart as he interceded for Israel in Numbers 14:15-19.

   •   This zeal is the force behind David's imprecatory prayers as he prays against his enemies, who were the Lord's enemies. He and the Lord were braided together in covenant so that the enemies of one were the enemies of the other.

   •   Zeal for God's glory in the earth was the primary force in the hearts of the early apostles as they took the gospel of the kingdom to the entire known world.

4.   This is an amazing place for a human being to come to in terms of voluntary sacrifice and selflessness. Our psalmist has made a turn in this second half of the journey from focusing on what is his inheritance in the gospel (what I get), to what is the Lord's inheritance in him (what He gets).

   •   He is our inheritance and our exceedingly great reward—that is awesome. What we have received in the gospel cannot be measured or fathomed, much less explained.

   •   However, we are also His inheritance. Is that any less awesome? Paul talks about the riches of the glory of His inheritance in the saints (Ephesians 1:18). In Ephesians 5:27, Paul shows us that *Yeshua* will present to Himself a bride without spot or wrinkle. *Yeshua* gets a bride!

   •   He is our God and we are His people. In the gospel, we obtain God as our God and He obtains us as His people. Our destinies are inseparable (see Revelation 21:3).

"Therefore I love Your commandments more than gold, yes, than fine gold. Therefore all Your precepts concerning all things I consider to be right; I hate every false way" (v. 127-128).

1.   "I love Your commandments" (*mitzvah*). For our psalmist to say this in context to a firestorm of backlash is amazing. Obeying God's commands is what brought him here in the first place.

2.   "Gold." Our psalmist is free from the love of this world and the lust of the eyes in particular (see 1 John 2:15-17). He cannot be bought. It is possible that the reactions affected our psalmist's finances or income in some way. How often through the ages have believers refused to compromise and, like our psalmist, have done justice and righteousness only to lose their source of income?

3.   "I hate every false (*sheqer*: untruth, sham, lie, deception) way." David will not resort to the same lying tactics of his enemies to protect or defend himself. He will wait on the Lord.

Concluding Thoughts

In verse 125 our psalmist chooses submission to a seemingly absent Master who is not backing him up in his obedience. Here are a few more thoughts on what God is doing here in *ayin*.

1. While we will always be servants of the Lord, there is a higher place than servant-hood and submission to Him. That place is a state of union with the Lord, where we actually love what He loves and are in agreement with His ways. That place could be referred to as friendship or sonship.

    *   A sevant's submission is however, the way to sonship: Hebrews 2:10, "It was fitting for Him . . . in bringing many sons to glory, to make the captain of their salvation perfect through sufferings."

2. The test: Do you want to go back? In Hebrews 11:15-16, God basically says that He will buy your ticket back if that is what you want. "And truly if they (pilgrims looking for a homeland or city) had called to mind that country from which they had come out, they would have had opportunity (*kairos*: window of opportunity) to return. But now they desire a better, that is, a heavenly country."

    *   The test: What is the promise worth? Will I be satisfied with less?

    *   From servanthood to sonship and friendship: A servant does not know what his master is doing (John 15:15). But he obeys.

    *   "I am Your servant; give me understanding, that I may know Your testimonies" (v. 125).

    *   What are You doing so that I can co-labor in the mission (John 5:19)? Obedi-ence was never about going to heaven but about pleasing the Father and accomplishing the mission. What happens when the Father is pleased? The heavens open.

        o   "This is My beloved Son, in whom I am well pleased" (Matthew 3:17).

        o   "The Father will reward you openly" (prayer, fasting, giving referred to in Matthew 6).

        o   Will I be satisfied living in safety, but with a closed heaven?

3. This is a good place to refresh the discussion of God's purposes in deliverance versus God's purposes in martyrdom in the "Concluding Thoughts" of chapter 13. Moses has a clear promise of what God will do, so we know Moses will live through Exodus chapter 5. David has a promise of becoming king of Israel, so we know he will live through King Saul's attempts on his life. However, there are times when faith and obedience lead to great sufferig and martyrdom. Ponder the following.

    *   The Apostle Paul, in Acts 20:22-24, knew that great suffering and probable death awaited him if he proceeded on to Jerusalem. His response in verse twenty-four is powerful: "But none of these things move me; nor do I count my life dear to myself, so that I may finish my race with joy." Paul ended up being martyred in Rome.

- *Yeshua*, in John 14:30-31 said, "The ruler of this world is coming, and he has nothing in Me. But that the world may know that I love the Father, as the Father has given Me commandment, so I do." *Yeshua* obeyed God and died.

- Accepting martyrdom reveals the bankruptcy and ultimate demise of Satan's kingdom. it is the exact opposite of the self-worship and self-preservation upon which Satan's kingdom is predicated.

- Ponder again Hebrews 11:33-35 as noted in chapter 13. Deliverance and martyrdom seem to be opposite outcomes, but in reality, both require death to the self-life because obedience requires death to self.

4.   Exodus 6—How did God persuade Moses to go back to Pharaoh?

- He renewed the promise to bring Israel into the Land of Promise (v. 1-5).

- God was *El-Shaddai* (the Almighty) to Abraham, Isaac and Jacob, but He was *YHVH* (God's Name) to Moses (v. 3).

- Go to the people and renew my promise (v. 6-9).

- Anguish of spirit and cruel bondage prevented their heeding of Moses.

- Go to Pharaoh (v. 10-12).

- *YHVH* gave a charge (*tsavah*: they saw the armies of Israel in v. 13-27).

- Moses' uncircumcised lips (v. 12, 30): "Behold, I am of uncircumcised lips, and how shall Pharaoh heed me?" If Moses is acknowledging the weakness of his flesh, this realization may be a good thing and not a negative complaint (see John 6:33).

The website *Hebrew for Christians* adds this concerning the Hebrew letter: "*Ayin* is sometimes described as having two eyes that connect to a common optic nerve that leads to the brain. The two eyes represent choice or the actions of the will (or the heart). We can choose whether to use the good eye or the evil eye to perceive things; we can choose to see the glass as half full rather than half empty."[1]

The Master has promised: "I will instruct you and teach you in the way you should go; I will guide you with My eye" (Psalm 32:8).

This is a prayer from Psalm 73 for when the wicked prosper against the righteous: "Nevertheless I am continually with You; You hold me by my right hand. You will guide me with Your counsel, and afterward receive me to glory. Whom have I in heaven but You? And there is none upon earth that I desire besides You. My flesh and my heart fail; But God is the strength of my heart and my portion forever" (Psalm 73:23-26).

Questions to Ponder

1. When has it seemed as if the Lord did not recognize or respond to your obedience?

2. How have you been tempted to stop waiting on the Lord and take matters into your own hands? What were the circumstances that seemed to justify that action?

3. Are there occasions when you have experienced such zeal for God's reputation and purposes that you willingly sacrificed yourself in order to see God glorified?

Chapter 19

Passionate Partnership

PEY

¹²⁹Your testimonies are wonderful;
Therefore my soul keeps them.
¹³⁰The entrance of Your words gives light;
It gives understanding to the simple.
¹³¹I opened my mouth and panted,
For I longed for Your commandments.
¹³²Look upon me and be merciful to me,
As Your custom is toward those who love Your name.
¹³³Direct my steps by Your word,
And let no iniquity have dominion over me.
¹³⁴Redeem me from the oppression of man,
That I may keep Your precepts.
¹³⁵Make Your face shine upon Your servant,
And teach me Your statutes.
¹³⁶Rivers of water run down from my eyes,
Because men do not keep Your law.

Pey—Psalm 119:129-136

In *nun*, our psalmist established his heart to serve the Lord despite the rigors of army life. *Pey* depicts the Lord's response to his life of service and partnership in mission.

"Your testimonies (*eduwth*) are wonderful (*pele'*)." This first phrase announces a new season in our psalmist's journey. *Pele'* is a Hebrew word which points to something marvelous, a marvel, something extraordinary or unusual and causing wonder. The root of *pele'* is *pala*, which basically means a miracle. *Pele'*, translated wonders in Exodus 15:11, references Israel's spectacular crossing of the Red Sea: "Who is like You, O LORD, among the gods? Who is like You, glorious in holiness, fearful in praises, doing wonders?" In *ayin*, when our psalmist's obedience provoked backlash, it seemed that the Lord was absent. Now in *pey*, God is very present and acting in power, and our psalmist is passionately engaged in the mission.

Recalling the definition of testimonies (*eduwth*) given in the introduction, we see that God's testimonies represent, repeat or do again, something that took place at a different time or existed in a different place. The word hints at a fresh revelation or communication from God to us, something experiential, manifested from heaven and re-presented on earth. *Yeshua* did on earth what He saw the Father doing in heaven (John 5:19-20). *Yeshua* said on earth what He heard the Father saying in heaven (John 12:49-50). Hence, God's communication to men was the testimony of *Yeshua* (see Revelation 19:10). *Yeshua* was "a Man attested by God to you by miracles, wonders, and signs which God did through Him in your midst" (Acts 2:22).

What a partnership! It was a passionate partnership in mission, a love-walk between the Father in heaven and His Son on earth. Eleven times in the gospel of John *Yeshua* referenced the Father's love for Him (John 3:35; 5:20 and others). Twice the Father shouted from heaven, "This is My Son, whom I love. With Him I am well pleased" (Matthew 3:17 and others). Four times *Yeshua* said that He loves the Father (John 14:31 and others). In John 8:29, *Yeshua* said, "I always do those things that please Him." In John 4:34, *Yeshua* said, "My food is to do the will of Him who sent Me, and to finish His work."

God's work or mission could be considered a divine conspiracy to bring heaven's rule to the earth—a conquest by love, if you will. In 2 Corinthians 6:1, the apostle Paul also claimed to be in partnership with the Lord in this same mission, a worker together with Him. The early apostles in Mark 16:20, "went out and preached everywhere, the Lord working with them and confirming the word through the accompanying signs." See Addendum 6, Slave of Righteousness, for more thoughts on passionate obedience.

We cannot help but recall *Yeshua's* words in Matthew 6:10 teaching us to pray, "Your kingdom come. Your will be done on earth as in heaven." This is a call to duplicate or reproduce on earth that which is in heaven. Our partnership is expressed by contending in prayer and obedience for exactly that. The great announcement that "the kingdom of heaven is at hand" (Matthew 4:17) is in itself a testimony that makes way for the Lord to confirm the word with signs following.

So our psalmist is deployed on the battlefield and in full-blown effective ministry in partnership with the Lord. When Moses passed the test of counterattack from Pharaoh in Exodus 5, and again faced Pharaoh with the word of the Lord, Aaron's rod became a serpent and the entire water supply of Egypt turned to blood (Exodus 7). The contest between the Lord and Pharaoh is on, as God now keeps the promise He made to Moses back in Exodus 3:20 when He said, "I will stretch out My hand and strike Egypt with all My wonders (pala')."

Pey, the seventeenth letter of our Hebrew alphabet depicts an open mouth:

1. Open, as if in astonishment and wonderment at something extraordinary.

2. Open as if to receive food and water to satisfy hunger and thirst. The hunger and thirst in this case is for intimacy with the Lord—to know Him more!

3.   Open, as the source of something (such as the mouth of a river). In this case the mouth is the source of delivering the Lord's testimonies, the speaking of His words, which are then confirmed by the manifestation of God's kingdom power through signs and wonders.

Let's join our psalmist as he continues on in his journey to maturity. We will loosely correlate our thoughts with the three points under *pey* above in a 2–4–2 pattern as follows:

- Impact: The kingdom of God showcased by signs and wonders (v. 129-130).

- Desire: Intimate partnership, the gift of grace (v. 131-134). See Ephesians 3:7.

- Partnership: Loving what God loves (v. 135-136).

Impact: The kingdom of God showcased by signs and wonders (v. 129-130).

"Your testimonies (*eduwth*) are wonderful; Therefore my soul keeps them" (v. 129).

1.   "Your testimonies" (*eduwth*: revelation on earth of what is in heaven).

2.   "Are wonderful" (*pele'* is a marvelous thing or a marvel, something extraordinary or unusual, something surpassing the expected and causing wonder, or separated by distinguishing action). *Pele'* occurs only here in our psalm. Its appearance suggests that our psalmist is experiencing God's power in effective ministry. Or, he may be recounting God's wonders in history. Here are some scriptures in which *pele'* (wonders) is employed:

- Exodus 15:11, "Who is like You, O LORD, among the gods? Who is like You, glorious in holiness, fearful in praises, doing wonders?"

- Psalm 77:11, 14, "I will remember the works of the Lord; Surely I will remember Your wonders of old. . . . You are the God who does wonders; You have declared Your strength among the peoples."

- Psalm 89:5, "And the heavens will praise (declare) Your wonders, O LORD."

- Psalm 78:12-13, "Marvelous things He did in the sight of their fathers, in the land of Egypt, in the field of Zoan. He divided the sea and caused them to pass through; And He made the waters stand up like a heap."

- Isaiah 9:6, "And His name will be called Wonderful, Counselor, Mighty God, Everlasting Father, Prince of Peace."

3.   "Therefore my soul (*nephesh*) keeps them." Verse 167 of our psalm says, "My soul keeps Your testimonies and I love them exceedingly." The soul expresses the whole inner self with all its desires and emotions.

- The ark of the covenant is called "the ark of the testimony" thirteen times in scripture.

- The stone tablets containing the Ten Commandments are referred to as "the tablets of the testimony."

- The tablets of the testimony were placed inside the ark of the testimony. This powerfully depicts the keeping of the testimonies of the Lord innermost (in the heart) and uppermost (in the mind). Nothing on earth is more precious or powerful than the revelation of that which is in heaven.

- Our psalmist is passionate about God and His kingdom.

"The entrance of Your words gives light; It gives understanding to the simple" (v. 130).

1. "The entrance (*pethach*: opening, unfolding, disclosure or revelation via declaration or proclamation) of Your words gives light."

   - The god of this age seeks to blind the minds of those who are perishing lest they see the light of the gospel (2 Corinthians 4:4).

   - 2 Corinthians 4:6, "For it is God who commanded light to shine out of darkness, who has shone in our hearts to give the light of the knowledge of the glory of God." Light enters the world, in general, and the hearts of people in particular, by the proclamation of the word of God. The revelation of the kingdom of God follows the proclamation of the gospel of the kingdom.

2. "Gives light" (*'owr*: makes luminous, illuminates, or causes to shine). This is impact. This word, translated shine in verse 135, occurs twice in this section, and only here. In both instances, the light of God comes to transform humans into friends of God.

3. "Understanding (*biyn*) to the simple" (*p\ethiy*: simplicity, naïveté, seducible, foolish). David agrees in Psalm 19:5, "The testimony of the LORD is sure, making wise the simple." The simpleton or fool throughout the Proverbs refers to one who wastes his life in carnality, seeking after temporal pleasures at the expense of eternal reward. God's testimonies have the power to turn a fool from his ways, and bring him into friendship with the Lord!

4. When anointed ministry duplicates on earth something from heaven, and darkened hearts see the light of God—that is a wonder to behold!

Desire: Intimate partnership (v. 131-134); See also the gift of grace (Ephesians 3:7)

"I opened my mouth and panted, for I longed for Your commandments" (v. 131).

1. "I opened my mouth (*peh*) and panted (*sha'aph*: to gasp, pant, to inhale eagerly, desire, to covet earnestly), for I longed for (*ya'ab*: desire, longing) Your commandments."

    - In verse 103 the psalmist experienced God's words as sweet to his taste, sweeter than honey to the mouth. Here he opens his mouth and longs intensely for more of God and His word. He desires intimacy with the Almighty God.

    - In Psalm 34:8, David writes: "Oh, taste and see that the LORD is good." It is amazing how the most satisfying and pleasurable experiences with the Lord only serve to awaken desire for more of the same.

    - In Jeremiah 2:24, *sha'aph* is used of a wild donkey in heat, ready to mate.

2. "Your commandments" (*mitzvah*: command, directive, charge, order). This is surprising. Who of us wants to be commanded to do something or be charged with a mission? Here, David is actually longing for God's commandments.

    - Recall *Yeshua's* words in John 4:34, "My food is to do the will of Him who sent Me, and to finish His work." Nothing is more satisfying or addictive than obeying God. How can this be? There are two aspects to the rewards of obedience:

        o   The reward of knowing or sensing the Father's pleasure at our obedience. In John 8:29, *Yeshua* said, "I always do those things that please Him."

        o   The breaking in of heaven's power. Obedience precipitates encounter. In Romans 6:16-22, Paul describes two ways to yield our members:

        o   We can yield to the lure of sin and experience death.

        o   We can yield to the lure of righteousness and experience holiness.

3. The implication is that we become slaves to whomever we yield. We get addicted to righteousness by yielding to the directive of the Holy Spirit. Obedience produces encounter with God and encounter produces hunger for more. The fruit of this love-walk is that God's mission to take back the created order is being realized. Read Addendum 6, Slaves of Righteousness, for a fuller discussion on this powerful truth.

4. This hunger for a directive from God could also be seen in context to the backlash illustrated in *ayin* from Exodus 5. There, after Pharaoh made things more difficult than ever, Moses was in a very challenging situation. He desperately needed to know what to do next. Here in *pey*, David is enjoying the impact of his obedience and wants to know what is next.

"Look upon me and be merciful to me, as Your custom is toward those who love Your name" (v. 132).

1. "Look upon (*panah*: to turn, to face, appear) me." The word, face (*paniym*) in verse 135 is a derivative of *panah*. Both words speak of the face of the Lord turning toward us. The issue is desire for nearness and intimacy.

2. "Be merciful" (*chanan*: literally to bend or stoop [so as to show kindness], to be gracious, show favor or pity). "Be gracious" might be the better translation. *Chen*, derivative of *chanan*, is translated grace thirty-eight times in the Hebrew Scriptures. In Ephesians 3:7-8, Paul writes about the "mystery of Christ" of which he "became a minister according to the gift of the grace of God given to me by the effective working of His power. To me, who am less than the least of all the saints, this grace was given, that I should preach among the Gentiles the unsearchable riches of Christ."

    •   God in His kindness made Paul a partner in the mission to reach the Gentiles with the gospel.

    •   How is human partnership with God in mission an expression of God's grace? Former enemies have been so utterly redeemed that they have become friends of God who now accept the rigors of war in order to see God's interests advanced on the earth.

    •   Discipleship is not about making it through this life and reaching heaven. It is about bringing heaven to earth in this life. It is about partnership with the Lord in His desire for the world. This mission gives us purpose.

3. "As Your custom" (*mishpat*: verdict, judgment). *Mishpat*, translated judgments elsewhere, points to the right rulings of the Lord as the King who decrees a thing so that wrong things are set right. God has decreed and will decree things on behalf of those who love His name. In other segments, we have discussed at length God's faithfulness in history to answer the cry of His people with powerful acts of redemption.

4. "Your name" (*shem*: reputation, fame, glory). *Shem* appears only here and in verse fifty-five of our psalm where our psalmist, hurting from betrayal, turns for comfort to God's reputation for bringing justice with these words: "I remember Your

Name in the night, O LORD." Those who love His name are those who have zeal for His glory in the earth. In other words, those who desire for God to be famous on earth are the ones who can expect to see the breaking in of God's judgments on their behalf.

- "Love Your name" is totally unique to this section and adds to the theme of desire, passion or zeal for God's glory.

- Who of us really has zeal for God's glory in the earth? Many people in scripture exhibited great zeal for the Lord at personal cost.

5. The Scriptures translation translates verse 132 this way: "Turn to me and show me favor, according to Your right-ruling, toward those who love Your Name."

"Direct my steps by Your word, and let no iniquity have dominion over me" (v. 133).

1. "Direct" (*kuwn*: to be erect, to set up, establish, be firm, be stable).

    - *Yeshua* depended on the Father to direct His every step. John 5:19 says, "The Son can do nothing of Himself, but what He sees the Father do; for whatever He does, the Son also does."

    - Psalm 17:5, "Uphold my steps in Your paths, (so) that my footsteps may not slip."

2. "Let no iniquity (*'aven*: trouble, sorrow, wickedness, vanity) have dominion (govern, domineer, exercise power or mastery over) over me."

    - *'Aven* is not the primary Hebrew word for sin and perverseness within the human heart. It is much broader and can simply refer to the trouble of life on a fallen earth. Our psalmist wants to be directed by the word of the Lord, not by negative circumstances.

    - *'Aven* could also refer to possible fault lines of iniquity yet within David's soul. Our psalmist wants to be ruled by neither inward iniquity nor outward trouble. He desires to be governed by the Lord Himself.

    - David prayed in Psalm 25, "Let not my enemies triumph over me." Also in Matthew 6:13 we see the prayer, "deliver us from the evil one."

    - Psalm 19:13, "Keep back Your servant also from presumptuous sins; Let them not have dominion over me."

3. David wants nothing to disrupt this passionate partnership with the Lord. A propensity to sin still resides in his flesh, and he needs humility to keep leaning upon the Lord.

"Redeem me from the oppression of man, that I may keep Your precepts" (v. 134).

1.   "Redeem (*padah*: ransom, deliver, rescue) me from the oppression of man."

     •   In the heat of kingdom warfare, the apostle Paul asked for prayer in 2 Thessalonians 3:1-2, "Pray for us, that the word of the LORD may run swiftly and be glorified, just as it is with you, and that we may be delivered from unreasonable and wicked men; for not all have faith."

     •   Moses certainly needed the Lord's rescue from Pharaoh in that great contest of the Exodus of Israel out of Egypt.

2.   "That I may keep Your precepts." Our psalmist desires to be redeemed from oppression to serve the Lord freely without hindrance. He really loves what God loves. This is what friendship and partnership are all about. This man can be trusted with great authority.

     •   Luke 1:74, "To grant us that we, being delivered from the hand of our enemies, might serve Him without fear."

     •   There is an ease with which the gospel can be preached when a nation's laws are righteous. In 1 Timothy 2:1-4, we are instructed to offer prayers and intercessions "for kings and all who are in authority, that we may lead a quiet and peaceable life in all godliness and reverence . . . in the sight of God . . . who desires all men to be saved and to come to the knowledge of the truth."

     •   The prevalence of a somewhat biblical worldview at the founding of America provided for a relatively righteous government with just legislation, paving the way for great prosperity over much of its 200-plus year history. That prosperity has financed the greatest missionary movement ever in the history of the earth. The paradox is that in times of prosperity, believers tend to lose their zeal for God and can become lukewarm (Revelation 3:17).

     •   Paradoxically again, it has often been in times of persecution that the gospel has advanced powerfully. Even so, today in nations where there is extreme persecution of Christians, there is also restriction in openly serving the Lord, and many are fleeing for their lives to other places. Those nations only grow darker and darker, at least for now, but ultimately that also seems to set the table for the advance of the gospel.

Partnership: Loving what God loves (v. 135-136).

"Make Your face shine upon Your servant, and teach me Your statutes" (v. 135).

1. "Make Your face shine (*'owr*) upon Your servant," was prayed by God's servants throughout the scriptures. It is the priestly blessing of Numbers 6:24-26. "The LORD bless you and keep you; The LORD make His face shine upon you, and be gracious to you; The LORD lift up His countenance upon you, and give you peace."

    *   Psalm 4:6, "There are many who say, 'Who will show us any good?' Lord, lift up the light of Your countenance upon us."

    *   This is *The Blessed Life*, when the light of God's countenance shines upon us and covers us with favor. Everything we need is imparted through His favor.

    *   This light (*'owr*) leads to the writing of God's law upon the human heart.

2. "Teach (*lamad*) me Your statutes (*choq*)." This prayer occurs ten times in all of scripture, eight of them in Psalm 119. *Choq* (statutes) emphasizes that which is engraved, unchanging, or permanent. Our psalmist is asking that God's word be engraved on his heart. This is the promise of the New Covenant that the Lord said He would make with His people.

"Rivers of water run down from my eyes, because men do not keep Your law" (v. 136).

1. Our psalmist is weeping because men do not value the word of God! His tears reveal his close friendship and partnership with the Lord.

2. Conversely, any jurisdiction that does honor the law of the Lord would be blessed and prosperous.

3. David's union with the heart of God is amazing. It is said of the Messiah in Psalm 45:7, "You love righteousness and hate wickedness; Therefore God, Your God, has anointed You with the oil of gladness more than Your companions." Biblical holiness is happy holiness (see Addendum 6 for further discussion).

Questions to Ponder

1. Recall some of your own times of exhilaration in partnership with the Lord. Review the times when you prayed and obeyed, and He responded in power to advance His kingdom. In other words, has your mouth ever been the source of a message that God confirmed with a sign and wonder?

2. Have you ever experienced such a zeal for God that it led to sacrifice and weeping for the sake of God's name?

3. Do you know what it is to experience great desire for God and His words (v.131)?

Chapter 20

Zeal for Righteousness

TSADDE

137Righteous are You, O LORD,
And upright are Your judgments.
138Your testimonies, which You have commanded,
Are righteous and very faithful.
139My zeal has consumed me,
Because my enemies have forgotten Your words.
140Your word is very pure;
Therefore Your servant loves it.
141I am small and despised,
Yet I do not forget Your precepts.
142Your righteousness is an everlasting righteousness,
And Your law is truth.
143Trouble and anguish have overtaken me,
Yet Your commandments are my delights.
144The righteousness of Your testimonies is everlasting;
Give me understanding, and I shall live.

Tsadde—Psalm 119:137-144

Our psalmist has come to an amazing and relatively rare place in his life; he has become a redeemed human being who has more zeal for God and God's purposes than he does for his own life. God has answered David's panting desire for more, and our psalmist finds himself consumed with zeal for righteousness and for the reputation of God's name (v. 132). Just as is spoken of the Messiah in Psalm 45:7, our psalmist loves righteousness and hates wickedness. Paradoxically, this passion precipitates greater conflict with the kingdom of darkness, and as the opposition intensifies, this increased zeal fortifies him to press the battle. In fact, the verses that precede Psalm 45:7 portray the Messiah as being at war for the cause of truth, humility and righteousness (Psalm 45:4).

In this segment David gives matchless adulation to the righteousness of God. Ultimately, this praise can be ascribed to *Yeshua*, the Righteous One who is worthy of praise (Revelation 5:12). Our psalmist is overcome with joy in his zeal and delight for the absolute rightness and trustworthiness of God and His word. These eight verses are distinguished by the occurrence of words like righteous, righteousness, upright, faithful, pure and truth. Two phrases in particular appear only in this scripture and punctuate this section with intense extolling and admiration of God's righteousness and the utter trustworthiness of all of His ways:

- Very faithful (v. 138).

- Very pure (v. 140).

Tsadde, the eighteenth letter of the Hebrew alphabet, speaks of a righteous person whose desires and needs are fulfilled in the Lord. A *tzaddik* in Hebrew is a righteous person. Proverbs 10:23-25 says, "To do evil is like sport to a fool, but a man of under-standing has wisdom. The fear of the wicked will come upon him, and the desire of the righteous (*tsaddik*) will be granted. When the whirlwind passes by, the wicked is no more, but the righteous (*tsaddik*) has an everlasting foundation." *Tsadde* can also speak of warfare or fighting; a righteous life will confront the evil of a fallen world system and incur its wrath, leading to a clash of values and aims.

The ancient pictograph of *tsadde* depicted a fish hook. The idea is that of being inescapably pulled or drawn toward something by strong desire—hooked. We noted in *pey* that we can be slaves of righteousness. Well, it happened to our psalmist. He was hooked. There is something compelling about a truly righteous person. The integrity of *Yeshua's* life was a powerful magnet. Multitudes were drawn to Him. Here in our psalm, David is also being pulled by a consuming love for God's Word: "My zeal has consumed (put an end to) me."

The love of righteousness

What is surprising about Psalm 45:7 noted above is that being anointed with the oil of gladness comes as a result of loving righteousness and hating wickedness. *Yeshua* loved righteousness and hated wickedness more than any man and therefore He was anointed with the oil of gladness more than His (Your) companions. The unmistakable hint is that our lives are joyful and full in proportion to our love for righteousness. See Addendum 6 regarding Happy Holiness. The degree to which we love righteousness is the degree to which:

1. We hate what He hates. Thus, love and hate are two sides of one coin.

2. We are in union with and have communion with Him.

3. We pray according to His will and have what we ask for. "Ask and you shall receive that your joy may be full" (John 16:24). See also 1 John 5:14-15.

Ironically, this life of fullness is precisely what precipitates opposition from the adversary. It exposes and confronts evil in the culture. *Yeshua's* life was filled with conflict. As He entered the towns of His day, demons would manifest. Whole regions became embroiled in controversy regarding His identity, miracles and agenda. Leaders converged upon Him with intentions to stop Him. Ultimately, they crucified Him.

Conversely, He was compelling and desirable as multitudes followed Him. Haggai calls Him "the Desire of All Nations" (Haggai 2:7). *Yeshua* was and is the most controversial figure ever to enter human history. He is simultaneously the most loved and the most hated man ever to appear in history. He is the ultimate test of every human heart. He came to divide the earth into two groups of people (see Luke 12:51-53), those who hate Him and those who love Him. Simeon's prophecy over the baby *Yeshua* in Luke 2:34 is as powerful as it is troubling: "Behold, this Child is destined for the fall and rising of many in Israel, and for a sign which will be spoken against."

It is this zeal for righteousness which compels someone to selflessly confront the injustice, corruption and decadence of his own community. It motivates him to confront the status quo and contend for righteous legislation and righteous leadership that will serve to promote peace and prosperity. In other words, anyone with this zeal for righteousness and for the glory of God will pick fights with the devil everywhere he goes—not because he loves controversy, but because he has zeal for God's name and compassion for those who are oppressed through the injustice of corrupt systems.

What we are contending for is for *Yeshua* to possess all that He paid for on the cross—that is the entirety of the created order under His kingship. The announcement in Revelation 11:15, at the second coming of Messiah, is what rightly became His at the moment on the cross when He said, "It is finished" (paid in full). "The kingdoms of this world have become the kingdoms of our Lord and of His Christ and He will reign forever" (Revelation 11:15). We contend for His righteous rule first in our own lives and in our families and then beyond to our community and nation. For now, "The kingdom of heaven is near" (Matthew 3:2), but one day He will rule it all. "Let Your kingdom come."

Zeal for God's glory is the highest motivation a believer can know. It is a mark of maturity to desire God's glory before one's own life. It is the key to overcoming the fear of man, the fear of death and all the self-preservation instincts that drive us to compromise in a politically correct society. To love what He loves and hate what He hates: this is union with Him to the highest degree and it is what gets our prayers answered, because we will ask for things "according to His will" (see 1 John 5:14-15). Answered prayer then results in fullness of joy (John 15:7; 16:24). This cycle both precipitates and perpetuates warfare with the kingdom of darkness, ultimately overcoming it. The Apostle Paul said it this way in Romans 11:36, "For of Him and through Him and to Him are all things, to whom be glory forever. Amen."

Let's join David in his journey again. We will outline our thoughts in two four-verse segments as follows:

- Loving righteousness—Extolling the Lord in overflowing joy (v. 137-140)
- Loving righteousness—Confident in battle (v. 141-144)

Loving righteousness—Extolling the Lord in overflowing joy (v. 137-140).

"Righteous are You, O LORD, and upright are Your judgments" (v. 137).

1. "Righteous are You, O LORD" is a massive and powerful declaration in the midst of a fallen world where the righteous are often hated and persecuted. This declaration was made by a suffering psalmist in Psalm 92:15 "The LORD is upright; He is my rock, and there is no unrighteousness in Him." This declaration has been made by many throughout scripture and throughout all of history as they experienced or witnessed the righteous dealings of a holy God in a fallen world.

2. When John saw the throne of God in Revelation 4:2-3, he saw "One on the throne . . . like a jasper." A jasper is a white, diamond-like crystal. It hints at God's white-hot purity. It speaks of His indescribable holiness and the absolute perfection of all of His ways and dealings with men. 1 John 1:5, "This is the message which we have heard from Him and declare to you, that God is light and in Him is no darkness at all" (burning purity in thoughts, intents and dealings concerning all people).

   - God's righteousness could include words such as righteous, upright, true, truth, faithful, pure, good, and perfect.
   - Psalm 25:8, "Good and upright is the Lord; Therefore He teaches sinners in the way."
   - Psalm 19:9, "The judgments of the Lord are true and righteous altogether" (Revelation 16:7; 19:2).
   - John 3:33, "He who has received His testimony has certified that God is true."

3. "Your judgments." God is righteous when judgment begins in His own house. He is righteous when He waits to judge the wicked (see Addendum 4). He is righteous when, at their repentance, He saves the wicked. He is righteous when He ultimately judges the wicked who refuse to repent. He is righteous when the saints are vindicated and delivered from the wicked and when they prosper and are promoted. He is righteous when the saints suffer martyrdom and loss in this age, receiving their reward in eternity.

"Your testimonies, which You have commanded, are righteous and very faithful" (v. 138).

1. "Testimonies" (*edah*): Just as *Yeshua* was a trustworthy representation of God on earth, so all of the Lord's testimonies are a faithful representation of what is in heaven. In our weakness, we can get it wrong and misrepresent who He really is or what He wants, but as we mature we will represent Him more fully and accurately.

2. "Righteous" (*tsehdek*). God's testimonies are just, right, leading to equity and prosperity.

3. "Faithful" (*emuna*: firmness, security, trustworthiness, fidelity). The phrase "very faithful" occurs only here in all of scripture.

4. What we are commanded to believe and practice is both righteous and very faithful.

"My zeal has consumed me, because my enemies have forgotten Your words" (v. 139).

1. "My zeal" (*qin'ah*: ardor, zeal, jealousy, to be zealous or jealous for something).

2. Isaiah 9:7, speaking of the certain establishment of God's government, says "The zeal of the LORD of hosts will perform this."

3. "Because my enemies have forgotten Your words" shows that our psalmist's zeal is not for personal glory or vengeance but for his enemies to glorify God. It is zeal for God's glory.

4. In Psalm 69:9, David speaks of bearing reproach and alienation for the Lord's sake, "because zeal for Your house has eaten me up." Others in scripture who are known for their zeal for the Lord include:

   - *Yeshua* in John 2:17, "Zeal for Your house has eaten Me up."

   - Phinehas in Numbers 25:11, "Because he was zealous with My zeal among them."

   - Jehu in 2 Kings 10:16, "Come with me and see my zeal for the LORD."

   - The Apostle Paul's zeal for God's glory is legendary. He gladly embraced an intense and disciplined life, suffering much because of zeal for the gospel.

   - The story is often told of two young Moravian missionaries who in the 1700s left Herrnhut, Germany and sold themselves into slavery in order to reach slaves with the gospel. When asked why they would waste their lives in this way, their famous answer still resounds: "That Jesus would get the reward of His suffering."

5. Can we observe our psalmist's recent shift from a focus on himself to a concern for the Lord's name and mission?

    •   "It is time for You to act, O YHVH; they have regarded Your law (*torah*) as void" (v. 126).

    •   "I hate every false way" (v. 128). The converse would be a love for God's truth.

    •   "Rivers of water run down from my eyes, because men do not keep Your law" (*torah*) (v. 136).

    •   "My zeal has consumed me, because my enemies have forgotten Your words" (v. 139).

6. Consider the Lord's own zeal or jealousy in Exodus 34:14, "For the LORD, whose name is Jealous (*Qanna'*), is a jealous God." Deuteronomy 4:24 says, "For the LORD your God is a consuming fire, a jealous (*qanna'*) God" (both *qanna'* and *qin'ah* are derived from the same root and mean essentially the same thing). *Qanna'* is divine zeal to protect that which is dearest and most precious to the Lord. Two things in particular:

    •   His own glory and name (or reputation); God's dealings with His own people were often said to be for"His name sake" (Psalm 23:3; Ezekiel 20:9; 36:22; Isaiah 42:8; Psalm 79:9).

    •   The devotion of His bride (James 4:5; John 17:24).

7. Holy jealousy is a fiery passion in the heart of God which entails both love and wrath. His love redeems and brings us into His embrace. But when we, His betrothed bride, give our affection to another lover, the Lord's jealousy is stirred up. There is wrath toward the seducer and zeal to win us back because of His love. Without wrath, there could be no love. As we have already discussed, the one passion pre-supposes the other.

"Your word is very pure; Therefore Your servant loves it" (v. 140).

1. In Psalm 12:6, David has fallen from favor in Saul's court and writes, "The words of the LORD are pure words, like silver tried in a furnace of earth, purified seven times."

    •   The phrase "very pure" occurs only here in scripture.

    •   See also Proverbs 30:5; Psalm 19:8; 1 Peter 2:2; John 15:3; Psalm 119:9; Ephesians 5:26.

    •   Pure words edify and are free of error, offense, prejudice, flattery, malice, slander, accusation and so forth (see James 3:17; Philippians 4:8).

2.   His words have to be purified in us. We are the furnace of earth (Psalm 12:6). The dross of false doctrine, wrong and idolatrous concepts of God, and of our own impure and wrong thoughts have to be removed. Psalm 105:19, "Until the time that His word came to pass, the word of the LORD tested him" (Joseph).

3.   To receive or hear the word of the Lord is to be entrusted with a fearful steward-ship. It requires a response. It tests our hearts. We will be purified or apostatized related to our response to the word of God.

Loving righteousness—Confident in battle (v. 141-144)

"I am small and despised, yet I do not forget Your precepts" (v. 141).

1.   "I am small" (*tsaiyr*: young, least, insignificant). God has a reputation for choosing the least likely through whom to display His power and goodness.

- God chooses the weak things to shame the mighty (1 Corinthians 1:27). See also Micah 5:2; Isaiah 60:22; Genesis 48:14.

- Gideon's disbelieving response to the angel's words, "Go in this might of yours, for you shall save Israel" was "O my Lord, how can I save Israel? Indeed my clan is the weakest in Manasseh; I am the least (*tsaiyr*) in my father's house" (Judges 6:14-15).

- David himself was the youngest of Jesse's eight sons and anointed to be king in Israel. In 1 Samuel 16:11 Jesse says, "There remains yet the youngest (small, insignificant, unimportant), and there he is, keeping the sheep."

2.   Despised (*bazah*: despise, hold in contempt, disdain). David experienced being despised or belittled in some way numerous times.

- As noted above, David was overlooked when the prophet came to anoint a king.

- He experienced contempt from his older brother (1 Samuel 17:28).

- Skepticism from King Saul: "You are not able . . . you are a youth" (1 Samuel 17:33).

- Scorn and contempt from Goliath: "When the Philistine (Goliath) looked about and saw David, he disdained (*bazah*) him; for he was but a youth" (1 Samuel 17:42).

- His own wife: "David danced before the LORD with all his might." Michal "despised him in her heart" (2 Samuel 6:20).

- "A broken and contrite heart—these O God, You will not despise" (Psalm 51:17).

3.   "Yet I do not forget (ignore, wither [in the keeping of]) Your precepts (*piqquwd*)."
     As noted in the introduction to the psalm, God's precepts are ever present to at-
     tend to us and preside over our lives. They are authorized by a righteous Father
     to attend to one's life and produce a kind of cause and affect related to our life's
     choices, so that we are helped to stay on the right path."

     •   Is our psalmist being careful to respond righteously to demeaning treatment?

     •   These presiding precepts would not only convict him of getting it wrong (if
          he did), but they would assure him of the truth of how God defines him. In
          this context of zeal for righteousness, the latter is the better idea.

     •   David, in 1 Samuel 17:45-47, though "but a youth," answers Goliath's taunts
          with amazing boldness and confidence. Can you sense zeal for righteousness
          in these words? "You come to me with a sword, with a spear, and with a
          javelin. But I come to you in the name of the LORD of hosts, the God of the
          armies of Israel, whom you have defied. This day the LORD will deliver you
          into my hand . . . that all the earth may know that there is a God in Israel.
          Then all this assembly shall know that the LORD does not save with sword
          and spear; for the battle is the LORD'S, and He will give you into our hands."

     •   Our psalmist is certainly putting his hope in the word of God!

"Your righteousness is an everlasting righteousness, and Your law is truth" (v. 142).

1.   What is righteous and true today always was and always will be righteous and
     true.

     •   This is about eternity and eternal truth; see verse eighty-nine.

     •   In Malachi 3:6, God says, "For I am the LORD, I change not."

     •   James 1:17 speaks of the goodness of the Father of lights, with whom there
          is no variation or shadow of turning.

     •   Psalm 36:6, "Your righteousness is like the great mountains." See also Psalm
          97:6.

2.   To live righteously in context to a world system which hates righteousness requires
     an eternal perspective. Consider the words of the three Hebrews to Nebuchad-
     nezzar when commanded by him to bow to his image or be thrown into a fiery
     furnace: "Our God whom we serve is able to deliver us from the burning fiery
     furnace, and He will deliver us from your hand, O king. But if not, let it be known
     to you, O king, that we do not serve your gods, nor will we worship the gold im-
     age which you have set up" (Daniel 3:17-18). How do we reconcile the seeming
     contradiction of these statements?

- "God is able to deliver." We typically have no problem believing this.

- "He will deliver us from your hand, O king." Will He? What does this mean in light of the next statement?

- "But, if not, let it be known to you, O king, that we do not serve your gods. Nor will we worship the gold image you have set up." This statement suggests that they did not know exactly what God would do. Will God always deliver the righteous?

- It seems that these men were seeing eternity and were really saying something like this: "Our lives are not in your hand, O king. There is a throne set above your throne and our lives are in the hands of that King of kings. If He does not deliver in this age, then in the age to come we will be vindicated and rewarded."

3. Ultimate and eternal deliverance of the righteous is sure. However, in this age there is a kind of dance or interplay between deliverance and martyrdom. Here is another refresher from that dance discussed back in *kaph*:

   - Deliverance showcases the superiority and power of the kingdom of God in the earth. Because the kingdom of God is at hand, many righteous men and women will be supernaturally delivered from their persecutors. Many righteous businesses are prospering because of their godliness. It pays to be righteous.

   - Conversely, many are those who suffer martyrdom and loss because they will not compromise righteousness. Martyrdom and loss showcase the nobility of a heart that will go to the death for love. Eternally, there will be great reward and all will be set right, but it requires an eternal perspective to stand strong.

4. Life on earth is like a 70-year internship preparing us for ruling with Him in the age to come, which is our real ministry and calling. To compromise righteousness now for the sake of relieving the pressure of persecution, or for the sake of sinful desires, will jeopardize our reward in the age to come, when *Yeshua* rules the whole earth in righteousness (see Isaiah 11:4-5).

"Trouble and anguish have overtaken me, yet Your commandments are my delights" (v. 143).

1. "Trouble and anguish." Both of these Hebrew words speak of relentless enemies that press us to the point of distress. These are the rigors of war.

- The Apostle Paul experienced relentless difficulty from the Judaizers who would follow him and stir up trouble (see Acts 17:5; 18:12).

- Paul also, at one point, under severe persecution and pressure despaired even of life. Read 2 Corinthians 1:8-10. In Acts 14:19, he was stoned and left for dead outside the city. In Acts 16, he was beaten and thrown into jail.

- *Yeshua* had constant trouble with the Jewish leaders of His day. They resisted Him continually, ultimately crucifying Him.

2. "Your commandments are my delights" (*shashua*: delight, enjoyment, pleasure). How can one delight in the Lord amidst trouble and anguish? Yet, our psalmist has found that place of delight:

- He found "rest from the days of adversity until the pit is dug for the wicked" (Psalm 94:13).

- He found a table of intimacy and delight in the presence of his enemies (Psalm 23:5).

- He found the fellowship of His (*Yeshua's*) sufferings (Philippians 3:10).

- In Acts 16:25, at midnight Paul and Silas were praying and singing hymns to God.

- 2 Corinthians 1:5 assures us that however much suffering abounds, so consolation (comfort and the sense of God's presence) also abounds.

"The righteousness of Your testimonies is everlasting; Give me understanding, and I shall live" (v. 144).

1. Not only is God's own righteousness everlasting (verse 142), but the righteousness of His testimonies is everlasting. "Heaven and earth will pass away, but My words will by no means pass away" (Matthew 24:35).

2. Proverbs 10:25 asserts that "When the whirlwind passes by, the wicked is no more, but the righteous has an everlasting foundation."

3. "Give me understanding." Again our psalmist is asking for friendship with God. Check the comparison with John 15:15. As we have already noted, there is something higher than submission to the will of God as an obedient servant. It is union with Him as a friend. As a friend, you love what He loves, think like He thinks, and know His ways. In 1 Corinthians 2:16, Paul said: "But we have the mind of Christ."

Concluding Thoughts

Imputed righteousness is different from imparted (attained) righteousness. "Abraham believed God, and it was accounted (*logizomai*) to him for righteousness. Now to him who works, the wages are not counted (*logizomai*) as grace but as debt. But to him who does not work but believes on Him who justifies the ungodly, his faith is accounted (*logizomai*) for righteousness, just as David also describes the blessedness of the man to whom God imputes (*logizomai*) righteousness apart from works: Blessed are those whose lawless deeds are forgiven, and whose sins are covered; Blessed is the man to whom the LORD shall not impute (*logizomai*) sin" (Romans 4:3-8).

The Greek work *logizomai* occurs six more times in Romans 4 and is definitely the key to what is being discussed: a righteousness that comes by faith apart from the *torah* (Romans 3:21-22). *Logizomai* is an accounting word meaning reckoned, computed, imputed, credited, or charged. It is a word dealing with the hard facts (truth) of numbers. Is this the righteousness we are discussing here in *tsadde*? The answer is "No." Let me explain.

We were in Adam when Adam sinned, therefore we sinned. Adam's sin was imputed to us. When the Messiah, the Last Adam, died, He bore our sins in His own body on the tree (1 Peter 2:24). That is, our sin was imputed to the Messiah, who was Himself without sin. All who believe in (have faith in) *Yeshua* as the Messiah—He who lived, died, was buried and rose again on the third day according to the scriptures (1 Corinthians 15:1-5)—are declared to be righteous by their faith. That is, the Messiah's righteousness is imputed to them and they are legally justified before God (Romans 5:1). Messiah's righteousness was counted as their righteousness. They have His righteousness in their account as a free gift that comes by faith.

This infinitely valuable gift now defines the believer and gives him not only right standing before God, but also the right to intimacy with God (Hebrews 4:16; 10:19-22). All of this is available before he actually overcomes any of the sin operating within his own flesh. But having righteousness imputed to us doesn't make us righteous. Imputed righteousness is potential righteousness which must be drawn upon (like money in a bank account) in order to actually live out that new identity and walk as *Yeshua* walked (1 John 2:6). We will call it attained righteousness. Our lives, both inwardly and outwardly, have yet to be conformed to the image of the Messiah.

Imputed righteousness is like money charged to your account in the bank. It has great potential. But attained righteousness is like money paid out of the account into your hands. This is what actually showcases Messiah to the world. It is the currency of the kingdom.

One can know the joy of sins forgiven with imputed righteousness, but only the power of attained righteousness can showcase *Messiah* to the world and qualify one for reward in the kingdom. The meek (Christ-like) inherit the earth, not the justified. Those who actually overcome and attain to some measure of true Christ-likeness will get the reward. Paul's crown of righteousness in 2 Timothy 4:8, is the victor's wreath (*stephanos*) which only an overcomer obtains: "There is laid up for me the crown of righteousness, which the Lord, the righteous Judge, will give to me on that Day, and not to me only but also to all who have loved His appearing."

Review in *mem* a study on the victor's wreath (*stephanos*). This attained righteousness is the righteousness which is the subject of our segment, *tsadde*.

Questions to Ponder

1. Can you recall the time when you knew the joy of sins forgiven and of having Messiah's righteousness imputed to your account? How secure are you in this standing?

2. Can you identify with our psalmist's zeal for and love of righteousness? How have you grown in zeal for God's glory?

3. What are some issues in your life that you have overcome? What are some areas in which you have attained greater righteousness and grown to be more like the Master?

Chapter 21

Pressing the Battle

QOOF

[145]I cry out with my whole heart;
Hear me, O LORD!
I will keep Your statutes.
[146]I cry out to You;
Save me, and I will keep Your testimonies.
[147]I rise before the dawning of the morning,
And cry for help;
I hope in Your word.
[148]My eyes are awake through the night watches,
That I may meditate on Your word.
[149]Hear my voice according to Your lovingkindness;
O LORD, revive me according to Your justice.
[150]They draw near who follow after wickedness;
They are far from Your law.
[151]You are near, O LORD,
And all Your commandments are truth.
[152]Concerning Your testimonies,
I have known of old that You have founded them forever.

Qoof—Psalm 119:145-152

David's zeal for righteousness engages him in an intense battle. Today, David is renowned as a man of war for his zeal to see the Lord's enemies subdued and to see the righteous possess the land.

Our Messiah's zeal for righteousness, as noted in *tsadde* from Psalm 45, is also referenced in Isaiah 42:2-4, 13. "He will bring forth justice for truth. He will not fail nor be discouraged, till He has established justice in the earth. . . . The LORD shall go forth like a mighty man; He shall stir up His zeal like a man of war. He shall cry out, yes, shout aloud; He shall prevail against His enemies."

When Phinehas saw immorality in the house of God, "he rose from among the congregation and took a javelin in his hand; and he went after the man of Israel into the tent and thrust both of them through . . . so the plague was stopped among the children of Israel" (Numbers 25:7-8). A present-day saint's zeal for righteousness may lead him to confront a local business concerning the magazines or television channel in the waiting room. Those loyal to God will confess the name of *Yeshua* in the workplace environment. They may confront injustice, such as an issue in which women, children, or a particular ethnic group are victimized and oppressed while those who traffic in hell's agenda profit at their expense.

In Acts 19:20, we are told that the word of the Lord grew mightily and prevailed against the idol-making industry in Ephesus. When Demetrius, a silversmith who made "no small profit" from this illegitimate business, saw what was happening, he mobilized the whole city against Paul to the extent that Paul's very life was endangered.

Seeking first God's kingdom and His righteousness with the zeal that our psalmist manifests in *tsadde* will inevitably ignite a reaction from our adversary. We have discussed this dynamic several times already. In Acts 2 and 3, after an initial advance by the early body of Messiah, Peter and John are suddenly arrested, detained and ordered to stop preaching. The battle is on as the adversary pushes back. Consider the believers' response upon Peter and John's release in Acts 4:23-24, "And being let go, they went to their own companions and reported all that the chief priests and elders had said to them. So when they heard that, they raised their voice to God with one accord."

A powerful intercessory prayer meeting ensues in which they pray Psalm 2:1-2 back to God. The raging of the nations against the Lord and His Messiah is referenced. Consider Acts 4:27-28: "For truly against Your holy Servant Jesus, whom You anointed, both Herod and Pontius Pilate, with the Gentiles and the people of Israel, were gathered together to do whatever Your hand and Your purpose determined before to be done." God has predetermined that we are to love and advance His righteous kingdom in hostile territory and in context to an adversary. Pushback is inevitable, but ultimate victory is assured.

What do they ask for in the prayer meeting? They ask for boldness to speak God's word. They ask for signs and wonders. The kingdom of God suffers violence, but "the violent take it by force." In verse thirty-one, heaven hears and responds: "And when they had prayed, the place where they were assembled together was shaken; and they were all filled with the Holy Spirit, and they spoke the word of God with boldness." Acts 5 is the result—greater advance than ever is made as even Peter's shadow heals the sick. Check it out.

This section of Psalm 119, *qoof*, has a number of new words and phrases which relate to the prevalent biblical call to watchfulness (wakefulness) and prayer (watch and pray). Thus, it connects to the theme of intercessory prayer referenced in this psalm. We list them here:

1. "Cry out" (*qara*: to call out to, call on, address by name in accosting someone, cry out, proclaim, recite, summon, appeal to, read). This occurs twice and only in *qoof* (v. 145, 146).

2. "Hear me" (*anah*: answer). The psalmist is really saying, "answer me" (v. 145).

3. "Dawning of the morning" (*nesheph*: morning or evening twilight), occurs only in verse 147.

4. "I cry out" (*shava'*: cry as if for help or freedom), occurs only in verse 147. The root word has to do with being free.

5. "I rise . . . and awake" (v. 147, 148) are the same Hebrew word, *qadam*. *Qadam* occurs twice in the psalm, and only here. It means to project oneself (precede, hence to anticipate, hasten, meet [usually for help]; come or be in front of, confront, go before).

6. "Night watches" (*'ashmurah*: a night watch). The 24-hour day was divided into watches. Guards were set to stay awake and watch army encampments and cities. This word occurs only here in verse 148 in our psalm.

7. "Hear my voice" (*shama' qowl*). These two words appear only here in verse 149.

8. "They (the wicked) draw near (v.150) and You (the Lord) are near (v. 151). "

The ancient pictograph of our nineteenth letter, *qoof*, depicts the back of the head and speaks of that which is following behind, coming after, the last or the least, what comes first and what follows after. In the wilderness, Israel followed the cloud by day and the pillar of fire by night. At the conquest of the land they followed the ark of the covenant borne on the shoulders of the priests. In both scenarios Israel followed the Lord and God's power was manifest. In the conquest, we especially see the place and role of human intercession in the coming of the kingdom of God. Intercessors follow God and the release of God's power follows their intercession (agreement with God). Note the following verses:

1. Joshua 3:3, "When you see the ark of the covenant of the LORD your God, and the priests, the Levites, bearing it, then you shall set out from your place and go after it" (*'achar*: follow afterwards). Note that the biblical priesthood is about the prayer ministry.

2. At the taking of Jericho, the priests, bearing the ark of the covenant, marched with the men of war and the people came after the ark of the LORD (Joshua 6:13).

3. Conclusion: The people possess what God promised (their inheritance) after intercession. Here is the sequence:

    *   Divine initiative: The Lord goes first. He has given His word.

    *   Human response to divine initiative: Human agreement via intercession.

- Divine response to human response: The breaking in of the kingdom of God in power.

Principle of order: What is first and what follows

The principle is this: "The heaven, even the heavens, are the Lord's, but the earth He has given to the children of men" (Psalm 115:16). At the beginning, humans were given stewardship of the earth, but then lost it to an usurper. Another government has taken over. Since God will only rule the earth through humans, the Word had to be made flesh (*human*). A Man, *Yeshua*, redeemed it back at the cross. He alone is worthy rule the earth. However, He will only rule with the redeemed who have been made kings and priests to our God (Revelation 5:10).

Both the scriptures and true prophetic words reveal the divine destiny which is brooding over the lives of people, families and nations—purposes of God that are revealed but not yet fulfilled. There are many statements in scripture concerning God's intentions and promises of what He will do. It all culminates in the bringing of His kingdom, setting wrong things right and filling the whole earth with His glory. But, as seen in Acts 4 and 5, He waits for the intercessors' cry before He acts. The release of kingdom power follows human agreement in intercession.

Let's examine a classic scripture on intercession in Isaiah 62:1-7. In verse one, God makes a promise concerning Jerusalem: "I will not rest, until her righteousness goes forth as brightness, and her salvation as a lamp that burns." Many scriptures address God's intention to make Jerusalem the capital city of the earth with Messiah, the Son of David ruling on David's throne. So what is God's *modus operandi?* He sets watchmen on the wall. Verses six and seven say, "I have set watchmen on your walls, O Jerusalem; They shall never hold their peace day or night. You who make mention of the LORD, do not keep silent, and give Him no rest till He establishes and till He makes Jerusalem a praise in the earth." Note the sequence, also identified above:

1. The Lord reveals His intentions for Jerusalem (divine initiative).

2. The watchmen (intercessors) make mention (recall, remind, rehearse) that intention and cry out for God to do what He said He would do (human response to divine initiative).

3. God moves in power to fulfill His promise (divine response to human response).

The themes of Isaiah 62:1-7 match up with themes in our segment on *qoof:*

1. Isaiah's phrases, "Never hold their peace" and "do not be silent" connect to David's words, "cry out" (v. 145, 146), "cry" (v. 147) and "hear my voice" (v. 149).

2. Isaiah's phrase, "day or night" connects to David's phrases, "rise before the dawn" (v. 147) and "awake through the night watches" (v. 148).

3. "Do not keep silent, and give Him no rest" is precisely what is happening in *qoof*.

4. "Make mention" (*zakar*: to name, remember, call to mind, recall, take to court, pay attention to, commemorate, recite, and rehearse). It's all about what God said in His word that He would do. An intercessor holds God to His word, reminding Him of the commitment He has made. This idea easily connects with phrases like "keep Your statutes" (v.145), "keep Your testimonies" (v. 146), "hope in Your word" (v. 147), "meditate on Your word" (v. 148), and "according to Your justice" (v. 149). Every verse in this segment references God's word in some fashion.

Yeshua's instructions on multiple occasions, to watch and pray, point to the need for alertness, wakefulness, expectation and prayer. This is the charge to the watchmen on the wall, the intercessors who night and day do not keep silent and give Him no rest until He establishes and makes Jerusalem a praise on the earth (Isaiah 62:6-7). In other words, they pray until God does what He said He would do—bring His kingdom to the earth. The great question is this: whose kingdom will govern the earth, God's or Satan's?

An initial reading of *qoof* might suggest that our psalmist has come to a place of desperation and great need because of phrases such as "cry out," "cry for help," and "save me." The statement in verse 150, "they draw near who persecute me" shows that David is feeling the pressure of the battle and may be in a tough place.

But the greater context in *tsadde* of zeal for righteousness, and a closer look at *qoof*, allow us to conclude that David has really become an intercessor. He is himself pressing the battle in prayer. He will not cede even one inch to the enemy. His zeal for the kingdom of God leads him to embrace the call of a watchman on the wall of his city. This is the primary strategy for seeing God's kingdom come and the next step in establishing God's righteous government.

Let's join our psalmist on his journey as he presses the battle in intercession to see God's kingdom come.

"I cry out with my whole heart; Hear me, O LORD! I will keep Your statutes" (v. 145).

1. "I cry out" (*qara*: to call out to, call on, address by name in accosting someone, cry out, proclaim, recite, summon, appeal to, read).

2. "With my whole heart" appears in our psalm six times. It implies full engagement without duplicity, wavering or distraction. Our psalmist is not half-hearted in his mission.

3.   "Hear" (*anah*: heed, pay attention, answer, respond, testify, speak). Our psalmist is accosting the Lord, addressing Him by His name and asking for a response. This is the function of an intercessor.

4.   "I will keep (*natsar*: to guard, watch, watch over) Your statutes." The use of this word connects with the calling of a watchman/intercessor who represents God and contends for His interests in the earth.

"I cry out (*qara*) to You; Save me, and I will keep Your testimonies" (v. 146).

1.   "Save" (*yasha*: to save, deliver, help, defend, avenge, rescue, liberate, give the victory).

     •   The root idea of *yasha* is liberation into a wide open place safety and freedom, which means deliverance from present oppression, resistance, corruption and warfare. It is the root word behind salvation (*y'eshuwah*) = *Yeshua* = salvation.

     •   *Yasha* occurs in verses 94, 117 and 146. We know that salvation belongs to the Lord (Psalm 3:8; Revelation 7:10), and that God is mighty to save (Isaiah 63:1). This is the cry of both the intercessors and the redeemed throughout the ages. Let God arise to bring salvation. Consider also Exodus 15:2, "The LORD is my strength and song, and He has become my salvation (*y'eshuwah*)."

2.   "I will keep (*shamar*: keep as great treasure) Your testimonies."

     •   *Shamar*, a more common synonym of *natsar* (verse 145), and although a bit less militant in its feel, is also translated watchman in places.

     •   David has been treasuring the word of God in his heart all along. Salvation at this point in the heat of battle keeps him alive to continue on loving God's word.

"I rise before the dawning of the morning and cry for help; I hope in Your word" (v. 147).

1.   "I rise before the dawning" translates to "I met the twilight."

2.   "And cry" (*shava*: cry out, shout as for help). The root idea is to be free; hence our psalmist is crying out for freedom from some kind of trouble or oppression. "Your kingdom come!"

3. "I hope in Your word" (*dabar*). The revealed word of God is the prayer manual for all intercessors as they make mention (*zakar*: recall, recount as a secretary reminds an executive of his commitments – Isaiah 62:6) to the Lord what He said, in His word, that He would do. Our psalmist places his hope in that word.

"My eyes are awake through the night watches, that I may meditate on Your word" (v. 148).

1. "My eyes are awake through the night watches." Our psalmist is clearly being set as a watchman and taking his place on the wall as an intercessor.

2. "That I may meditate on Your word" (*imrah*). In the conflict, can the enemy dislodge the prophetic promises of God, and his hope in those promises, from our psalmist's heart? Not if he keeps those promises alive in his heart and mind via meditation.

"Hear my voice according to Your lovingkindness; O LORD, revive me according to Your justice" (v.149).

1. "Hear my voice." God hears the cry of His people.

    *   See Exodus 2:24; Psalm 3:4; 4:3; 6:9; 17:6; 18:6; 28:6; 31:22; 34:4, 6, 17; 38:15; 40:1; 55:17-19; 65:2; 69:33; 102:19-20; 106:44; 116:1; 120:1; 145:19.

2. "According to Your lovingkindness." God is famous for His lovingkindness. See Psalm 25:6 and Exodus 34:6. God's heart moves at the cry of His people.

    *   Again we will reference *Yeshua's* parable of the widow and the unjust judge (Luke 18:1-8): It is a parable of contrasts. We are not widows without intimacy, recourse or provision and God is not the unjust judge who cares nothing for righteousness. Rather, we are His own elect, His own special treasure. He is a heavenly Father who loves His children. God's heart will be moved by the cry of His elect who cry out day and night. He is a righteous Judge who has an ultimate zeal for righteousness.

    *   Even if He waits to deliver us, and bears long with us (Luke 18:7), we can enjoy intimacy with a beautiful God, who is Love, while we cry out for justice on the earth. This is the privilege that sustains all intercessors in the warfare.

    *   The great secret to sustaining night and day prayer as the set watchmen (Isaiah 62:6) until God answers (He often seems to delay answering) is to enter into intimacy with and enjoyment of the Bridegroom God who is already here by His Spirit. Isaiah 62:5, "As the bridegroom rejoices over the bride, so shall

your God rejoice over you." This immediately precedes Isaiah 62:6, where the watchmen cry out night and day. Intimacy empowers perseverance in prayer.

3.   "O LORD, revive me according to Your justice" (*mishpat*: judgments). Remember that judgment and deliverance are two sides of one coin. Both the righteous and the wicked are rewarded when God's kingdom comes and He arises to set wrong things right. Our psalmist has allowed God's word to judge his own life and now he is confident that He will be on the deliverance side of justice when God arises in power. The wicked, on the other hand, who draw near in the next verse, will be judged.

"They draw near who follow after wickedness; They are far from Your law" (v. 150).

1.   "They draw near who follow after wickedness" (*zimmah*: plan, device, evil plan or mischievous purpose). There is an evil plan with malicious intent against our psalmist, and he is feeling the pressure but is putting his hope in the Lord.

2.   "They are far from Your law." The words near and far, used in contrast, occur only here in the entire psalm. Being far from the law of the Lord places them in jeopardy of loss when God answers our psalmist's prayer for justice.

"You are near, O LORD, and all Your commandments are truth" (v. 151).

1.   "You are near, O LORD. "God's primary commitment to all who would follow Him is "I will be with you."

   •   God prepares a table before us in the presence of our enemies. When you see trouble on every side, start looking for a table at which to eat with *Yeshua*.

   •   This could be the fellowship of His sufferings referenced by Paul in Philippians 3:10.

2.   "All Your commandments (*mitsvah*) are truth" (*emeth*: utterly dependable and established).

   •   Remember, our psalmist has obeyed the Lord's command only to encounter warfare and persecution.

   •   It is also obedience to God's commands that precipitates the breaking in of God's power in salvation and answered prayer.

"Concerning Your testimonies, I have known of old that You have founded them forever" (v. 152).

1. "I have known of old" (*qedem*: front, fore part, aforetime). Our psalmist knew from the start that the Lord's testimonies were eternal.

2. "You have founded (*yasad*: set, establish, found, fix) them forever" (*owlam*: perpetual, forever). Psalm 19:7, "The testimony of the LORD is sure, making wise the simple."

3. Our psalmist believes the declaration found in Psalm 93:3, "The floods have lifted up, O LORD, the floods have lifted up their voice; The floods lift up their waves. The LORD on high is mightier than the noise of many waters, than the mighty waves of the sea. Your testimonies are very sure."

More on Intercession

In Mark 11:17, *Yeshua* quotes Isaiah 56:7, "My house shall be called a house of prayer for all nations." Prayer will mark and define the end-time body of Messiah, both corporately and individually. We will be primarily a people of prayer. Though there will be powerful evangelism, discipleship, teaching, ministry to the poor and much more, prayer will define the body of Messiah. Ultimately, when, in intercession, the Spirit and the bride say "Come!" (Revelation 22:17), He will come!

In each generation God builds a house of prayer in which intercessors cry out for restoration, a revival of righteousness and the establishing of His government. He raises up intercessors who are so joined to Him that His burden becomes their burden. God's word becomes their promise and hope. The subsequent release of God's power follows the seeming weakness of human intercession or agreement. These intercessors stand in the gap and intercede for the very things that God has on His heart to do. More examples include the following:

1. Modern revivals have consistently been linked to someone crying out for revival.

    *   The famous Moravian missionary movement of the 1700s was empowered by night and day prayer that lasted for 120 years. Their slogan was "If no one is praying, no one will work."

2. Anna and Simeon were watching for the kingdom before *Yeshua* was born (Luke 2:25-38). Anna, a warring intercessor, "did not depart from the Temple, but served God with fastings and prayers night and day." The promised Messiah was not born in a vacuum, solely as a sovereign act of God. He was born on the wings of human agreement (partnership) in intercession.

3. David's tabernacle was the night and day prayer ministry that preceded and fueled restoration and revival in Israel in the days of David, Solomon, Jehoshaphat, Hezekiah, Josiah, Ezra and Nehemiah. See 1 Chronicles 15-16; 2 Chronicles 3-5; 20; 29-30; 35:1-19; Ezra 2:65; 3:1-13; Nehemiah 12:27-47.

4. The apostles and the early body of Messiah gave themselves to prayer night and day, and when God answered from heaven, the kingdom of God came in power (1 Thessalonians 5:17; 2 Timothy 1:3).

5. Daniel's prayer in Daniel 9 is connected to Ezra 1:1, where "the LORD stirred up the spirit of Cyrus king of Persia, so that he made a proclamation" to release the Jewish people to return to their homeland. Jeremiah had prophesied seventy years in Babylon, but God waited to act until Daniel, an intercessor, cried out for God's promise to be fulfilled.

6. Elijah's prayers both stopped and produced rain (see James 5:17-18 and 1 Kings 18:42-45).

7. The message of *qoof* can also be illustrated by the war between righteous Abijah, with Judah's 400,000-man army, versus wicked Jeroboam, with Israel's 800,000-man army (2 Chronicles 13). Judah cried out to the Lord and the priests blew the trumpets (in intercession) turning the battle against Jeroboam and delivering Abijah's army from a trap. The release of God's power followed those who were following Him. Check it out.

Questions to Ponder

1. Has your zeal for righteousness ever stirred you to take a stand for justice in a way that precipitated wrath from the enemy?

2. Has the burden of the Lord ever motivated you to intercession? How has God answered your cry?

3. Are you willing to be available to the Lord in intercession in order to see His interests advanced in your world?

Chapter 22

Enduring the Heat

RESH

¹⁵³Consider my affliction and deliver me,
For I do not forget Your law.
¹⁵⁴Plead my cause and redeem me;
Revive me according to Your word.
¹⁵⁵Salvation is far from the wicked,
For they do not seek Your statutes.
¹⁵⁶Great are Your tender mercies, O LORD;
Revive me according to Your judgments.
¹⁵⁷Many are my persecutors and my enemies,
Yet I do not turn from Your testimonies.
¹⁵⁸I see the treacherous, and am disgusted,
Because they do not keep Your word.
¹⁵⁹Consider how I love Your precepts;
Revive me, O LORD, according to Your lovingkindness.
¹⁶⁰The entirety of Your word is truth,
And every one of Your righteous judgments endures forever.

Resh—Psalm 119:153-160

Resh, the twentieth letter of the Hebrew alphabet, depicts the head of a person. It can mean person, head or summation. It can point to that which is the highest, most important, first or authoritative (headship). In this case, it is as if evil is coming to a head.

In *qoof* our psalmist embraced his call as an intercessor, praying day and night, as the primary strategy for the advance of the kingdom of God on earth, "Your kingdom come!" *Yeshua* taught us to seek first God's kingdom and His righteousness (Matthew 6:33). Our psalmist has been fully engaged in warfare to see God's kingdom come. All the while, in verse 150, those who follow after wickedness are drawing near. Now, here in *resh*, they converge on the psalmist in order to stop him and to counter this advance of God's kingdom. The first line says it all: "Consider (see) my affliction and deliver me."

David has experienced affliction before, way back in verse fifty, but here in *resh* we have an unprecedented conflagration of evil as many persecutors and enemies converge to afflict him. It seems that we can perceive Nebuchadnezzar's fury toward

Shadrach, Meshach, and Abed-Nego (Daniel 3:19) when these three Hebrews refused to bow to his image. Three of the four enemies listed here have showed up before in David's life, but never together. In fact, no two of them ever showed up in the same segment. It is as if the furnace is seven times hotter for our psalmist as the competition heats up over whose government will rule the earth.

We can detect a progressive intensification of their efforts against him.

1. "The wicked" (*rasha*: criminal, ungodly, wicked) in verse 155: This is their final appearance out of six times in the psalm, and salvation is far (*rachowq*: distant, remote) from them. Can you perceive a progression of hardening until salvation is only a remote possibility?

    •   In verse 53, they forsake God's *torah*.

    •   In verse 61, they robbed our psalmist.

    •   In verse 95, they lay in wait to destroy our psalmist.

    •   In verse 110, they lay a snare for David.

    •   In verse 119, we learn that they cannot ultimately prevail.

    •   Here in *resh*, salvation is only a remote possibility for them as, much like Pharaoh of old, they have hardened their hearts and intensified their pursuit of David.

2. "Persecutors" (*radaph*: pursue with evil intent), mentioned in verse 157. As with the wicked, these too seem to have intensified their pursuit of David with evil intent.

3. "Enemies" (*tsar*: adversary, foe or oppressor who causes constraint and forces you into a tight or narrow place which restricts freedom) in verse 157.

4. "The treacherous" (*baqad*: to act treacherously or deceitfully) in verse 158.

5. "Many" (*rab*: much, many, great, abounding, numerous, mighty). This Hebrew word *rab* appears here for the first time in our psalm. This shows the escalation of the warfare. This word occurs in verse 156, describing God's tender mercies as being great (*rab*). *Rab* occurs twice in *resh*, hinting at the fullness of evil, and twice in *shin*, hinting at the fullness of righteousness. In the parable of the wheat and the tares (Matthew 13), *Yeshua* taught that both the wheat (sons of the kingdom) and the tares (sons of the evil one) would mature in the same field (earth) and in the same time-frame (end of the age).

Three times in this segment our psalmist says "revive me" as he actively waits on the Lord according to Isaiah 40:31 so as not to lose heart in the battle. "But those who wait on the LORD shall renew their strength; They shall mount up with wings like eagles, they shall run and not be weary, they shall walk and not faint." He is strengthening himself in the Lord His God as he endures the persecution from his enemies and awaits the Lord's deliverance.

Another clue regarding what is happening in *resh* is the phrase in verse 154, "plead my cause" with its companion word, redeem (*ga'al*). These words add the dynamic of a legal battle and introduce the subject of the kinsman-redeemer (*go'el,* from *ga'al*). The kinsman-redeemer, among other things related to restoring losses for relatives, was to act as the avenger of blood when wrongful death came to a family member (Numbers 35:19). Consider our two key words:

- "Plead my cause" (*riyb* [verb] *riyb* [noun]): to strive, contend, quarrel, or dispute, especially in court; conduct a case or lawsuit.

- "Redeem" (*ga'al*): redeem, avenge, act as a kinsman.

Consider some other scriptures which employ these words:

- Proverbs 23:10-11 warns us not to take advantage of the fatherless, for their Redeemer (*Go'el*) is mighty; He will plead their case.

- Jeremiah 50:34 warns all of Babylon that Judah has a strong Redeemer (*Go'el*). "Their Redeemer is strong; The LORD of hosts is His name. He will thoroughly plead their case."

- Lamentations 3:58-60, "O LORD, You have pleaded the case for my soul; You have redeemed (*ga'al*) my life. O LORD, You have seen how I am wronged; Judge my case. You have seen all their vengeance, all their schemes against me."

Our psalmist is doing exactly what the widow did in *Yeshua*'s parable of the widow and the unjust judge (Luke 18:1-8). Her prayer was "Get justice (or avenge) for me from my adversary." This was a legal battle. So it is with our psalmist as he goes to the Righteous Judge and sues for justice. This is not a personal vendetta in which he wants to see a flesh and blood enemy suffer. He has proven that he has more zeal for God's glory than he does for his own life. Vengeance belongs to the Lord. He will repay. Our role is to love people and trust the Lord. For David, this is a prayer for the triumph of divine justice, for the release of the oppressed and for the kingdom (government) of God to come to the earth.

With that, let's join David in his journey.

"Consider my affliction and deliver me, for I do not forget Your law" (v. 153).

1. "Consider" (*ra'ah*: see, look at, inspect) occurs three times in *resh* in verses 153, 158 and 159. This is a prayer that God Who Sees would indeed see what is happening. See also Genesis 16:13; 22:14.

- Noah found grace in the eyes of the Lord (Genesis 6:8).

- Psalm 9:13, "Have mercy on me, O LORD! Consider (*ra'ah*) my trouble from those who hate me, You who lift me up from the gates of death."

- Psalm 25:19-20, "Consider (*ra'ah*) my enemies, for they are many; And they hate me with cruel hatred. Keep my soul, and deliver me."

- "The eyes of the LORD roam to and fro throughout the whole earth, to show Himself strong on behalf of those whose heart is loyal to Him" (2 Chronicles 16:9).

2. "My affliction." This affliction is in context to a world system which hates light. John 3:19-20 prepares us in the mission to be light to a world which hates light. "And this is the condemnation, that the light has come into the world, and men loved darkness rather than light, because their deeds were evil. For everyone practicing evil hates the light and does not come to the light, lest his deeds should be exposed."

   - This convergence of enemies shows that our psalmist is being deemed a threat.

   - *Yeshua* was very clear about coming persecution (see Matthew 5:10-12; 10:16-19; John 15:18-25).

3. "Deliver" (*chalats*: remove, draw out, rescue, equip or arm for war). *Chalats* occurs only here in our psalm.

   - It means far more than "get me out of here." In fact, considering the context and all the possible meanings of *chalats*, we see a hint of persevering prayer that is seeking the Lord for the strength to press the battle until the victory comes.

   - A thorough study of this Hebrew word will show that of forty-four occurrences, twenty are in context to warfare or the presence of an army. Seven times in the NKJV the word is translated "armed for war." Here are two other uses of *chalats*:

     o Psalm 50:15, "Call upon Me in the day of trouble; I will deliver (*chalats*) you."

     o Psalm 91:15, "He shall call upon Me, and I will answer him; I will be with him in trouble; I will deliver (*chalats*) him and honor him."

   - Our warring God delivers us when He arises for war on our behalf.

4. "I do not forget (*shakach*: ignore, wither from, forget, mislay) Your law." One of the great temptations, when encountering resistance, is to compromise the goal

of the mission and make an agreement of "peace" with the enemy. Our psalmist is not withering under the heat of the warfare. Consider the following examples:

- Israel's propensity to give land (their inheritance) for peace.

- Three times Pharaoh tried to talk Moses into accepting less than complete and full deliverance (see Exodus 8:25; 10:8-11; 10:24).

"Plead my cause and redeem me; Revive me according to Your word" (v. 154).

1. "Plead (*riyb*: strive, contend for) my cause" resembles Luke 18:3, "Give me justice from my adversary."

2. "Redeem" (*ga'al*: redeem, act as kinsman-redeemer, avenge, revenge, ransom, deliver).

   - *Ga'al* occurs more than one hundred times in scripture, but only one time in this psalm. A primary role of a kinsman-redeemer is to redeem, provide for and avenge those who have no recourse of their own. Vengeance is the Lord's.

   - Boaz' provision for Naomi, in the book of Ruth, gives a classic example of what a kinsman-redeemer is and does.

3. "Revive" (*chayah*: to live, have or sustain life). The KJV translates *chayah* as "quicken me." David is persevering in prayer and asking to be sustained and to have life. He is strengthening himself in the Lord.

   - The great test and question is this: What will the righteous do if God delays in delivering them from the wicked? When the wicked prosper against the righteous, what is God doing? Review Addendum 4.

   - Isaiah 40:27 "Why do you say, O Jacob, and speak, O Israel: 'My way is hidden from the Lord, and my just claim is passed over by my God?'"

4. Waiting on the Lord is the key and is exactly what our psalmist is doing.

   - Psalm 27:14, "Wait on the LORD; Be of good courage, and He shall strengthen your heart; Wait, I say, on the LORD!"

"Salvation is far from the wicked, for they do not seek Your statutes" (v. 155).

1. "Salvation is far from the wicked." These wicked have persisted in evil and have hardened their hearts. The light of David's righteous responses along the way did not lead them to repentance, as God designed, even though He is not willing that any perish!

- Psalm 85:9, "His salvation is near to those who fear Him, that glory may dwell in our land."

2. "They do not seek Your statutes" (as do the righteous). They are pursuing the very things the righteous are to be against.

    - Psalm 24:6, "This is Jacob, the generation of those who seek Him, Who seek Your face."

    - Remember, Jacob became Israel by prevailing in prayer! "Your name shall no longer be called Jacob, but Israel; for you have struggled with God and with men, and have prevailed" (Genesis 32:28).

"Great are Your tender mercies, O LORD; Revive me according to Your judgments" (v. 156).

1. "Great (*rab*: many, much, great) are Your tender mercies (*racham*)." God's answer, when our enemies multiply, is to multiply His mercies toward us. There is grace for this level of warfare. While He waits to deliver us, we can enjoy His embrace at the table He has prepared for us in the presence of our enemies.

    - God is famous for great mercy (*racham*). See Isaiah 55:7; 63:7; Psalm 51:1; 86:5, 13, 15. *Racham* appears in the psalm only here and in verse seventy-seven.

    - Our psalmist is enjoying great intimacy in the midst of warfare as can all of God's own elect "who cry out day and night to Him for justice" while waiting for the kingdom to come (Luke 18:7). This is the honor of the saints (read Psalm 149).

2. "Revive me according to Your judgments" (*mishpat*).

    - "Revive." This is the second of three occurrences in this segment. Our psalmist really is waiting upon the Lord to renew his strength according to Isaiah 40:31.

    - Recall our extensive discussion of this word *mishpat*, which is linked with the decree of a ruler that sets things in motion to establish justice. The acts of God in history are linked to His judgments and our psalmist is strengthening himself by remembering that God acted in the past and will act again.

    - Again, Luke 18:7-8, "And shall God not avenge His own elect who cry out day and night to Him, though He bears long with them? I tell you He will avenge them speedily (suddenly)."

3. When God issues the decree and breakthrough comes, it is sudden and powerful. Pharaoh's resistance against Moses served to prolong Israel's time of deliverance,

and their faith was put to the test. That resistance, however, only served in the end to render the deliverance all the more spectacular. Furthermore, in the delay, many Egyptians joined Israel and got saved.

- Remember deliverance and judgment as two sides of one coin: For the Lord to deliver our psalmist would mean the defeat of his enemies.

"Many are my persecutors and my enemies, yet I do not turn from Your testimonies" (v. 157).

1. "Many are my persecutors (*radaph*: run after, follow after, pursue) and my enemies" (*tsar*: narrow, a tight place, opponent, adversary, oppressor)."

   - Our psalmist is being hunted down by someone with evil intent and is constrained because of this adversary.

   - Our adversary is employing every possible tactic because his time is short (Revelation 12:12).

2. "Yet I do not turn from Your testimonies." This is powerful. Consider these scriptures:

   - Psalm 44:18, "Our heart has not turned back, nor have our steps departed from Your way."

   - Job 17:9, "Yet the righteous will hold to his way, and he who has clean hands will be stronger and stronger."

   - Acts 20:23-24, "The Holy Spirit testifies in every city, saying that chains and tribulations await me. But none of these things move me; nor do I count my life dear to myself, so that I may finish my race with joy."

"I see the treacherous, and am disgusted, because they do not keep Your word" (v. 158).

1. "I see (*ra'ah*: behold) the treacherous" (*bagad*: to act or deal treacherously, deceitfully).

   - The root of this word means to cover or act covertly.

   - This is the first and only occurrence of *bagad*. This represents another level of evil.

2. "And am disgusted" (*quwt*: to loathe, be grieved, detest). Our psalmist is getting close to the prayer in Psalm 139:19-22, "Oh, that You would slay the wicked, O God! Depart from me, therefore, you bloodthirsty men. For they speak against You wickedly; Your enemies take Your name in vain. Do I not hate them, O LORD,

who hate You? And do I not loathe those who rise up against You? I hate them with perfect hatred; I count them my enemies." We discussed this world of imprecatory prayers at some length in *yod*. Here are a few critical reminders as we ponder this kind of praying:

- Perfect hatred and righteous anger are never personal or vindictive, but are always about zeal for God's glory.

- God loves those who are resisting us and trafficking in hell's agenda to the destruction of people's lives. We are to both love the person and also have zeal for righteousness.

- This is a perfect place to refresh the thoughts on imprecatory prayers connected to verse seventy-eight, all the way back in *yood*.

- Our real enemies are not flesh and blood. Ephesians 6:12, "For we do not wrestle against flesh and blood, but against principalities, against powers. . ."

3. "They do not keep Your word." It is a rare mark of spiritual maturity to grieve more over insults to God than over wrongs to oneself. Oh, to be thus consumed with zeal for the Lord.

"Consider how I love Your precepts; Revive me, O LORD, according to Your lovingkindness" (v. 159).

- "Consider (*ra'ah*) how I love." In verse 153 it was "consider my affliction," but in this verse, it is "consider my affection."

- "Revive me, O LORD, according to Your lovingkindness." This is the third occurrence of the word revive as our psalmist is strengthening himself in the Lord. Remember *Yeshua's* words in Luke 18:1, "Men always ought to pray and not lose heart." Consider them all together as our psalmist's method of not losing heart in the battle:

  o Verse 154: "Revive me according to Your word" by pondering God's promises.

  o Verse 156: "Revive me according to Your judgments" by pondering God's faithfulness and acts of power in history that brought deliverance to His people.

  o Verse 159: "Revive me according to Your lovingkindness" by pondering God's love, which is legendary and endures forever.

"The entirety *(ro'sh)* of Your word is truth, and every one of Your righteous judgments endures forever" (v. 160).

1. "Entirety" (*ro'sh*: head, chief, summit, top, highest, front, first, principle). This Hebrew word appears only here in our psalm and most certainly connects with the letter *resh* and its meaning discussed at the head of this chapter. This could be translated "from the head" or "from the beginning." In fact, the KJV puts it this way: "Thy word is true from the beginning." See again verses eighty-nine, ninety and 138 of our psalm.

2. What a declaration as David establishes with absolute certainty that God's word is:

    *   Truth (*'emeth*: stability, certainty, firmness, trustworthiness, faithfulness).

    *   Righteous (*tsedeq*: right, equity, rightness, justice).

    *   Enduring (*owlam*: antiquity, everlasting, perpetuity).

3. What a place to land, as many persecutors, or great persecutors and enemies, converge to cause great trouble for our psalmist. All of hell may rage against us but God's word endures forever. Isaiah put it this way in Isaiah 40:6, 8: "All flesh (including our persecutors) is grass. . . . The grass withers, the flower fades (because the breath of the LORD blows on it), but the word of our God stands forever."

4. In the great end-time drama, just before the coming of Messiah, when the tares (sons of the wicked one referred to in Matthew 13:38) come to maturity and evil runs seemingly unchecked in its quest to obliterate righteousness, we will need an unrelenting confidence in the word of God. Though it is warred against and at times seemingly defeated, it will ultimately prevail as it did in Acts 19:20, "So the word of the Lord grew mightily and prevailed."

5. *Yeshua* is the Word of God. "And He . . . was called Faithful and True, and in righteousness He judges and makes war" (Revelation 19:11).

Concluding Thoughts

The harvest signals the end of the age. *Yeshua's* parable about the wheat and the tares shows us that both the wheat (sons of the kingdom) and the tares (sons of the evil one) come to maturity in the same field and in the same timeframe, the end of the age (Matthew 13:24-43).

As Moses foreshadows the first coming of Messiah, to work redemption through the death of the Passover Lamb and to deliver Israel out of Egypt (sin), so Joshua's conquest to possess the Promised Land and establish a righteous government foreshadows the second coming of Messiah in conquest of the earth to establish His kingdom (see

Revelation 11:15). Even as the iniquity of the Amorites was not yet complete when Abraham received the promise of the land (Genesis 15:16), likewise the righteousness of the children of Israel was not complete. Hence, it would be years until the conquest of the land, and this would allow for both the tares and the wheat to come to fullness.

At the time of the crossing of the Jordan River in conquest of the land in Joshua 3, there is an enlightening parenthetical statement in verse fifteen, "for the Jordan overflows all its banks during the whole time of harvest." The flow of the Jordan into the Dead Sea depicts the flow of death and darkness in the earth, which was cut off and "rose in a heap very far away at Adam" when the priests stepped into it (Joshua 3:16). At that time the flow of the Jordan was at flood stage, hinting at the maturity of evil. So at the end of the age, when death and darkness seem to be unrestrained and evil is mature, there will arise a people who step into the darkness and drive it back. It is at the time of the harvest, when the righteous come to maturity and the greatest harvest of souls ever is reaped into the kingdom of God.

Isaiah 60:2 tells us that the glory of the LORD will be seen upon His people at the very time when darkness shall cover the earth and deep darkness the people.

Intercessory prayer as spiritual warfare—Flesh and blood are not our enemy

This battle for righteousness must be won in the heavenly realm before we can see God's kingdom manifest on earth. In Exodus 17:8-16, we have a classic illustration of this truth. Joshua was in the valley fighting Amalek while Moses, Aaron and Hur were on the top of the hill—in the heavenlies—with the rod of God. Verse eleven says, "so it was, when Moses held up his hand (in perpetual prayer), that Israel prevailed; and when he let down his hand, Amalek prevailed." He was ruling in the heavenlies with the rod of God. The only way for Israel to prevail in the valley of a fallen world was through perpetual intercession.

Demonically energized structures and ideologies trap billions in darkness in our world. All false religious systems must be confronted with the gospel of the kingdom. They must be resisted, exposed and ultimately overthrown, not because God hates their adherents, but because He loves them. The multi-billion dollar pornography industry which is destroying untold numbers of marriages and the souls of millions must be hated, resisted and ultimately toppled by the coming of God's kingdom. The militant homosexual agenda for gay marriage and the mainstreaming of a gay lifestyle as an acceptable alternative must be resisted, dismantled and overthrown, not because God hates homosexuals, but because He loves them and desires to show them, along with all of sinful mankind, His great salvation. The abortion industry in our nation must be resisted and dismantled, not because God hates abortionists, but because He loves them and their victims. The dismantling of these structures by the coming of the kingdom will not only deliver a myriad of victims from this holocaust of human life, but help jolt the lifestyles of thousands of pushers at the head (*roshe*) of these structures who have profited at this expenditure of human life, that they, too, should (perhaps) seek the Lord, in the hope that they might grope for Him and find Him (Acts 17:27).

Historically, systemic poverty in a region flows from corruption in high places, thus oppressing and helping to destroy the lives of millions. In 1 Timothy 2:1-4, the Apostle Paul instructs us to "first of all pray for kings and all who are in authority, that we may lead a quiet and peaceable life in all godliness and reverence. For this is good and acceptable in the sight of God our Savior, who desires all men to be saved and to come to the knowledge of the truth." We are in a war for souls and God wants righteous influential structures in a society to foster and bless the preaching of the gospel of the kingdom so that all men may be saved.

In all of our discussion about forcefully advancing the kingdom of God in the face of the men and women at the head of these structures, and who traffic in hell's agenda to steal, kill and destroy in our communities, we must remember that the real enemy is never flesh and blood. *Yeshua* came to seek and to save the lost, including those who hate us and violently resist us in our mission of seeing God's kingdom come, seemingly at their expense.

In Ephesians 6:12, we have these familiar words: "For we do not wrestle against flesh and blood, but against principalities, against powers, against the rulers of the darkness of this age, against spiritual hosts of wickedness in the heavenly places." Also, consider 2 Corinthians 10:4-5, "For the weapons of our warfare are not carnal but mighty in God for pulling down strongholds, casting down arguments and every high thing that exalts itself against the knowledge of God."

All of these demonic structures must be defeated in the heavenlies in intercession (*qoof*) before we can hope to see them lose their power to hold men in darkness on the earth. God's intent is that the manifold wisdom of God might be made known by the body of Messiah to the principalities and powers in the heavenly places (Ephesians 3:10).

When these structures begin to collapse, as in Ephesus during the time of Paul and Demetrius (Acts 19), those with the most to lose may well turn against us. Although, on their part, their hatred of us may be personal, our hatred must be the perfect hatred according to Psalm 139:22 (see notes on verse seventy-eight in *yood*). Though we may be sinned against, we are never justified in sinning back. Though some of *Yeshua's* words to the leaders of His day were blistering in their indictment of the corruption and hypocrisy of His opponents, they were nonetheless truthful and designed to help them repent. He was never vindictive, nor was it ever about Himself. It was always about His love for those who were oppressed by the demonic structures of His day and His zeal for truth and righteousness.

When they attacked *Yeshua* personally, He did not defend Himself, but contended for truth and righteousness. *Yeshua*, when He was reviled, "did not revile in return . . . but committed Himself to Him who judges righteously" (1 Peter 2:23). Consider again *Yeshua's* words: "Love your enemies, bless those who curse you, do good to those who hate you, and pray for those who spitefully use you and persecute you." Or recount the words of Romans 12:20-21, "If your enemy is hungry, feed him; If he is thirsty, give him a drink; For in so doing you will heap coals of fire on his head. Do not be overcome by evil, but overcome evil with good."

When it comes to corrupt governments, we have Paul's instruction in Romans 13:1-7 to factor into our zeal for the kingdom of God. Peter also, tells us in 1 Peter 2:17, "Fear God. Honor the king." And so, we pray. We pay our taxes. We are "subject to governing authorities" and we are those who, in our zeal for righteousness, "Do what is good" (Romans 13:1, 3).

We are not leading rebellions. That does not mean that we don't confront or witness to those in government. And, it does not mean that there won't be times when the fear of God requires that we have Peter and John's response to the authorities when ordered to stop preaching. "Whether it is right in the sight of God to listen to you more than to God, you judge. For we cannot but speak the things which we have seen and heard" (Acts 4:19-20).

Resh then, gives us insight into how to persevere in an hour when evil seems to be winning and the blood of martyrs is flowing in a great end-time onslaught of the wicked against the righteous.

Questions to Ponder

1. Review David's declaration in verse one hundred sixty. How has the truth of that confession held you during a difficult time of testing?

2. In what ways can you perceive the maturing of both good and evil in the earth? What are you doing to ensure that you continue to grow zealous for righteousness?

3. What have your responses been when confronted with great evil? Have you ever experienced what it is to love those who promote an evil for which you have a hatred?

4. "Revive me" or "sustain my life" has been a staple prayer of our psalmist which appears three times here in *resh*. Have you ever strengthened yourself in the Lord in difficult circumstances with a similar prayer?

Chapter 23

Examine Yourself

SHIN

¹⁶¹Princes persecute me without a cause,
But my heart stands in awe of Your word.
¹⁶²I rejoice at Your word
As one who finds great treasure.
¹⁶³I hate and abhor lying,
But I love Your law.
¹⁶⁴Seven times a day I praise You,
Because of Your righteous judgments.
¹⁶⁵Great peace have those who love Your law,
And nothing causes them to stumble.
¹⁶⁶ LORD, I hope for Your salvation,
And I do Your commandments.
¹⁶⁷My soul keeps Your testimonies,
And I love them exceedingly.
¹⁶⁸I keep Your precepts and Your testimonies,
For all my ways are before You.

Shin—Psalm 119:161-168; His wife has made herself ready

Our psalmist has clearly come to a place of significant fullness and maturity. He is tasting the power of *The Blessed Life*, the observance of which provoked him to begin this journey in the first place. This life is filled with joy, unflagging zeal for righteousness and unrelenting confidence in the word of God. At the same time, it is a life which totally threatens the world's systems, hence it is embroiled in fierce conflict and warfare from the adversary.

The longing cry of our psalmist's heart for *The Blessed Life*, stated in Psalm 119:5-7 in *aleph*, is manifestly fulfilled here in *shin*. Compare the following:

1.   Verses five and seven: David longs to have his ways directed by God's word, but the learning of God's ways was yet in the future (v. 7). Almost every verse in *shin* indicates quantifiable growth and fulfillment of that longing. Here are a few noteworthy quotes:

   • "I hate and abhor lying, but I love Your law" (v. 163).

- "I do Your commandments" (v. 166).

- "My soul keeps Your testimonies" (v. 167).

- "I keep Your precepts and Your testimonies, for all my ways are before You" (v. 168).

2.   The shame that David had experienced when first looking into the word of God, expressed in verse six, now gives way to the following:

- "My heart stands in awe of Your word" (v. 161).

- "I rejoice at Your word" (v. 162).

- "Great peace with God and man" (v. 165).

- "I love them (Your testimonies) exceedingly" (v. 167).

3.   The statement, "I will praise (future) You with uprightness of heart" expressed in verse seven becomes "Seven times a day I praise (present tense) You" (v. 164).

"I," "me" and "my" occur twelve times in this section as our psalmist assesses his spiritual health. He seems to be examining himself according to 2 Corinthians 13:5, "Examine yourselves as to whether you are in the faith. Test yourselves. Do you not know yourselves that *Yeshua* Messiah is in you?" The following phrases specify areas in which our psalmist has seen growth, quantifiable transformation and triumph over sin in his life.

- "My heart stands in awe of Your word" (*dabar*), verse 161.

- "I rejoice at Your word" (*imrah*), verse 162.

- "I hate and abhor lying," verse 163. Contrast this with verse twenty-nine.

- "I love Your law" (*torah*), verses 163 and 165.

- "I praise You (seven times a day) because of Your righteous judgments," verse 164.

- "I hope (wait with expectancy) for Your salvation," verse 166.

- "I do Your commandments," verse 166.

- "My soul keeps Your testimonies," verse 167.

- "I love them (Your testimonies) exceedingly," verse 167.

- "I have kept Your precepts and Your testimonies," verse 168.

- "All my ways are before You," verse 168.

Our 21st Hebrew letter, *shin*, depicts a tooth. It can symbolize any of the following: eat, bite, consume, destroy, plunder (as in spoils of war), or shine (as whitened teeth). These ideas all connect to the following themes in this segment:

1. The mature eat the solid food of obedience and righteousness (v. 166). "I do Your commandments."

    - *Yeshua* said in John 4:34, "My food is to do the will of Him who sent Me and to finish His work."

    - Hebrews 5:13-14, "For everyone who partakes only of milk is unskilled in the word of righteousness, for he is a babe. But solid food belongs to those who are of full age (mature), that is, those who by reason of use have their senses exercised to discern both good and evil."

2. The overcomer or victorious soldier rejoices in victory. In verse 162 the psalmist is rejoicing as one who finds great treasure (*shalal*: spoils of war):

    - The clear hint is that he has overcome and is gathering the plunder.

    - In Numbers 14:9, Joshua and Caleb attempt to encourage Israel with these words: "Do not . . . fear the people of the land, for they are our bread."

3. The "great peace" (*shalom*: completeness, soundness, welfare, peace, safety, happiness) of verse 165 is significant. Righteousness, peace and joy, the characteristics of the kingdom of God (Romans 14:17), are all part of *shalom*. The implication is that the enemy's kingdom is destroyed and plundered and God's kingdom has come. 1 John 3:8 says, "For this purpose the Son of God was manifested, that He might destroy the works of the devil."

4. Our psalmist is certainly shining brightly in this stage of maturity and fruitful ministry.

As we saw in *resh*, the tares (sons of the wicked one) are coming to maturity and are seeking with great treachery to stop the forceful advance of the kingdom of God and obliterate the righteous from the earth. However, as we see here in *shin*, the wheat (sons of the kingdom) are also coming to maturity, and bringing great light into that great darkness. In fact, the fullness of the tares may precede and help bring about the maturity of the wheat.

In Daniel 3 we have a prophetic rehearsal of a great end-time drama under the anti-Messiah, or the beast (Revelation 13). Nebuchadnezzar, foreshadowing the beast, basically said, "bow (to my image) or burn" (Daniel 3:15). The beast issues a similar edict in Revelation 13:15, where he will "cause as many as would not worship the image of the beast to be killed."

When the three Hebrews refused to bow, Nebuchadnezzar was full of fury and commanded the furnace to be heated seven times hotter than usual. All through the ages, the righteous, who would not bow to the world's idolatrous systems, have encountered the fires of persecution. In Acts 14:22, Paul strengthens the souls of the disciples with these words: "We must through many tribulations enter the kingdom of God." We know at least a little about the refiner's fires (Malachi 3:3) which serve to purify the saints.

Nebuchadnezzar's fiery furnace, seven times hotter, foreshadows the great tribulation under the rule of the beast at the end of the age. It is just more of the same: persecution and tribulation multiplied by seven. Daniel 11:35 reads, "And some of those of understanding shall fall, to refine them, purify them, and make them white, until the time of the end; because it is still for the appointed time."

Here in *shin*, we see a psalmist who is rejoicing as one returning with the spoils of war. The persecution continues, but is not receiving David's attention. Instead, he is trembling in awe and amazement at the power of God released into earth. Extravagant praise, great rejoicing, fiery love for God and blessed hope of the glorious appearing of Messiah fill his life. Is it possible that the fires of *resh* have helped him in his journey to maturity? He has become a mature believer, joining those who "have overcome by the blood of the Lamb and by the word of their testimony, and they did not love their lives to the death" (Revelation 12:11).

Let's join David in his journey and marvel at the man who has become so much like the Master. *Yeshua* said in Matthew 10:25, "It is enough for a disciple that he be like his teacher, and a servant like his master." Remember Romans 8:29, "For whom He foreknew, He also predestined to be conformed to the image of His Son, that He might be the firstborn among many brethren."

"Princes persecute me without a cause, but my heart stands in awe of Your word" (v. 161).

1. "Princes." The only other appearance of this word is in verse twenty-three where they spoke against our psalmist. But here they persecute or follow hard after, and that with malignant intent. As discussed before, it is often the leaders (princes), those in high places who have a vested interest in this world system, who are threatened by the announcement of a coming King and His government (Matthew 27:18).

    *   Those at the top of corrupt structures, whether political, economic, religious, or social, are those who have the most to lose when people come into the kingdom of God. They are the ones who carry out the worst kind of persecution.

    *   It was a silversmith who "made no small profit" from the idolatry of Diana worship in Ephesus who started the riot against Paul (Acts 19:21-34).

- When Herod heard the coming of the King of the Jews, he unleashed a terrible edict to kill all male children from two years old and under (Matthew 2:16).

- When the gospel of the kingdom is preached and the harvest is reaped in power, thus eroding the root system of these corrupt structures, the persecution begins.

- In Psalm 2:2 it is the kings of the earth who set themselves against the Lord and against His Messiah.

- A gospel that speaks only of having sins forgiven and going to heaven is not the message that precipitates this kind of persecution. The gospel of the kingdom, which speaks of a Jewish King coming to rule the earth with a rod of iron, is the gospel which enrages and threatens the present rulers.

- The great challenge to those in power is to acknowledge and submit to the King of kings and humbly steward their power under His Lordship.

2.   "Without a cause." Our psalmist's claim is not to sinless perfection, but to having a righteous cause. There is a great theme about integrity and uprightness of heart throughout the scriptures that men with weak flesh like yours and mine, men who stumble in many ways, claimed to possess. Their hearts, as our psalmist's heart here, were set upon the Lord. They loved righteousness and hated wickedness. Though sin will precipitate trouble, their difficulties were not primarily due to their sins but were actually often due to their righteousness.

- Paul and Silas landed in a Philippian jail because they obeyed the Lord.

- Check out these verses: Genesis 20:5; 1 Kings 9:4; Psalm 7:8; 18:20, 24; 35:27; 78:72.

3.   "But my heart stands in awe (*pachad*: to fear, tremble, revere or dread, to startle as by a sudden alarm, to shake) of Your word."

- *Pachad* occurs only here in the entire psalm and speaks of our psalmist's trembling in awe and amazement at the power of God's word.

   o   Proverbs 28:14 says, "Happy is the man who is always reverent (*pachad*), but he who hardens his heart will fall into calamity."

   o   Isaiah 66:2 teaches us that the one upon whom the LORD will look is the "one who trembles at My word."

- Our psalmist seems to be witnessing a supernatural phenomenon connected to the proclamation of the word, which has his heart trembling in astonishment. What could he be seeing?

o   The Lord working with them, confirming the word through the accompanying signs (Mark 16:20)?

o   A great harvest at the anointed preaching of the word (Acts 2:41)? The entire city of Nineveh repented at the preaching of Jonah.

o   Men like Stephen, full of faith and power, performing great signs and wonders so that they were not able to resist the wisdom and spirit by which He spoke (Acts 6:8, 10)?

o   The power of the sword of the Spirit, which is the word of God, to resist and confront systemic evil?

o   The prophetic end-time Bride of Messiah referred to in Joel 2:28-30, and led by the two witnesses of Revelation 11:3-6?

"I rejoice at Your word as one who finds great treasure" (v. 162).

1.   "I rejoice" (*suws*: exult, display great joy) at Your word. Exult, triumph, revel at the word!

2.   "As one who finds (*matsa'*: attains to) great treasure (*shalal*: prey, plunder, spoil, booty)."

   •   This is the first and only appearance of *shalal* in our psalm.

   •   This word is about plundering the enemy and acquiring (*matsa'*) the spoils of war! The KJV actually translates shalal as spoil. Remember, the Hebrew letter *shin* means to consume, destroy, plunder or spoil.

   •   What are the spoils of war? Souls in a great harvest? Regional transformation?

3.   Great (*rab*) is the third of four occurrences of this word, all of which appear together in *resh* and *shin*, here at the end of the journey. The fourth appears in verse 165. A quick look at all four suggests at a great drama at the end of the age as both the wheat (the righteous) and the tares (the wicked) come to full maturity.

   •   Great mercies (v. 156)

   •   Great persecutions (v. 157)

   •   Great treasure or pluder (v. 162)

   •   Great peace (v. 165)

"I hate and abhor lying, but I love Your law" (v. 163).

1. "I hate (*sane'*: hate, odious) and abhor (*taab*: loathe as an abomination, detest) lying."

    - Lying and falsehood is the very antithesis to God's essential nature as the one true God who is called Faithful and True and who is righteous in all His ways. The Holy Spirit is called the Spirit of truth in John 14:17; 15:26; and 16:13. John said, "I have rejoiced greatly that I have found some of your children walking in truth." Our psalmist has endured much testing as the wicked and the proud forged a lie against him early in the journey (v. 69, 78, 86 and 118).

    - Lying and falsehood is the foundation of Satan's kingdom and the very essence of his nature. Ponder these scriptures and thoughts concerning our adversary:

        o   John 8:44, "He (the devil—*diabolos*: slanderer) was a murderer from the beginning, and does not stand in the truth, because there is no truth in him. When he speaks a lie, he speaks from his own resources, for he is a liar and the father of it."

        o   The entire world system, with all of its enticements and pursuits, is based on lies.

        o   As the accuser of the brethren, our adversary seeks to get us to believe lies about God and lies about ourselves in order to bring us into bondage. *Yeshua* said, "And you shall know the truth and the truth shall make you free" (John 8:32).

    - To hate lying involves more than not speaking lies with our lips. It has to do with being true. Do you remember these words from verse one? "Blessed are the undefiled (*tamiym*: complete, full, perfect, sound, sincere, upright) in the way who walk in the law of the Lord."

    - This kind of person, though greatly blessed, terrifies the world, because he has won the battle for truth in his own soul. This person sees through things because he is himself transparent, and fearlessly calls them as they really are.

2. "But I love Your law (*torah*)."

    - Talk about personal transformation and answers to prayer. This is precisely what our psalmist prayed way back in verse twenty-nine, "Remove from me the way of lying and grant me Your law (*torah*) graciously."

    - It was prophesied of the Messiah in Psalm 45:7, "You love righteousness and hate wickedness." Our psalmist has become like Him.

"Seven times a day I praise You, because of Your righteous judgments" (v. 164).

1. "Seven times a day I praise (*halal*: to shine or flash forth, make a show, boast, rave, praise, celebrate, act like a madman, be clamorously foolish) You."

   - *Halal* appears 165 times in scripture, but only here and in verse 175 of this psalm, both at the very end of the journey. It is the most powerful, expressive, emotional and animated of all Hebrew words for praise.

   - Seven times points to seven as the great number of completeness, fullness and spiritual perfection. The whole aim of the Christian life is to be conformed to the image of His Son (Romans 8:29), who is Himself the measure of perfection (maturity). Ponder these scriptures on fullness:

     o Ephesians 3:19, "That you may be filled with all the fullness of God."

     o Colossians 2:9-10, "For in Him dwells all the fullness of the Godhead bodily; and you are complete in Him, who is the head of all principality and power."

2. "Because of Your righteous judgments."

   - David has embraced God's judgments in his own life, the setting right of wrong things within his own soul. Now God is manifesting righteous judgments in the earth and bringing salvation to many others. The joy of harvest is here.

   - The great confession of the bride at the end of the age is this: "For true and righteous are His judgments" (Revelation 19:2).

   - In Luke 10:21, when *Yeshua* saw Satan fall like lightning from heaven, it says that *Yeshua* rejoiced (*agallial*: exult, rejoice exceedingly, jump for joy) in the Spirit.

3. A mature body of Messiah, which has come to fullness, will certainly reap the harvest in power with great rejoicing. Psalm 126:6 says it this way: "He who continually goes forth weeping, bearing seed for sowing (the sacrifice of those who submit to the fire of God's dealings), shall doubtless come again with rejoicing, bringing his sheaves with him (harvest)."

"Great peace have those who love Your law, and nothing causes them to stumble" (v. 165).

1. "Great peace (*shalom*: completeness, soundness, welfare, peace, safety, happiness) have those who love Your law (*torah*)." This is the only place in our passage that this phrase occurs. There is no other reference to shalom in the entire psalm.

2.   *Shalom* is the result of wrong things being set right by the coming of God's king-
     dom. Romans 14:17 says that the kingdom of God is a matter of righteousness and
     peace and joy in the Holy Spirit. All three attributes are included in the meaning
     of *shalom*.

   - Peace always follows righteousness.

     o   Isaiah 32:17, "The work of righteousness will be peace, and the effect
         of righteousness, quietness and assurance forever."

     o   In the age to come, when Messiah rules the earth from Jerusalem, the
         law (*torah*) will go out of Zion and there will be *shalom* for a thousand
         years. Our psalmist already tastes, in this age, the *shalom* of that future
         age, because wrong things are set right in his life (see Hebrews 6:5).

   - *Yeshua*, in John 14:27 said: "Peace I leave with you, My peace I give to you;
     not as the world gives do I give to you." Again in John 16:33, we have these
     words: "These things I have spoken to you, that in Me you may have peace.
     In the world you will have tribulation; but be of good cheer, I have overcome
     the world."

   - "Great peace have those who love Your law (*torah*)" and "Blessed are the
     undefiled in the way who walk in the law (*torah*) of the LORD." God will rest
     His case with the human race one day. His ways truly do lead to life and
     blessing and *shalom*, and the whole world will ultimately acknowledge it.

3.   "Nothing causes them to stumble" (*mikshowl*: stumbling-block, offense, fall).

   - No degree of injustice, insult or treachery could cause *Yeshua* to stumble
     in His walk. Nor could any degree of enticement toward compromise cause
     Him to stumble in His walk. He truly did overcome the world (John 16:33).

   - God's answer to great (*rab*) evil and persecution in the earth (in *resh*), is a
     people who have great (*rab*) peace. These overcomers will not be intimidated
     or enticed by great evil, nor can they be made to take up offense and become
     embittered by injustice, thus stumbling in their faith. "And the God of peace
     will crush Satan under your feet shortly" (Romans 16:20).

**"LORD, I hope for Your salvation, and I do Your commandments. My soul keeps
Your testimonies, and I love them exceedingly. I keep Your precepts and Your
testimonies, for all my ways are before You" (v. 166-168).**

1.   "I hope (*sabar*: to inspect, examine, wait, hope, wait upon) for Your salvation."
     Sabar is a focused anticipation of a future certainty.

- *Sabar* occurs only here in our psalm. Doing the verb tense and literal meaning, the phrase could read thus: "I have fully focused my expectation upon and am watching for Your salvation. "

- This is precisely the attitude of New Testament believers as they await the promise of *Yeshua*'s return. Titus 2:13 explains that they are "looking for (focused anticipation) the blessed hope (expectation of future certainty) and glorious appearing of our great God and Savior Jesus Christ."

2. "I do Your commandments." Do you remember the teaching about the listen–keep–do" progression? Our psalmist has gone from keeping the word to actually doing it. He has become a doer of the word (James 1:22).

   - This is *Yeshua* in John 4:34, "My food is to do the will of Him who sent Me."

   - "The bride has made herself ready and is arrayed in fine linen, clean and bright, for the fine linen is the righteous acts of the saints" (Revelation 19:7-8).

   - Reread Hebrews 5:13-14, noted above.

3. Can we perceive a progression to full obedience in the life of our psalmist?

   - I have inclined my heart to perform Your statutes (v. 112).

   - I have done justice and righteousness (v. 121).

   - I do Your commandments (v. 166).

4. "My soul keeps Your testimonies and I love them exceedingly." In verse twenty-five, his soul was cleaving to the dust of this world. The very desires and passions of our psalmist's heart have been changed.

   - Now, David loves what God loves and hates what God hates with intensity.

   - Love for God's word (v. 97) has grown to, "I love them exceedingly" (*m\eod*: with force or abundance).

5. "All my ways are before You."

   - Remember the cry of our psalmist way back in verse five: "Oh, that my ways were directed to keep Your statues."

   - Recall from *dalet* our psalmist's battle between his own ways and God's. It seems that God's ways have become his ways. He has been transformed.

   - Romans 12:2, "And do not be conformed to this world, but be transformed by the renewing of your mind, that you may prove what is that good and acceptable and perfect will of God."

Concluding Thoughts

Shin represents a shift in focus:

Our psalmist has clearly done what Paul instructs in 2 Corinthians 13:5, "Examine yourselves as to whether you are in the faith. Test yourselves. Do you not know yourselves that Jesus Christ is in you?" This represents a shift in focus from his calling in the advance of the kingdom to the issue of his character—what he has become. Remember that our nature is inherited, but our character is formed under pressure over time until we become just like our Master.

Remember from *tsadde* that having righteousness imputed to us does not make us righteous. Imputed righteousness is the potential to attain unto righteousness. Our psalmist has now attained to quantifiable righteousness as enumerated here in *shin*.

More thoughts on verse 164: "I praise You because of Your righteous judgments."

The subject of God's righteous judgments is the most difficult arena for humans to come into agreement with God. God's war on sin can strike us as excessive. His dealings with His own children can seem intense and unloving. In Isaiah 63 we see Messiah, with the day of vengeance in His heart, treading the winepress as He judges the nations. In verse five He says, "I looked and there was no one to help." He goes on to say, "Therefore My own arm brought salvation for Me."

In Revelation 19:2, after the judgment of Babylon, John sees Babylon burning. He hears the loud voice of a great multitude (like the sound of many waters and mighty thunderings) saying, "Alleluia! Salvation and glory and honor and power to the Lord our God! For true and righteous are His judgments, because He has judged the great harlot." Here too, as in our psalm, great joy and praise are expressed in context to the subject of God's judgments.

The phrase "righteous judgments" appears five times in Psalm 119. Consider them again:

1. Verse 7 (*aleph*): "O that my ways were directed. . . I will praise You with uprightness of heart, when I learn Your righteous judgments." This hints at the dealings of God against the sin operating within David's own heart.

2. Verse 62 (*chet*): "At midnight I will rise to give thanks to You, because of Your righteous judgments."

   • This seems to point to God's dealings in history as our psalmist waits for God to judge those who have betrayed him.

   • In the fullness of time, God consistently turns the tables on oppressors and sets the oppressed free through great judgments.

3.   Verse 106 (*nun*): "I have sworn and confirmed, I will keep Your righteous judgments."

       •   Taking an oath of allegiance, our psalmist promises to uphold God's definition of right and wrong. This counters our human tendency to interpret God's word (relative to our own issues) in a way that excuses our accommodation of that which God actually hates.

4.   Verse 160 (*resh*): "The entirety of Your word is truth, and every one of Your righteous judgments endures forever."

       •   This is a powerful confession of faith as all David's enemies converge with evil intent.

5.   Verse 164 (*shin*): "Seven times a day I praise You, because of Your righteous judgments."

       •   David has come to the place in which he actually, from the heart, loves what God loves and hates what God hates. This is amazing grace manifested.

Another thought on verse 165, "Great peace have those who love Your law. Nothing causes them to stumble."

It seems impossible to overstate the power of this verse. Can you imagine a group of people who have come to such total union with God that nothing can offend them? No degree of injustice, insult or treachery can embitter their hearts, and no degree of enticement to sin or promise of enrichment from the world can cause them to compromise. They are indeed those with great peace who love His law. The bride has made herself ready!

Questions to Ponder

1.   Have you ever examined yourself, as Paul instructed in 2 Corinthians 13:5? Do it now.

2.   How have you become like *Yeshua*? What areas of your life demonstrate real growth?

3.   How well, in this broken world, have you guarded your heart from bitterness, cynicism and hardness? Does your heart still pound with love for God and His word?

4.   The greatest in the kingdom is like a little child (Matthew 18:4). Is your heart still childlike, open and trusting and able to love others?

Chapter 24

Blessed Are the Meek

TAV

¹⁶⁹Let my cry come before You, O LORD;
Give me understanding according to Your word.
¹⁷⁰Let my supplication come before You;
Deliver me according to Your word.
¹⁷¹My lips shall utter praise,
For You teach me Your statutes.
¹⁷²My tongue shall speak of Your word,
For all Your commandments are righteousness.
¹⁷³Let Your hand become my help,
For I have chosen Your precepts.
¹⁷⁴I long for Your salvation, O LORD,
And Your law is my delight.
¹⁷⁵Let my soul live, and it shall praise You;
And let Your judgments help me.
¹⁷⁶ I have gone astray like a lost sheep;
Seek Your servant,
For I do not forget Your commandments.

Tav—Psalm 119:169-176

"It was granted her to be arrayed in fine linen, clean and bright" (Revelation 19:8).

Tav is the twenty-second and final letter of the Hebrew alphabet. The ancient pictograph portrays a cross and speaks of a mark, sign or covenant. It symbolizes ownership, making a covenant, or joining two things together in a covenant relationship. *Tav* is translated as mark in Ezekiel 9:4, where a "man clothed with linen" was commanded to "put a mark (*tav*) on the foreheads of the men who sigh and cry over all the abominations that are done within Jerusalem." In verse six we learn that everyone was killed except those with the *tav* on their foreheads. This mark protected them.

In the book of Revelation, both the Lord and the beast are observed setting their mark of ownership on people's foreheads. Those marked by the Lord were protected from the judgments which were poured out on the earth. In 1 Corinthians 6:19-20, Paul says, "Or do you not know that your body is the temple of the Holy Spirit who is in you, whom you have from God, and you are not your own? For you were bought at a price." Also, in Ephesians 1:13 we see a mark on God's people, "having believed, you were sealed (marked with a seal) with the Holy Spirit of promise."

Throughout scripture, circumcision, a mark that required the shedding of blood, represents a covenant with the Lord. Paul writes, "You were also circumcised with the circumcision made without hands, by putting off the body of the sins of the flesh, by the circumcision of Christ" (Colossians 2:11). This too required the shedding of blood—*Yeshua's* blood. Consider *Yeshua's* words at the Last Supper: "This is My blood of the new covenant, which is shed for many for the remission of sins" (Matthew 26:28). This covenant between God and His people is really about the circumcision of the heart; hence, with changed hearts and with the *torah* written upon our hearts, we become like our Master Himself. This Christ-likeness is the mark of every mature believer.

In *shin* David has identified substantial transformation in his life—quantifiable conformity into the likeness of the Master Himself. The wheat (sons of the kingdom) has matured and it is harvest time. If the phrase, "the bride has made herself ready," from Revelation 19:7 describes *shin*, then this phrase from Revelation 19:8 describes *tav*: "And to her it was granted to be arrayed in fine linen, clean and bright, for the fine linen is the righteous acts of the saints."

This begs a question: Did the bride make herself ready or was it granted (gifted) her to be arrayed thus? It is as if our psalmist is making another assessment of his transformation and, in humility, attributing it all to God's grace. The truth is that our choices and co-operation with the Lord are very important. We will never fulfill our destiny without exercising our will and choosing the right path. Conversely, it is also true that it is "God who gives us the victory" (1 Corinthians 15:57) and that without Him we can do nothing (John 15:5).

We are, on the one hand, jars of clay (2 Corinthians 4:7) and mere dust (Genesis 2:7). On the other hand, we are the very image of God in the earth, having His glory and Spirit within, expressed as "Messiah in you, the hope of glory" (Genesis 1:27; Colossians 1:27). Ephesians 1:23 speaks of "the church, which is His body, the fullness of Him who fills all in all." "The Word became flesh" in John 1:14, and manifested the glory of God, "for in Him dwelt all the fullness of the Godhead bodily" (Colossians 2:9). Human beings, yes, mere humans, are created to showcase the glory of God on the earth.

"But God has chosen the foolish things of the world to put to shame the wise, and God has chosen the weak things of the world to put to shame the things which are mighty" (1 Corinthians 1:27). The Lord defeats His enemies through mere humans. Consider Psalm 8:1-2, "O LORD, our LORD, how excellent is Your name in all the earth, who have set Your glory above the heavens! Out of the mouth of babes and nursing infants You have ordained strength, because of Your enemies, that You may silence the enemy and the avenger." God told Paul in 2 Corinthians 12:9, "My grace is sufficient for you, for My strength is made perfect in weakness."

The Shulamite, in the Song of Solomon, at the end of her journey to maturity, is described thus: "Who is this coming up from the wilderness (in triumphant victory [see Song of Solomon 6:10]), leaning (for help and strength) upon her beloved?" (Song of Solomon 8:5). This demonstrates both triumph and leaning.

These two seemingly paradoxical attitudes of heart and mind are unmistakable in *tav*. One is associated with the truth that we are created in the image of God and the other with the truth that we are but jars of clay—mere humans (see Psalm 103:14).

Here in *tav*, our psalmist is demonstrating boldness with humility, strength in weakness, confidence (in the Lord) yet having "no confidence in the flesh." By these attitudes, he is displaying the primary character trait of the kingdom of God, meekness. Consider the following scriptures associated with each truth:

1. The image of God: A mature son who walks in the fullness of the Spirit's power with boldness, in triumph and in confident faith, like *Yeshua,* who in Acts 10:38, went about doing good and healing all who were oppressed by the devil. See also 2 Corinthians 2:14.

    - "I can do all things through Messiah who strengthens me" (Philippians 4:13).

    - In Song of Solomon 8:5, the Shulamite is seen coming up (*alah:* ascending) in triumph from the wilderness of a fallen world where she had endured much tribulation.

    - His wife has made herself ready (Revelation 19:7).

    - Jacob became Israel, "for as a prince hast thou power (to prevail) with God and with men" (Genesis 32:28 KJV). He overcame his flesh and walked in a new nature.

    - "Trust in the LORD with all your heart" (Proverbs 3:5) shows confidence in the LORD.

2. Jars of clay (dust): A child of God who knows his weakness and walks in humility, gentleness, and gratefulness, completely leaning upon the Master. Humility is probably the virtue from which all other virtues flow. The Son of God, *Yeshua,* said of Himself, "I am gentle and lowly of heart" (Matthew 11:29).

    - "Without Me you can do nothing" (John 15:5).

    - In Song of Solomon 8:5, the Shulamite is seen "leaning upon her beloved."

    - "It was granted her to be arrayed in fine linen, clean and bright" (Revelation 19:8).

- Israel, a "prince with God," walked with a limp (in his flesh) ever after his encounter with God (Genesis 32:31).

- "Lean not on your own understanding" (Proverbs 3:5) reiterates that we are to claim no confidence in the flesh.

Tav can also speak of desire or longing. Consider Job's cry in Job 31:35 (KJV), "Oh that one would hear me! Behold, my desire (*tav*) is, that the Almighty would answer me." The mark of Job in that hour of his life was a desire to receive an answer from the Lord. A crescendo of fervent petition is evidenced in this segment by the following words:

- "Let" occurs five times, giving expression to great longing.

- "Cry" (*rinnah*: a cry of triumph) occurs only here in the psalm.

- "Supplication" (*t^echinnah*) occurs only here in the psalm.

- "Help" (*azar*) occurs twice as our psalmist acknowledges his need of the Lord.

Although there is some overlap, we can loosely outline our thoughts under these two headings:

- Verses 169-172: In the image of God: Bold and triumphant—kings and priests to God

- Verses 173-176: Jars of clay: Humble and dependent—the meek will inherit the earth

Let's join David in this final stage of his journey.

Image of God: Bold and triumphant (v. 169-172)

"Let my cry come before You, O LORD; Give me understanding according to Your word" (v. 169).

1. "Let my cry" (*rinnah*: a ringing cry; a shrill or ringing sound, shout of joy, cry of proclamation or praise, cry of entreaty or supplication, cry of grief).

    - *Rinnah* is translated ten different ways throughout the NKJV: cry, singing, rejoicing, joy, gladness, proclamation, shouting, sing, songs, and triumph. *Rinnah* occurs thirty-three times in scripture, seven of which could be perceived as negative such as in a cry of desperation, pain or grief.

    - The root word, *ranan*, occurs fifty-two times in scripture, none of which carry a negative connotation. *Ranan* means to overcome, to cry out, shout for joy, give a ringing cry. Ponder several occurrences of *rinnah* in the scriptures:

        o   Psalm 47:1, "O, clap your hands all you peoples! Shout to God with a voice of triumph" (*rinnah*)!

- o Psalm 126:2, "Then (after a powerful restoration) our mouth was filled with laughter and our tongue with singing (*rinnah*)."

- o Psalm 61:1-2, "Hear my cry, (*rinnah*) O God; Attend to my prayer. From the end of the earth I will cry (call out in prayer) to You, when my heart is overwhelmed; Lead me to the rock that is higher than I."

- o Psalm 17:1-2, "Hear a just cause, O LORD, attend to my cry (*rinnah*); Give ear to my prayer. . . Let my vindication come from Your presence."

- The conclusion of this study shows that this cry is not so much one of desperation, pain or grief, as it is a ringing cry, primarily of the following:

  - o Triumph, joy, rejoicing and singing.

  - o Entreaty, supplication (for help and support in the face of weakness) and/or longing for, desiring the Bridegroom (as in "even so, Lord Jesus, come").

2. "Come before (*qarab*: draw near, approach) You (*paniym*: face), O LORD." Literally, "Let my ringing cry (of triumph or longing) approach near to Your very face, O LORD."

3. "Give me understanding according to Your word." This is our psalmist's fifth request for understanding. He wants to know the very heart of God: what God thinks, what He feels and what He is saying.

    - Revelation 19:10, tells us that "the testimony of Jesus is the spirit of prophecy."

    - *Yeshua* said in John 15:15, "I have called you friends, for all things that I heard from My Father I have made known to you."

    - 1 Corinthians 2:9-10, "Eye has not seen, nor ear heard, nor have entered into the heart of man the things which God has prepared for those who love Him. But God has revealed them to us through His Spirit. For the Spirit searches all things, yes, the deep things of God."

"Let my supplication come before You; Deliver me according to Your word" (v. 140).

1. "Let my supplication (*t\echinnah*: favor, graciousness, supplication for favor, mercy, pardon) come before You."

    - This Hebrew word appears only here in our psalm. Solomon employs it eight times in his prayer of dedication of the temple as He sought God's favor toward the temple and the people of Israel. It is about God hearing and answering the prayers of His people, causing them to shine with His favor.

Chanan is the root, and means to be gracious, show favor or mercy (seen in verses 29, 58 and 132).

- Joshua 11:20 employs the first use of this Hebrew word. It is about the cities of Canaan which fought against Israel's conquest, rather than make peace. "It was of the LORD to harden their hearts, that they should come against Israel in battle, that He might utterly destroy them, and that they might receive no mercy" (*t\echinnah*). This word is really about a prayer for favor from God.

- David is asking for God's presence as a cloak of favor, which will ultimately show forth God's glory through his life. Ponder Moses' prayer in Exodus 33:15-16, "If Your presence does not go with us, do not bring us up from here. For how then will it be known that Your people and I have found grace (derived from the same root as *t\echinnah*) in Your sight, except You go with us? So we shall be separate, Your people and I, from all the people who are upon the face of the earth."

- Answered prayers display God's glory on earth and mark us as His favored ones.

2. "Deliver (*natsal*: to snatch away, deliver, rescue, take out, save) me according to Your word." *Natsal* appears in verse forty-three as "take not the word of truth utterly out of my mouth." Recall from *resh* and *shin* that our psalmist is experiencing great zeal for righteousness while being embroiled in fierce conflict and warfare from his treacherous adversaries.

    - "According to Your word." Our psalmist references a promise of deliverance from the word of God. This is his expectation and longing.

    - This could parallel the longing cry of the bride, "Even so Lord Jesus come."

3. The prophets had revelation of a supernatural re-gathering of God's elect from the ends of the earth at the end of the age, a kind of rapture of the saints. Because of the Hebrew word choice (*natsal*), we can't help but reference Paul's teaching on the rapture in 1 Thessalonians 4:13-17. After all, our journey is a journey to maturity, both individually and corporately. A mature bride without spot or wrinkle, who, in the heat of this end-time battle has made herself ready, will surely be caught up to meet the Lord in the air at His coming. This is the blessed hope of every believer (Titus 2:13).

"My lips shall utter praise, for You teach me Your statutes. My tongue shall speak of Your word, for all Your commandments are righteousness" (v. 171-172).

1.   "My lips shall utter (*naba*: to flow, pour out, gush forth, spring or bubble up) praise" (*t\ehillah*). *T\ehillah* (laudation, praise, glory, hymn of praise) is the noun form of *halal*, which we studied in verse 164. It is the Hebrew word for extreme praise.

2.   "For You teach me Your statutes." Eight times throughout this journey, David has asked God to do just that (something we have interpreted as a cry for friendship as per John 15:15). Now he essentially says, "You do it!" This is David's reason for uttering extreme praise (*t\ehillah*) with his lips. God has answered his prayer!

3.   "My tongue shall speak (*anah*: respond, answer, testify) of Your word." Our psalmist is in love with the Lord and His word. Like Peter and John in Acts 4:20, he cannot keep silent. "For we cannot but speak the things which we have seen and heard."

4.   "All Your commandments (*mitsvah*: an imperative decree or order) are righteousness."

     •   Recall our introduction on *mitzvah*. God's *mitzvah* determines what is right concerning our lives and how we are to live before Him and each other.

     •   Our psalmist, possibly near the end of his life or at least at a stage of substantial maturity, is not regretting the journey of obedience to the Lord's commands. On the contrary, he is acknowledging that the Lord's commands, which totally directed what he did with his life and which at times precipitated great warfare, criticism and difficulty, were, in fact, righteous.

     •   "To declare that the LORD is upright; He is my rock, and there is no unrighteousness in Him" (Psalm 92:15).

     •   Recall the revelation of verse ninety-six, "Your commandment (*mitzvah*) is exceedingly broad" (extremely liberating, not restricting).

5.   These are the confessions of a triumphant son or daughter of God who is walking in bold faith. That person will not be silenced.

Jars of clay: Humble and dependent (v. 173-176)

"Let Your hand become my help, for I have chosen Your precepts" (v. 173).

1.   "Let Your hand."

     •   The hand of God speaks of His manifest power in acting to deliver His people. In Psalm 98:1, "His right hand and holy arm have gained the victory" (in the deliverance of Israel from out of Egypt with power).

- In verse seventy-three of our psalm, God's "hands have made and fashioned me."

2.   "Become my help" (*azar*: to help, succor, support, surround, protect, aid).

   - *Azar* occurs two times in this segment, distinguishing it from all the others.

   - Our psalmist is acknowledging that without the Lord, he can do nothing. God said it this way to Paul in 2 Corinthians 12:9, "My grace is sufficient for you, for My strength is made perfect in weakness."

   - The mature bride in Song of Songs 8:5 is leaning (in weakness) upon her beloved.

3.   "I have chosen Your precepts."

   - In verse thirty our psalmist says, "I have chosen the way of truth."

   - This hints at our role in this journey to maturity. The dignity and power of being human is that we can choose. And our choices determine whether or not we fulfill our destiny. "His wife has made herself ready" (Revelation 19:7). She chose Him.

   - Conversely, it was granted (gifted) her to be arrayed in fine linen (Revelation 19:8).

   - The King to His mature bride, in the Song of Songs, says "I awakened you." It is all about Him. However, over and over again, in the journey she chose Him. With her will, she said, "yes" to the journey. It is about her too.

"I long for Your salvation, O LORD, and Your law is my delight" (v. 174).

1.   "I long for (*ta'ab*: to desire) Your salvation (*y\eshuwah*)." The psalmist is longing for *Yeshua*.

   - In all of scripture, *ta'ab* appears only here, and in verse forty of our psalm, where David says, "I have longed for (*ta'ab*) your precepts."

   - *Y\eshuwah* is the most comprehensive Hebrew word for salvation. It includes healing, victory, welfare and deliverance, and is the word which gave *Yeshua* His name, as in, "Call His Name *Yahshua* (*Yah* saves), for He shall save. . . ." (Matthew 1:21).

   - His longing is not so much a feeling of "get me out of here" as it is the longing of the bride for the Bridegroom. Our psalmist's delight in and enjoyment of the law of the Lord has awakened in him a deep longing for the fullness of the very salvation which he has already had a taste of in this age. We have been "enlightened, and have tasted the heavenly gift, and become partakers of the Holy Spirit, and have tasted the good word of God and the powers of the age to come" (Hebrews 6:5).

- Ponder the words of John Piper in his book, *Hunger for God.* "We have tasted the powers of the age to come. . . We have tasted it so wonderfully by His Spirit, and cannot now be satisfied until the consummation of joy arrives. . . We have been aroused by the aroma of Jesus' love and by the taste of God's goodness in the gospel of Christ (I Peter 2:2-3)."[1] Piper continues: "Faith means both delighting in the (past) incarnation and desiring the (future) consummation. It will be both contentment and dissatisfaction. And the dissatisfaction will grow directly out of the measure of contentment we have known in Christ."[2] He explains that "Christian fasting is . . . a hunger for God awakened by the taste of God freely given in the gospel."[3]

2. "Your law (*torah*) is my delight" (*shashua*: enjoyment, pleasure, delight). See verse ninety-seven.

"Let my soul live, and it shall praise You; And let Your judgments help me" (v. 175).

1. "Let my soul live and it shall praise (*halal*) You."

- *Halal,* as previously noted, is the most comprehensive Hebrew word for full and extreme praise. See the notes on verses 164 and 171.

- Of three occurrences, two are in this last segment. Praise comes to fullness as we mature in Him. Praise is also a powerful weapon in spiritual warfare. At the end of the age, when the false prophet has commanded all to worship the image of the beast or die (Revelation 13:15), there will be a people who will not bow, but will have extravagant praise for *Yeshua*. They will love Him more than they love their own lives (Revelation 12:11).

2. "Let Your judgments (*mishpat*) help (*azar*) me."

- "Let Your judgments." The heat is still on in the conflict of kingdoms. Our psalmist is asking for the judgments of God to set wrong things right. He has zeal for righteousness. Recall that the breaking in of God's judgments is salvation (for which he is longing) for the righteous, and judgment for the wicked—two sides of one coin.

- "Help me." When Moses confronted Pharaoh, God's power backed Moses up and the judgments "helped" Moses.

"I have gone astray like a lost sheep; Seek Your servant, for I do not forget Your commandments" (v. 176).

1.   "I have gone astray" is stated in the perfect tense, which means it is a completed action. Apparently our psalmist is about to step into the age to come and is done with going astray. It is also a way of acknowledging that it was grace, not merit, which brought this victory.

2.   This seems like a surprising way to end the journey, but it reflects a profound humility on the part of our mature psalmist. He is walking with a limp, for it is not about his own merit and strength but about the grace of God.

3.   A mature apostle Paul claimed to be the "chief of sinners" (1 Timothy 1:15). Though his sin did not define him, Paul still saw himself as the chief of sinners. He knew that in his flesh dwelt no good thing, and that he had to discipline his body to avoid being disqualified. 1 Corinthians 9:27, "I discipline my body and bring it into subjection, lest, when I have preached to others, I myself should become disqualified."

4.   He who is forgiven much loves much. The revelation of my sinfulness and my love for God goes hand in hand. Never forget from where He brought you or to where He has taken you to. This realization generates humility and gratefulness (see 1 Timothy 1:12-17).

5.   "Seek your servant." Our capacity for indulging in evil is terrifying. Our propensity to stray persists. We need the Lord until the end.

6.   Consider again John 15:16, "You did not choose Me, but I chose you and appointed you that you should go and bear fruit."

Concluding Thoughts

A few more thoughts on the paradox of meekness can be seen in Revelation 4. John sees twenty-four elders on thrones (ruling with Him), clothed in white robes (righteousness) with crowns (*stephanos*: a victor's wreath) of gold on their heads. They represent the redeemed who have overcome and are seated with Him on His throne (Revelation 3:21). In verse ten they are seen casting their crowns before the throne and proclaiming His worthiness and merit, not their own. Yes, they overcame, and yes they chose His way by their own free will. However, in 1 Corinthians 15:57, Paul ends that great resurrection chapter with these words: "But thanks be to God, who gives us the victory through our Lord Jesus Christ." His grace has given us the victory. God has given them the victory.

In Luke 17:10, after the servant accomplished great things in full obedience to his master, consider *Yeshua's* words: "So likewise you, when you have done all those things which you are commanded, say, 'We are unprofitable (unmeritorious) servants. We have done what was our duty to do.'" Ultimately, it is not about our merit.

No matter how far we have come or how anointed we may be in ministry, as long as we are in this body, sin still operates within our flesh and renders us weak. The same propensity to wander referenced back in *bet* is still with us. Paul warns in 1 Corinthians 10:12, "Let him who thinks he stands take heed, lest he fall." In Philippians 3, Paul deemed himself to not yet have attained the goal, "I press on that I may lay hold . . . I press toward the goal for the prize" (Philippians 3:12, 14). In 1 Corinthians 9:27, Paul guards himself against falling with these words: "I discipline my body and bring it into subjection, lest, when I have preached to others, I myself should become disqualified." We are utterly dependent upon His grace, while still needing to choose to do our part.

There will be yet another body prepared, the corporate body of Messiah, which will fill the earth with glory in these last days. God's power, presence, beauty and the glory of His character and nature (Hebrews 10:5-6; Psalm 40:6-8) will be displayed through weak human flesh. Fullness is when dust displays glory. This is our calling: jars of clay filled with God's Spirit.

"Blessed are the meek, for they shall inherit the earth" (Matthew 5:5). The meek (not simply the justified or those declared legally righteous) shall inherit the earth.

Meekness is the primary positive virtue of the kingdom and the one to be most sought after. Meekness is associated with gentleness and humility. It is the restraint of one's power for a higher redemptive cause. This is not to be confused with weakness or a relaxed personality. Meekness is the cultivation of a spirit of servanthood (submitted power and ability) even in the face of adversity and mistreatment.

Self-control is also a major ingredient or mark of meekness. A truly meek person can steward great authority and wealth without being seduced by it. Although the meek possess the ability to serve their own self-interests with these resources, they remain submitted to the Lord. Hence, they can be trusted with power.

Yeshua is the ultimate example of meekness. He could have used His power to deliver Himself, come down from the cross and destroy His enemies (Matthew 26:53), but He remained submitted to His Father. He knew who He was as the Son of God. Although He had the power to save Himself, He prayed, "nevertheless, not as I will, but as You will" (Matthew 26:39). Therefore *Yeshua* could say, "All authority has been given to Me in heaven and on earth" (Matthew 28:18).

Consider the power of the two witnesses in Revelation 11:3-7, "And I will give power to my two witnesses, and they will prophesy . . . clothed in sackcloth (humility). These are the two olive trees and the two lampstands standing before the God of the earth. And if anyone wants to harm them, fire proceeds from their mouth and devours their enemies. And if anyone wants to harm them, he must be killed in this manner. These have power to shut heaven, so that no rain falls in the days of their prophecy; and they have power over waters to turn them to blood, and to strike the earth with all plagues, as often as they desire. When they finish their testimony, the beast that ascends out of the bottomless pit will make war against them, overcome them, and kill them."

Why did the two witnesses allow themselves to be killed?

Being clothed in sackcloth speaks of humility and demonstrates submitted power. The witnesses' power was submitted to God. Like *Yeshua*, they would not use it to save themselves.

The most mature among us are often regarded by the measure of their anointing or by the extent of their ministry and influence. Who considers the quality of one's interior life as the primary measure of a person's maturity? Who considers that God truly looks upon the heart? Who stops to ask, "How tender and responsive is my heart to God? How submitted to and teachable am I in the ways of God?"

The human being is the most sought after venue for the display of glory, both by heaven for showcasing God's glory and by hell for displaying the devil's "glory" or character. We choose who will fill us and possess our faculties as human beings.

Questions to Ponder

1. When have you experienced the boldness and triumph of moving in the anointing of the Holy Spirit and subsequently seen the power of God demonstrated?

2. In what ways can you identify with the ongoing operation of sin within your members and the propensity to wander from the path of life?

3. Have you ever lost a game on purpose because you loved the other person? When have you restrained yourself in setting right something that was wrong for the sake of another person's good or because of the will of God? This is meekness.

Supplemental Teaching

Addendum 1

Keeping the Word

Consider for a moment the power of a seed to reproduce life. The word of God is like a seed with life in it from another realm. It is the testimony of God sown into the earth. How precious is it? In the parable of the sower and the seed (Mark 4), the seed of the word comes under great attack. Why? Because it has the capacity to reproduce on earth what is in heaven. 1 Peter 1:23 says that we were "born again, not of corruptible seed, but of incorruptible (seed), by the word of God." How then can we be certain that the word of God will produce heaven in and through us? Or we could ask: how will it form Messiah in us so that we are conformed into His image?

A verse in Deuteronomy 7 shows the principle of keeping the word. Moses has just recounted the covenant at Sinai as God's marriage vow to Israel. Israel's part of this "marriage" comes in verse twelve. "Then it shall come to pass, because you listen to these judgments, and keep and do them, that the LORD your God will keep with you the covenant and the mercy which He swore to your fathers" (Deuteronomy 7:12).

How or under what conditions will the children of Israel be able to inherit, enjoy and remain in the Promised Land (the covenant and mercy which He swore to their fathers)? Salvation was a free gift by faith in the Passover Lamb during the Israelites' exodus from bondage in Egypt. To possess the promise would require faith-filled obedience and perseverance. Let's explore the significance of these three verbs and their order: listen, keep, do (perform or obey).

Our tendency is to begin our journey by striving diligently to obey God's word. What if that is impossible? The truth is that I cannot obey God's word or fulfill God's will for my life because as Paul said, "For I know that in me (that is in my flesh) nothing good dwells; For to will is present with me , but how to perform what is good I do not find" (Romans 7:18). In essence Paul says, "I want to perform all God's will and do what is good, but I cannot. As noble as it seems to strive for obedience, that would mean that we are beginning at the end. Let's explore the progression of listen, keep and do.

1. **Listen** is the Hebrew word *shama*, the primary biblical word for hearing or listening. It occurs more than 1,100 times in the Hebrew scriptures. The KJV translates it as hearken. Some translations translate it obey. Obviously it implies intent of the heart to obey, but it means to hear. Hearing God requires that we draw near to God and hear His voice before we have actually performed His word. The power

of the cross lies in this, that before I am perfect (mature), while I am yet struggling with sin in my members, I can with boldness enter the Holiest by the blood of *Yeshua*, by a new and living way (Hebrews 10:19-20). Through intimacy with the Lord, I can hear and receive the seed (words) from heaven that have power to reproduce heaven on earth (in my own earth first). So then, faith comes by hearing and hearing by the word (*rhema*) of God (Romans 10:17).

2.   **Keep** is the Hebrew word *shamar* (a synonym of *natsar* translated as keep in Psalm 119:2). It means to keep or guard, to post a sentry or hedge about as with thorns so as to keep safe. Again, the implication is that something precious must be protected. Having heard the word of God, I am now to keep it as a great treasure. It will be attacked. The enemy will seek to steal or destroy this seed with heaven's life in it.

Let's illustrate:

-    While enslaved in Egypt, the children of Israel received a promise, a seed, from God about a land flowing with milk and honey. As they began the journey toward that Promised Land, the first place they came to was the wilderness, which was the exact opposite of the promise. Now what?

-    The enemy comes and attacks that seed with the age-old question of Genesis 3:1, "Did God really say . . . ?" Instead of keeping God's word, Israel believed the enemy's lie that God had brought them out of Egypt to die in the wilderness (Exodus 16:3). This should have been the time to guard God's word against theft and confess their faith in His promise. This was not the time to abort the seed, but the time to keep it as the very seed with potential to bring itself to pass. Yet Israel aborted the seed that had the life they were promised within it. Consequently, they perished in the wilderness. Only Joshua and Caleb, who remained steadfast in believing God's promise, entered in.

-    Paul's charge to Timothy: "According to the prophecies (seed of the word) previously made concerning you (his promise), that by them you may wage the good warfare" (1 Timothy 1:18). This is a great example of keeping the word.

3.   **Do** is the Hebrew word *asah*. It means to perform, accomplish or do something. I cannot perform (obey) the word of God, but the word kept in me accomplishes what I cannot do in my own strength.

-    Consider Mary's encounter with Gabriel in Luke 1:26-38 as an allegory illustrating the keeping of the word until Messiah is formed in us.

o   "You shall conceive in your womb, and bring forth a son, and shall call His name *Yeshua*" (v. 31). Mary received the word as a seed from God through Gabriel with these words: Let it be to me according to your word (*rhema*) (v. 38).

o   How is Mary going to bring forth *Yeshua*? How are you and I going to bring forth Messiah to the world? We will do it the same way Mary did, by receiving heaven's seed into the womb of our spirit, then keeping (guarding, protecting, nourishing) it as something precious until it comes to full term.

o   As Mary's body conformed to the seed that was in her womb, so our lives will conform to the seed that is in ours. I am sure it was hard work to give birth to the baby *Yeshua*, but Mary did not strive to produce Him within her and when it was time to deliver the baby, nothing could stop him from being born.

A final note on Israel: Yes, they disobeyed God's command to cross over and possess the land, but more than that, they did not have the capacity to do so. They were not "pregnant" with the expectation of victory. They had not kept the promise of God alive within. They had aborted the seed of the word of God and received a lie (a seed) from the enemy. It is no accident that in Mark 4:24, after the parable of the sower and the seed, Yeshua warns us thus; "Take heed what you hear." There was no word of God within them to draw upon for faith. When the strong man comes knocking on your door, it is too late to go to the gym and try to build up strength for the fight.

Consider Gabriel's final words to Mary in Luke 1:37, "For with God nothing will be impossible." Literally in the Greek, Gabriel said, "With God, no word (*rhema*) shall be powerless (without *dunamis*)."

The word of God has the power to bring itself to pass in us if we will keep it. The life is in the seed, not in us. *Yeshua* said in John 6:53 "Unless you eat the flesh of the Son of Man and drink His blood, you have no life in you." Then in John 6:63 He follows up with these words: "The words that I speak to you are spirit, and they are life." The power is in the word of God. I cannot perform or fulfill the word, but the word within in me can. My job or calling is to keep, protect and guard as great treasure, the word of God. Read Proverbs 2:1-5.

Addendum 2

Mount Zion: Dwelling of God Among Men
A Teaching Connected to *Bet* (Psalm 119:9-16)

God's passion to dwell among men is legendary. He is portrayed in scripture as constantly seeking a dwelling place on the earth (Psalm 132:13-14; Isaiah 66:1-2). God desires to meet with humans. One can almost hear the sheer delight in God's voice at the great announcement of Revelation 21:3, "Behold, the tabernacle of God is with men, and He will dwell with them, and they shall be His people. God Himself will be with them and be their God." *Yeshua's* passion for us is revealed in John 17:24 when He prays, "Father, I desire that they also whom You gave Me may be with Me where I am." This is precisely the focus of *bet*, the second segment of Psalm 119.

Consider these poignant words in Exodus 19:4-6; "I bore you on eagles' wings and brought you to Myself. . . . You shall be a special treasure to Me above all people; for all the earth is Mine. And you shall be to Me a kingdom of priests and a holy nation." Immediately after Israel's deliverance from slavery in Egypt (their "salvation"), they headed for Mount Sinai, where Moses received the pattern for the Tabernacle. In Exodus 25:8, God instructed Moses, "Let them make Me a sanctuary, that I may dwell among them." In verse twenty-two of the same chapter, the LORD continues with, "And there I will meet with you, and I will speak with you from above the mercy seat." This is the house (*bet*) that Israel would build to host the Lord.

Whether it is the altar of a patriarch, or the tabernacle of Moses, or David's tabernacle, or Solomon's temple, or the New Covenant temple of our own bodies (1 Corinthians 6:19) in which the Holy Spirit dwells, or if it is the body of Messiah which "grows into a holy temple in the Lord, in whom you also are being built together for a dwelling place of God" (Ephesians 2:21-22)—it is a temple or sanctuary prepared as the place on earth for God to live with His people. This is where He will meet with, speak with and intimately encounter humans.

All along Israel's journey up to the land of Canaan, there was a location in view referred to as the "place where the Lord chooses to make his name abide" (Deuteronomy 12:5, 11, 21; 14:23). This was Mount Zion in Jerusalem. It was here that God's presence would more permanently rest in the temple among His people. It was the location of both David's tabernacle (2 Samuel 5:6-9; 6:1-19) and Solomon's temple, and if you believe in a literal 1000-year millennial reign of the Messiah, it is the place of the millennial temple described in Ezekiel 40 to 46. Many scriptures speak of the Lord dwelling in Zion, and of Zion being a place of encounter, unceasing praise, intimacy and delight. Consider the following scriptures:

- Psalm 9:11, "Sing praises to the LORD, who dwells in Zion! Declare His deeds among the people."

- Psalm 65:1, "Praise is awaiting You, O God, in Zion; and to You the vow shall be performed."

- Psalm 76:2, "In Salem also is His tabernacle and His dwelling place in Zion."

- Psalm 132:13-14, "For the Lord has chosen Zion; He has desired it for His dwelling place: 'This is My resting place forever; here I will dwell, for I have desired it.'"

- Joel 3:21, "For the LORD dwells in Zion." See also Joel 3:17.

- Zechariah 1:14, "I am zealous for Jerusalem and for Zion with great zeal."

- Psalm 87:2, "The Lord loves the gates of Zion more than all the dwellings of Jacob."

- See also Psalm 74:2; 99; Isaiah 8:18; 31:4, 9; 60:14-15; 62:1; Jeremiah 6:2; Zechariah 2:8; 8:3.

The geography of Mount Zion teaches us several spiritual truths. Consider the following:

1. Mount Zion is the preeminent place or high place of the city (and nation). David's zeal to bring up the ark of God to Mount Zion was His zeal to see the Lord again have the preeminence in Israel (see Colossians 1:18). In fact, Jerusalem itself is on the mountains (Psalm 125:1). One always has to ascend, or go up to Jerusalem from every location in Israel (see 1 Kings 12:27-28) or, for that matter, anywhere in the world (see Ezra 1:3-4; 7:13; Psalm 24:3; Isa 2:3; Micah 4:2; Zechariah 14:16).

2. Mount Zion is also the central place or heart of the city. David's zeal to bring up the ark of God to Mount Zion was his zeal to have the Lord again be the center of Israel's affections and worship (see Colossians 3:2). In Ezekiel 5:5 (ESV), we learn that the city itself is in the center of the earth. "Thus says the LORD God: 'This is Jerusalem. I have set her in the center of the nations, with countries all around her.'"

3. Mount Zion is a lowly hill in Jerusalem, not at all impressive as a mountain (Psalm 68:16). This teaches us that the Lord dwells in the high place of the lowly—that is, among the humble who have a broken spirit and a contrite heart (Isaiah 57:15; Psalm 51:17). These humble ones however, must give Him both the preeminent place and center place of their lowly lives. In the New Covenant, a believer's body is God's temple (1 Corinthians 6:19) which symbolizes the high place of the mind and the center place of the heart—our thoughts and affections (or worship)

respectively. God will not play second fiddle to any other love or priority. He will not be one among many lovers.

In 2 Samuel 5:6-10, David had to remove the Jebusites (that which treads on the holy place) from Mount Zion to prepare for bringing up the ark of God. This is precisely what building our lives into a house for God's presence with the seven planks described in *bet* does. It displaces that which defiles and fills our minds and hearts with His presence and His word. 2 Corinthians 10:4-5 (ESV) teaches us about this war for the mind and heart. "For the weapons of our warfare are not of the flesh but have divine power to destroy strongholds. We destroy arguments and every lofty opinion raised against the knowledge of God, and take every thought captive to obey Messiah, being ready to punish every disobedience, when your obedience is complete."

David brought up the ark of God, placed it in the "tabernacle of David" (1 Chronicles 16:1; 2 Samuel 6:17) and deployed, at tremendous expense, the priesthood to minister to the Lord night and day during his entire reign of thirty-three years from Jerusalem (1 Chronicles 16:4, 6). His number one priority was to place the Lord on the "high place" and in the center of the life of Israel. This was the place that the Lord desired and certainly the place He was worthy of. It is the place where the Lord chooses to make his name abide. See Psalm 132:13-14.

The job description or occupation of the priests was to "minister (*sharath*: attend to the presence) to the LORD" with the fat (which speaks of worship) and the blood (which speaks of prayer and intercession) of the sacrifices (Leviticus 3:16-17; Ezekiel 44:15). The priestly tribe was set apart to the Lord for one thing—that of hosting the presence of the Lord in Israel's midst by ministering to Him through worship and intercession (Numbers 3:5-13, 45; 28:1-2; 1 Chronicles 15:11-15; Deuteronomy 10:8).

Likewise, in the New Covenant, the redeemed have become "priests to (our) God" (Revelation 1:6; 5:10). The priests have authority in heaven—that is the right to enter the presence of God (see Hebrews 4:16; 10:19-22; Ezekiel 55:14). The kings have authority on the earth—that is power to extend the kingdom of God (see Matthew 28:18-20; 10:1; Luke 10:17-18).

Hebrews 12:22-23 speaks of the redeemed as having become the city (or dwelling) of God. "But you have come to Mount Zion and to the city of the living God, the heavenly Jerusalem, to an innumerable company of angels, to the general assembly and church of the firstborn who are registered in heaven." In Revelation 21:9-10, John was shown the bride of Messiah as a city, Jerusalem's heavenly counterpart, the holy Jerusalem, descending out of heaven from God. This city is both the dwelling of God with men and the dwelling of redeemed men with God (Revelation 21:3). He is in us and we are in Him. This is ultimate union with God. See John 17:21.

Two anointed offices functioned on and from Mount Zion:

- The priesthood, which related to the temple and the presence of God.

- The kingship, which related to the throne or kingdom.

Not only was the priesthood functioning in the temple on Mount Zion but also God's throne (government) was functioning, albeit through the king of Israel. The ark of the covenant in the temple was God's throne upon the earth. In Isaiah 66:1, the LORD says, "Heaven is My throne, and earth is My footstool." Consider the following scriptures:

- Psalm 2:6, "Yet I have set My King on My holy hill of Zion."

- Psalm 110:2, "*YHVH* shall send the rod of Your strength out of Zion. Rule in the midst of Your enemies!"

- Isaiah 16:5, "In mercy the throne will be established; One will sit on it in truth in the tabernacle of David, judging and seeking peace and hastening righteousness."

- Ezekiel 43:7 (about the temple), "This is the place of My throne and the place of the soles of My feet, where I will dwell in the midst of the children of Israel forever."

- Psalm 99:1-5, "The LORD reigns. . . . The LORD is great in Zion. . . . Exalt the LORD our God, and worship at His footstool—He is holy." See also Isaiah 24:23; Micah 4:7; Psalm 132:7.

The entire government of Israel flowed out from Mount Zion. Everything that is of the kingdom (government) of God flows from this mountain where the Lord, who is the King (see Psalm 93, 96-99 and 103:19) is hosted by the priesthood. Consider the following scriptures:

- Psalm 14:7, "Oh that the salvation of Israel would come out of Zion!" See also Psalm 53:6.

- Psalm 20:2, "May He send you help from the sanctuary, and strengthen you out of Zion."

- Psalm 50:2, "Out of Zion, the perfection of beauty, God will shine forth."

- Psalm 110:2, "Send the rod of Your strength out of Zion. Rule in the midst of Your enemies."

- Psalm 128:5, "The Lord bless you out of Zion, and may you see the good of Jerusalem."

- Psalm 134:3, "The Lord who made heaven and earth bless you from Zion!"

- Isaiah 2:3, "Out of Zion shall go forth the law, the word of the Lord from Jerusalem" (see also Micah 4:2).

- Joel 3:16, "YHVH also will roar from Zion, and utter His voice from Jerusalem" (Amos 1:2).

God's presence, then, is hosted in the temple upon this mountain, and God's government is extended out from His throne upon this mountain. Many scriptures point to the truth that the Messiah, the "Son of David" (*Yeshua*), will return to the earth. He is to be worshipped (a priestly function) upon this mountain and He is to rule the earth (a kingly function) from this mountain. He, the Son of David, of whom the Davidic kings were but a dim foreshadowing, is to sit on David's throne forever (2 Samuel 7:12; Zechariah 6:12-13; Jeremiah 3:17; Isaiah 9:7; 16:5; Luke 1:32; and other scriptures). No wonder this is the most contested and warred-over piece of real estate on the earth. Whoever's name is lifted up here in worship is the one whose government will fill the earth. The priesthood hosts His presence and the Kingship extends His rule over the earth. The war is ultimately over who will rule the earth.

This warfare over Mount Zion depicts the warfare for the mind and the heart of every believer. It is as if every human being has their own personal Mount Zion. If our enemy can fill our minds and hearts with his thoughts and passions (such as bitterness, the fear of man, anger, hatred, unbelief, greed, lust, pride, and so forth) as the Jebusites did in 2 Samuel 5:6-8, then he can control or exercise lordship over our lives. The war is not only about who will rule the earth, but about who will rule your earth, that is, your body which is to be His temple.

God's longing to dwell among men is reflected back to Him by our longing for His presence. If God's passion to dwell among men is legendary, David's passion to see the Lord have a dwelling place in Zion is also legendary—and is powerfully revealed in Psalm 132:1-5. Saul, in all of his supposed forty years as king of Israel, never bothered to seek the Lord (1 Chronicles 10:14). In contrast, the first thing David did as king was to bring up the ark of God to Mount Zion. And, the first priority of every believer should be to prepare his life as a sanctuary of the Lord.

Addendum 3

The Heart of Man

The heart (*leb* or *lebab*) in the Hebrew Scriptures is the center of the human being as a free moral agent. *Lebab* is not so much the seat of one's desires, emotions and feelings as it is the seat of a person's thoughts, intellect, will, and motives or intentions.

By comparison, the soul (*nephesh*) expresses the whole inner self, with all the desires (Deuteronomy 12:15), emotions, and personal characteristics that make each human being unique. For example, the psalmist sings in Psalm 103:1 (KJV), "Bless the LORD O my soul (*nephesh*), and all that is within me bless his holy name." It is the soul that interprets the input or stimuli from the world and consequently feels fearful, rejected, safe, happy, sad, angry, or other emotions. Desires are felt in the soul, but the heart shapes one's character, choices and decisions.

The heart of unregenerate man is described in Jeremiah 17:9 as "deceitful above all things and desperately wicked" (see also Genesis 6:5). This heart tends not to seek the Lord as our psalmist has set his heart to do. Rather, it is utterly self-seeking and looks everywhere except to the Lord for life and fulfillment. However, once a person turns to the Lord and is "born of God" (John 1:12-13), he has the promise of a new nature and a new heart. This is a tremendous transformation! See 1 John 3:20; Jeremiah 31:33-34; Ezekiel 11:18-20; 36:26; Deuteronomy 30:6; Hebrews 8:10; 10:16.

As believers, how are we to view our hearts? As deceitful and wicked? As righteous and pure? As a work in process? The truth is, all of those are correct. Paul said in Romans 7:17-19, "But now, it is no longer I who do it, but sin that dwells in me. For I know that in me (that is, in my flesh) nothing good dwells; for to will is present with me, but how to perform what is good I do not find. For the good that I will to do, I do not do; but the evil I will not to do, that I practice."

We have been born from above and have become partakers of the divine nature (2 Peter 1:4; 2; 2 Corinthians 5:17). The seed of God is within us (1 Peter 1:23; 1 John 3:9) and we have a new identity in Messiah. Therefore, the sin that yet lodges in our members, while it does not define us, must be overcome if we are to walk *The Blessed Life*. The question of how to overcome the sin in our members is precisely what building our house for the presence of God is all about. He does in us what we cannot do.

As stated in the chapter on *bet*, we are not advocating for a dead end of introspection in a kind of naval-gazing search for wrong motives and attitudes in our hearts. Hebrews 4:12 tells us that the word of God will do that for us: "For the word of God is living and powerful, and sharper than any two-edged sword, piercing even to the division of soul and spirit, and of joints and marrow, and is a discerner of the thoughts and intents of the heart." Furthermore, "the Spirit of truth, has come, He will guide you into all truth" (John 16:13). We are focused upon the Lord and looking for righteousness, not sin. We define ourselves according to our new nature.

Nevertheless, a believer needs to be humbly aware of the sin yet operating within his members and be ready to confess it by saying the same thing that God says whenever it is detected or exposed by the word and the Spirit. We know that God is greater than our hearts (1 John 3:20).

One of the ways our hearts deceive us is illustrated by an encounter I had with Manny, a graduating high school senior. I asked Manny, "So, what is next for you after graduation?" His answer was, "I am going to Amsterdam." His answer mirrored the intentions of numerous of the lawless students in our urban school. They thought there were too many rules restricting their fun and too many policemen enforcing those rules. "Why?" I asked him. Without hesitation, Manny said, "I am looking for truth." At that moment, whether it was the Holy Spirit or just because I had had enough of this "Amsterdam thing," I boldly said, "I doubt it. Most of us don't want truth. What we want is an ideology, or Bible verse, that justifies the lifestyle we have already set our hearts upon."

Believers too can set their hearts on things (good or bad) outside of the will of God, and pray, rationalize, apply biblical promises and work toward those things, all the while being unwilling to hear the truth. We often have a lot of dying to do toward our own desires, while we learn that "Blessed are the undefiled in the way, who walk in the law of the LORD." Our calling is to contend in faith for all of the promises of God concerning our lives (as Israel had to fight for the Promised Land), while being careful to grasp for nothing more than that which is truly ours in the Lord. Consider these scriptures:

- The Lord looks on the heart (1 Samuel 13:14; 16:7; 2 Chronicles16:9).

- 2 Chronicles 16:9, "For the eyes of the LORD run to and fro throughout the whole earth, to show Himself strong on behalf of those whose heart is loyal to Him."

Addendum 4

Judgments *(Mishpat)*

For the sake of review, we duplicate here the segment on *mishpat* (judgments) from the introduction. This word relates to government. It is a judicial sentence that decrees a decision or verdict. It can be favorable or unfavorable. In The Scriptures translation, this is translated right rulings, which is exactly what it is, the right rulings of a king who decrees a thing that is right. *Mishpat* occurs twenty-two times in Psalm 119.

1. Kings in Israel were said to "judge (*shaphat*, the verb form of *mishpat*) Israel" (1 Samuel 8:5-6, 20). "And all Israel heard of the judgment (*mishpat*) which the king (Solomon) had judged (*shaphat*); and they feared the king, for they saw that the wisdom of God was in him to administer justice" (*mishpat*) (1 Kings 3:28).

2. When a righteous king decrees a thing or renders a verdict, things are set in motion to put wrong things right and to make a distinction between the righteous and the wicked (Exodus 11:6-7). The oppressed are released and the oppressors punished. Peace (*shalom*) is the result of righteous government as both the wicked and the righteous are rewarded rightly. God's judgments are the King's right rulings which lead to redemptive acts of power.

3. The Lord, the righteous Judge, is unrelenting in His war against sin. He wants to destroy (judge) sin within His children as any father would want to destroy the disease that is killing the son whom he loves. He wants to set wrong things right within us.

4. We are not under the judgment of God, but the sin we cling to is. God's judgments first come to us as His word to help us "judge ourselves (so that) we would not be judged (by God). For when we are judged, we are chastened by the Lord, that we may not be condemned with the world" (1 Corinthians 11:31-32).

5. Hebrews 4:12 tells us that the word of God is living, powerful and sharp as it pierces, divides and it is "a discerner (judge) of the thoughts and intents of the heart."

6. Hebrews 5:13-14, "For everyone who partakes only of milk is unskilled in the word of righteousness, for he is a babe. But solid food belongs to those who are of full age, that is, those who by reason of use have their senses exercised to discern (judge) both good and evil."

7. *Mishpat* can also refer to the rights belonging to someone (Exodus 23:6).

Declaring God's Judgments – Concerning Psalm 119:13

1. When we recount God's judgments (*mishpat*), we recount the Lord's great deliverances of Israel from oppression throughout history. As we do this, faith comes for our own deliverance from difficulty. God is the same yesterday, today and forever. We note a two-fold pattern:

    •   God waits. There are times of oppression, testing and difficulty as the wicked seem to prevail over the righteous or prosper at the expense of the righteous. This test is designed to accomplish something in the people of God. We will examine this more closely.

    •   God acts. At the right time, the Lord arises and speaks, and gives the ruling that judges or separates the wicked from the righteous. The righteous are delivered and the wicked are punished as both are rewarded according to their deeds. This is precisely what occurs globally at the second coming of *Yeshua* predicted in 2 Thessalonians 1:6-10.

2. This two-fold pattern is evident in almost every deliverance and breakthrough of God on behalf of His people that is recorded in scripture.

    •   The restoration of Joseph to his family.

    •   The placement of David on the throne of Israel.

    •   The many deliverances in the days of the judges of which the deliverance under Gideon is characteristic.

    •   The six "palace stories" of the first six chapters of the book of Daniel (Daniel and the lion's den for example).

    •   The second coming of Messiah will be after a time of great trouble fostered by wicked leadership on the earth. At His coming, the kingdoms of this world will become the kingdoms of our Lord and of His Messiah and He shall reign forever and ever (Revelation 11:15). He will turn the tables on the anti-Messiah and his wicked cohorts and, by the word of His mouth (Isaiah 11:4; Revelation 19:15), set wrong things right. Both the wicked and the righteous will be rewarded by His judgments (right rulings). But for now, He waits (see 2 Thessalonians 1:6-10).

Further Discussion on the Judgments (*Mishpat*) of God

We need to discuss the judgments of God at some length because we will need this foundation all through our journey. God's judgments, used as a synonym for God's word, come to us to divide and discern between right and wrong within our own lives.

As we submit to the word of God and repent, sin is judged within us. However, so is our righteousness in Messiah and our true identity as sons of God revealed and affirmed. A judgment can be negative or positive.

At the early stage of *gimel* (v. 20), as a stranger in the earth, our psalmist is already feeling the heat of the world's hatred toward the righteous. *Yeshua* said, "If they persecuted Me, they will also persecute you" (John 15:20; Psalm 119:23). As the meek of the earth, hated by the world, we are at times allowed to experience great persecution, while the wicked (temporarily) overcome the righteous (as in Daniel 7:21-22). This is hopefully because the righteous will not compromise righteousness and play the same kind of self-promoting games that others may play. This injustice greatly tests our hearts, exposing all kinds of unrighteous instincts rooted in our own pride, fear and carnality.

Typically, the point at which the offenses come, we become indignant because of the injustice that has just occurred. Every carnal instinct within us is aroused. We now have several options:

1. Retaliate or humiliate that person by judging him and pointing out to everyone how bad or wrong he really is to have done what he did.

2. Justify our wrong response by pointing out the terrible injustice of what occurred.

3. Crawl into a corner in self-pity and wait for the rapture.

4. Allow the word of God to judge us (discern, separate out that which is sinful within ourselves), repent and judge ourselves (1 Corinthians 11:31) according to His judgments.

I hope it is obvious which option is right. *Yeshua* said, "It is impossible that no offenses come" (Luke 17:1). If we will seize the opportunity afforded us by the exposing of our own carnality, and repent, we have just set the table for a massive display of God's power in the earth as our Righteous Judge arises in power to set all wrong things right. Doing so requires that we allow God's word to come to us as judgment and separate the good from the bad in our own lives. Remember, He loves righteousness and hates wickedness (Psalm 45:7). Although we are not appointed to wrath, the degree to which we whom God loves cling to the sin which is destroying us, to that degree we will experience the judgments of God.

God cannot righteously judge sin in the world until He judges the sin in His own house. "For the time has come for judgment to begin at the house of God; and if it begins with us first, what will be the end of those who do not obey the gospel of God?" (1 Peter 4:17). God constantly employed nations more wicked than Israel to discipline His people before He would judge that nation.

So, how does this work again? Let us look at *Yeshua*, "Who, when He was reviled, did not revile in return; when He suffered, He did not threaten, but committed Himself to Him who judges righteously" (1 Peter 2:23). The only truly righteous Man ever to walk the face of the earth died at the hands of sinners in a most treacherous way. Talk about injustice or offense. Yet, He loved His enemies. He prayed for those who abused Him and prayed, "Father, forgive them. . ."

Yeshua, as He faces the cross, tells His disciples, "The ruler of this world is coming, and he has nothing in Me" (John 14:30). *Yeshua's* response to His enemies throughout His suffering proved that there was no sin in Him. He trusted *Abba* to determine how far the suffering would go. It appeared that the Father was not going to give a ruling on His behalf. Would *Yeshua* have to save Himself? He refused to call the legions of angels that were at His disposal. When He was reviled and insulted, He returned words of kindness. Would God arise on His behalf? "Where are You, LORD? Why have You forsaken Me? I thought that righteousness and justice are the foundation of Your throne (Psalm 89:14)? How can a righteous King allow this perversion of justice? Vindicate me. Deliver Me." Yet God waited—until it was too late, or so it seemed.

"Suddenly, there was a great earthquake; for an angel of the Lord descended from heaven, and came and rolled back the stone from the door, and sat on it. His countenance was like lightning, and his clothing as white as snow. And the guards shook for fear of him, and became like dead men" (Matthew 28:2-4). The table was set at the cross for a massive display of power as God vindicated His Son's righteous life. It now became manifest who was right and who was wrong. This is the effect of judgment (*mishpat*).

A massive truth was coined by the late Virgil Johnson. I heard him speak at our local church in the late 1980's and his powerful one-liner stuck with me: "it takes the snake to expose the snake in me." Offense and injustice, which are the work of the enemy, serve to expose the sin in us. In fact, to the degree that injustice provokes our carnality, to that degree God is justified in allowing injustice and offense to touch us. If we will judge the sin within, then God can righteously show His power on our behalf and judge sin in the world—the very sin that was employed against us. The drama is the contest between light and darkness. Our enemy wants us to get offended at a God who would allow such injustice and undeserved difficulty. He wants us to "Curse God and die!" God wants us to recognize our carnality and judge the sin within our own members. Hence, the sin in the world is a great key to our own formation. This is the wisdom of God to allow Satan to rage against His beloved children in a fallen world.

When God finally arose to vindicate enslaved Israel as belonging to Himself, and moved in power on their behalf, He made (as Judge) a difference or distinction between "My people and your (Pharaoh's) people" (Exodus 8:23). When the drama was over, the oppressed were freed and the oppressors who would not repent were judged. In the short term, injustice prevailed against Israel, testing their hearts. In Deuteronomy

4:20, Egypt was the iron furnace of formation in order for Israel to become the Lord's inheritance. But ultimately, who was right and who was wrong was manifest as God worked a mighty deliverance.

One final approach to this truth can be found in Psalm 92:7: "When the wicked spring up like grass, and when all the workers of iniquity flourish," what is God doing?

1.   God is judging sin in His people. The Judge exposes that sin through the injustices that abound so that we can allow the judgments of His word to purify us to become just like His Son. Read again 1 Corinthians 11:31-32 and 1 Peter 4:17.

2.   God is allowing time for repentance. He is working on behalf of those who are persecuting the righteous. He wants them to witness the Messiah-like responses of His child and repent. He is not willing that any perish. The scenario of injustice and offense sets the table for a display of Christ-likeness that will draw sinners to repentance. Romans 12:19-21, "Beloved, do not avenge yourselves, but rather give place to wrath; for it is written, 'Vengeance is Mine, I will repay,' says the LORD. Therefore, if your enemy is hungry, feed him; If he is thirsty, give him a drink; For in so doing you will heap coals of fire on his head. Do not be overcome by evil, but overcome evil with good." The strength of these verses demonstrated in real life is how Saul of Tarsus, witnessing the stoning of Stephen, became the Apostle Paul.

3.   God is allowing the iniquity to become complete or full. When Israel finally entered the land of Canaan to destroy the inhabitants, two things had come to fullness:

     •   Israel had come to full glory and power as the righteous army of the Lord.

     •   The iniquity of the Amorites was complete (Genesis 15:16). They had fully made their choice to not repent, and it was right for God to judge. This is the principle of Messiah's judgment of the anti-Messiah at the second coming. What God disallowed in Genesis 11 at the tower of Babel, He will allow at the end of the age.

The wheat (sons of the kingdom) and the tares (sons of the evil one) both mature in the same field at the same time setting the table for a great end-time drama (Matthew 13:24-43). When the angels reap the harvest at the end of the age, a great separation will take place as the reapers gather out of His kingdom all things that offend, and those who practice lawlessness and will cast them into the furnace of fire (Matthew 13:41-42). This is the final judgment.

Let's seize the opportunity in this fallen world where sin and injustice abound, to judge sin within ourselves and entrust our vindication to our heavenly Father, trusting Him to give a right ruling at the right time.

Addendum 5

The Fear of the Lord
A Study of the True and Holy Fear of God

It seems that the grace and love of God are focused on so much in contemporary Christendom that fearing God is seen to be antithetical to loving Him. This is a grave error. Love and fear are not opposite nor are they mutually exclusive. In fact, the one pre-supposes the other. To truly love is to fear and to truly fear is to love. One cannot exist without the other. Yes, fear is about being in awe of God and about reverencing Him, but fear also means fear—as in being afraid.

Consider an excellent excerpt from the writings of Rick Joyner of Morning Star Ministries:

"And he (Adam) said, 'I heard the sound of Thee in the garden, and I was afraid because I was naked; so I hid myself'"(Genesis 3:10).

The first mention of fear in the Bible is in the above verse. There is a pure and holy fear of God, and there is an unholy fear. This is the unholy fear of God that leads to further corruption of the soul, and causes us to run from Him instead of to Him.

The holy fear of God would never cause us to attempt to hide from Him. The holy fear of God is rooted in the knowledge that He is God and no one can hide from Him. It acknowledges that He is all knowing, and we at best know very little. The holy fear of God is the 'beginning of wisdom' (see Proverbs 9:10) because it acknowledges that we need help from Him to know anything accurately.

The unholy fear of God is rooted in the poisonous fruit of the tree of Knowledge of Good and Evil. This fear is not rooted so much in who God is but in our own self-centeredness. This is the fear that causes us to try to hide from God and one another. This causes the facades and pretensions that so dominate the relationships of fallen men."[1]

Listen to the cry of God's heart from Deuteronomy:

- Eleven times God says, "that you would love Me."
- Four times He adds, "that you would cling to Me." "Cling to me in love" is implied.
- Fourteen times God desires "that you would fear Me."
- Deuteronomy 10:12, "And now, Israel, what does the LORD your God require of you, but to fear the LORD your God, to walk in all His ways and to love Him, to serve the LORD your God with all your heart and with all your soul."

- Deuteronomy 13:4, "You shall walk after the LORD your God and fear Him, and keep His commandments and obey His voice; you shall serve Him and hold fast to Him."

Many scriptures speak of the benefits of fearing God. Take some time to look up a few of these verses:

- Proverbs 1:7 and 9:10 teach us that the fear of the Lord is the beginning of both knowledge and wisdom respectively.

- Psalm 128:1, "Blessed (*esher*: happy) is everyone who fears the LORD." See Psalm 34:7, 9; 85:9; 103:11; 111:5, 10; 115:11; 145:19; 147:11; Proverbs 10:27; 14:26-27; 15:16; 19:23; 22:4; Exodus 1:21; Acts 13:26.

One way to think about fear of the Lord is to be afraid to grieve a father's love.

We could illustrate fear and love in the context of a healthy home situation. A child will often run to greet his father at the door. The child does not run for cover or cower in fear. But, if the child has sinned and deserves discipline, he will not rest until all is set right. He may well cling to Dad, trembling, until all is made right and they are reconciled. It is all about love, but fear is the other side of the coin.

The stronger the bond, the more fear is involved in confessing a sin against that love. If the father does nothing, there is something wrong with his love. Proverbs 13:24, "He who spares the rod hates his son. Whom the LORD loves, He chastens."

How about a marriage? Don't you fear hurting your spouse? I cannot even imagine the breaking of the marriage covenant of love or the ensuing terror in confessing it. Fear and love go together. In the case of covenant unfaithfulness there would be terrible fear in bringing out the truth. But if reconciliation is ever to occur, truth must be brought to light and dealt with.

Yes, I know about 1 John 4:17-18, "Love has been perfected among us in this: that we may have boldness in the day of judgment; because as He is, so are we in this world. There is no fear in love; but perfect love casts out fear, because fear involves torment (fear of the Day of Judgment). But he who fears (that Day) has not been made perfect in love (parenthesis added for clarity).

1. First, this is about having confidence in the Day of Judgment, not about having the true fear of God as portrayed in scripture. If we have received His discipline and been reconciled to Him in this age, we will have nothing to fear on that day. Fear Him now and overcome sin, or fear Him later.

   - In Exodus 20:20 Moses said to the people, "Do not fear; for God has come to test you, and that His fear may be before you, so that you may not sin."

2.   In 1 Corinthians 3:9-15, Paul warns believers to "take heed (fear God) how you live your life in this age, because it will be tested or evaluated by the fire of God on that Day" (judgment). Again, fear Him now or fear Him then. You choose!

Yes, God forgives sin, but even that is so that we will fear Him. Psalm 130:3-4 says, "If You, LORD, should mark iniquities, O LORD, who could stand? But there is forgiveness with You, that You may be feared." Do you know what it cost to obtain your forgiveness? The Father paid a terrible price, the death of His Son on a cross. One who can casually sin, thinking, "God will forgive," neither loves nor fears God!

C. S. Lewis wrote of Aslan in The Chronicles of Narnia, "He is not a tame Lion,"[2] and again, "He is not safe, but He is good!"[3] He is holy and the inherent power in Him is infinite. His eyes of fire see right through us. He knows everything about us. This is cause for fearing God. His lovingkindness draws us. His inherent power causes us to tremble. It is conceivable that one could experience both sheer delight and sheer terror simultaneously, while burying one's face and hands in the glorious "mane" of the Lion of Judah.

The good news is, "God loves you." The bad news is, "God loves you." How can it be? The most powerful being in the universe, Who is a consuming fire of holy passion, and whose Name is Jealous, has set His love upon you and bound you to Himself in an unbreakable covenant, and He will not share you with another. Consider Paul's words in 1 Corinthians 10:21-22, "You cannot drink the cup of the Lord and the cup of demons; you cannot partake of the Lord's table and of the table of demons. Or do we provoke the Lord to jealousy? Are we stronger than He?"

Consider Isaiah 66:2, "But on this one will I look: On him who is poor and of a contrite spirit, and who trembles at My word." There is a vast difference between mere familiarity and true intimacy. We approach the Lord casually and blithely according to our own timetable and needs as if He exists for us. Godly fear and holy awe seem to have been replaced by a yawn of familiarity. The consuming fire of God has been reduced to a fire we can kindle at will for our own warmth and light. True intimacy speaks of love and affection, but leads to trembling. Consider the following New Testament scriptures:

1.   Acts 5:11, Ananias and Sapphira: "Great fear came upon all the church and upon all who heard these things."

2.   Revelation 1:17, "When I saw Him (*Yeshua*), I fell at His feet as dead."

Consider and use this outline for further meditation and study on your own.

The privilege and the peril of having God in the house—See Isaiah 29

1.   Scriptures to read:

    •   Sinners in Zion are afraid (Isaiah 33:14).
    •   Who can endure. . . He will be a "swift witness against. . . " (Malachi 3:1-5).
    •   Seventy men died in Beth-Shemesh (1 Samuel 6:20).
    •   Ananias and Saphira in Acts 5.
    •   Uzzah's death in 2 Samuel 6:7-9.
    •   Who can endure it? (The day of the LORD) (Joel 2:11).
    •   The death of Nadab and Abihu in Leviticus 10.

2.   If we want the blessing, we need the presence. If we want the presence, we must regard Him as holy!

    •   The ark was to be carried on poles so that no one could touch it.
    •   The ark was to be carried by Levites, a people of one thing.
    •   Moses was barred from the land because He did not "hallow God in the eyes of the children of Israel" (Numbers 20:12).

3.   Two fears are implied in Numbers 1:53, where the Levites protect the people from the holiness of God and they protect the sanctity of the sanctuary from the defilement of the people:

    •   Fear of His holy presence—"Who can dwell with everlasting burnings?" (Isaiah 33:14.)
    •   Fear of His absence—Who can even exist without Him? We would be utterly alone in the universe with no recourse!

Addendum 6

Slaves of Righteousness
A Teaching on Passionate Obedience
(See *Pey*: v. 129-136)

Psalm 119:131, "I opened my mouth and panted, for I longed for Your commandments." Our psalmist's intense longing for the commandments (*mitsvah*) of the Lord seems surprising. The Hebrew word mitsvah means command, directive, charge, or order. How can one so pant after and long for a command? Who of us wants to be commanded to do something or be charged with a mission? Might not that commission affect our goals in life? Yet *Yeshua's* entire goal in life was to please the Father. In John 8:29, *Yeshua* said, "I always do those things that please Him."

Yeshua said in John 4:34, "My food is to do the will of Him who sent Me." When facing the cross in John 14:31 He says, "That the world may know that I love the Father, and as the Father gave Me commandment, so I do." How can someone become addicted to the commands of the Father? The two-fold answer is simple but powerful, as it connects to the two primary needs of every human being:

- Identity: "Who am I?"

- Destiny and purpose: "Why am I here?" and "Where am I going?"

Every time *Yeshua* obeyed a command of the Father, He experienced the following:

1. The Father's pleasure upon His heart. This heart to heart intimacy connects with His identity as the Son of God—He who was with God from the beginning (John 1:1-2). *Yeshua* knew who He was and maintained that intimacy.

2. The breaking in of God's power to advance their joint mission to re-establish the kingdom of heaven on earth connects with His purpose as the Son of Man living among men (John 1:14).

What a life *Yeshua* lived on the earth as a Man. It was a passionate partnership in mission, a "love-walk" between the Father in heaven and the Son on earth. Eleven times in the gospel of John, *Yeshua* referenced the Father's love for Him (John 3:35; 5:20 and many more). Twice the Father shouted from heaven, "This is My Son, whom I love. With Him I am well pleased." Four times *Yeshua* referenced His own love for the Father (John 14:31 and others) as the primary motivation for doing what He did.

In Psalm 19:8 we have these familiar words: "The commandment (*mitsvah*) of the LORD is pure, enlightening the eyes" (or bringing light to the eyes). As noted in the introduction of Psalm 119, God's commands are pure because they are not self-serving but are designed to help us enter into our destiny as sons of God. Picture a father giving his young son some money and then giving this directive: "Son, go to the corner store and buy a gallon of milk." Provided things are healthy between father and son, this boy would go to the store with purpose, with light in his eyes, if you will. Obeying this directive then gives him a two-fold pleasure:

1. Opportunity to please his father, and experience his father's pleasure as only a son can.

2. Opportunity to enjoy the milk that just entered into his world from another place.

Every true believer is seated in the heavenlies in Messiah (Ephesians 2:6) with the privilege of access to God and of intimacy with Him as sons of God. This is our identity. Do you know who you are? Every believer lives on earth and has a destiny related to the mission of seeing the kingdom of heaven come to earth. Do you know your purpose?

Obedience to specific commands opens the door for the breaking in of heaven's power and the release of signs and wonders. In John 5:19-20, we learn that *Yeshua* did only those things He saw the Father doing. He said, "The Son can do nothing of Himself." Hence, as the Father directed, so *Yeshua* would do. Then the Father would back up that obedience with a release of heaven's power, and a healing or a miracle would take place. Acts 10:38 speaks of how "God anointed *Yeshua* of Nazareth with the Holy Spirit and with power, who went about doing good and healing all who were oppressed by the devil, for God was with Him." What a partnership between heaven and earth.

The breaking in of heaven's power to confirm a servant's obedience serves to display and advance God's kingdom on earth. Elijah's prayer for fire on Mount Carmel started like this: "LORD God of Abraham, Isaac, and Israel, let it be known this day that You are God in Israel and I am Your servant, and that I have done all these things at Your word." The miracle of fire from heaven confirmed Elijah's obedience that day. This is the process by which our capacity and desire for more of God increases.

Paul tells us in Romans 6:16-22, "We become slaves to whomever we obey." We can be slaves of sin leading to death or slaves of obedience unto righteousness. "Furthermore, when we were slaves of sin we were free in regard to righteousness. But, having been set free from sin, you became slaves of righteousness." How can a human being, who has sinful passions operating in his own soul, become a slave of righteousness? By yielding to the Father's invitation to do the right thing by obeying His command.

One becomes addicted to drugs little by little. The more he yields, the more he needs more to get the same impact. In other words, his capacity for the drug increases and so does his desire. We become addicted to righteousness in exactly the same way. Yield to Spirit's directive "temptation" to do something such as share the gospel with someone, testify to God's goodness, pray for a sick person or respond in a Messiah-like way to a difficult person. You will experience the two-fold reward of obedience and will begin to become a slave of righteousness.

Believers are not trapped by sinful passions because their desires are too strong to overcome. They are trapped because their desires are too weak and too easily satisfied with lesser things. Our deliverance from sinful passions will not come by fighting sinful passions. It will only come by tasting something better and getting addicted to that superior pleasure of walking in partnership with God. Go ahead, press through your fear and do what the Father has just commanded. Present your members as instruments of righteousness. You just might have an addictive encounter with the Lord.

Biblical holiness is "happy holiness"

David's restraint and self-control are not some kind of legalistic effort to move God on his behalf, nor a morbid show of religious self-denial or strict teeth-gritting adherence to some law. They flow from love for God and are unto the transcendent pleasures of knowing God and His ways even more. Self-denial is always encouraged in the context of a greater personal advantage such as the pleasures of following *Yeshua* and being received into God's eternal kingdom. It is not an end in itself, which would simply make it a religious show.

Michel Sullivant expounded on this theme during a message titled *Happy Holiness*.[1] He explained that God gives us all things to enjoy but not to worship. We must learn to trace the pleasure and joy of such things back to the Giver. We are to be lovers of God and enjoyers of the pleasures He gives, "not lovers of pleasure rather than lovers of God" as in 2 Timothy 3:1-5. We should be seekers of the true and lasting pleasures by seeking to be lovers of God. When we inordinately seek after temporal (even legitimate) pleasures, we betray the fact that we are worshipping and serving the creature and the creation rather than the Creator.

Sullivant went on to explain that there is a proper asceticism (from the word where we get the word athlete) called for within the New Testament doctrine of sanctification. Mortifying our earthly members does not mean that we are to literally pluck out our eyes or commit suicide! It means that we are to utilize and employ self-control by the Spirit's power to crucify (abstain from) the sinful manifestations of human desires that have gone out of bounds. This is to be accomplished through the biblically substantiated and time-tested methods of self-discipline ordained by God to help bring our mental and bodily powers into alignment with the powers of God's kingdom.

There is a form of religion called dualism in which the visible, material and natural realm is viewed as intrinsically evil, while only the invisible spiritual realm is good. One expression of dualism, a heresy known as Gnosticism, plagued the early body of Messiah. One extreme of this thinking led some to consider the body as irrelevant leading to moral license, while another extreme of the same thinking led others to promote a wrong asceticism (bodily disciplines) as a means of becoming spiritual. The truth is that both the material and the spiritual realms have been created by God as good, even though they have been invaded by Satan, his angels and human sinfulness. The natural realm is to be redeemed and sanctified by a submission to and a surrender of its resources and powers to the reign of the Holy Spirit and the kingdom of God.

Yeshua taught that we are in the world but not of the world. Detachment from the world is the only way to engagement in the world without entanglement in the world. Worldliness occurs when our natural human passions dominate our lives. Our desires become disordered and inordinate and are twisted into sinful lusts of body and mind. God is the originator of pleasure, not the devil. Satan only perverts the good things of God by tempting us to hold them without regard to their proper place in the heart of God and His overall economy of things. "The pride of life" views our God-given limited self-subsistent power as a license for autonomy rather than as a gift and stewardship from God that is to be offered back to Him in voluntary love.

Endnotes

Acknowledgements

1. Frank T. Seekins, Dr., *Hebrew Word Pictures: How Does the Hebrew Alphabet Reveal Prophetic Truths?* (Frank T. Seekins, 2012).

Chapter 1

1. Dallas Willard, *The Divine Conspiracy: Rediscovering our Hidden Life in God* (New York, Harper Collins Publishers, 1998) p. 142.

2. *The Babylonian Talmud* (In the public domain), Shabbat 31a

3. J. Preston Eby, *The Kingdom of God Book One* (Dallas, TX, Lighthouse Library International, 2014).

4. Francis Frangipane, *"The Power of a Transcendent Life."* Message can be read online at http://francisfrangipanemessages.blogspot.com/2005/07/the-power-of-transcendent-life-part-2.html

5. Ibid.

Chapter 2

1. Lionel Cabral, *God is Love, Booklet 1*, (Lionel Cabral, 1994) p. 16.

Chapter 3

1. J. Alec Motyer, *The Prophecy of Isaiah: An Introduction and Commentary* (Downers Grove, IL, InterVarsity Press, 1993).

Chapter 4

1. Don Nori, *"Biblical Meditation."* I copied this excerpt in the 1980's from a short article on Biblical Meditation by Don Nori.

Chapter 6

1. J. Preston Eby, *Echoes from Eden Part Two* (J. Preston Eby, The Savior of the World Series, 2014).

2. Alan Vincent, Transcribed from a series of messages given in the late 1990's.

3. Steve Sabol, *"Knights of the 21st Century Newsletter"* (Lebanon, PA, 2014).

Chapter 7

1. John Piper, *Desiring God* (Colorado Springs, CO, Multnomah Publishers, 1986) p. 10, 50.

2. V.P. Hamilton, R.L. Harris, G. L Archer Jr. and B.K. Waltke (Eds.), *Theological Wordbook of the Old Testament* (Chicago, Moody Press, Electronic edition 1999) p. 908.

3. C. S. Lewis, *The Lion, the Witch and the Wardrobe* (New York, NY, HarperTrophy, a Division of HarperCollins Publishers, 1950) p. 200.

4. Ibid, p. 86.

Chapter 11

1. Allen Hood, *"Sweet Aroma of Meekness,"* Part 3, Message given in Kansas City, 2004.

Chapter 17

1. C. S. Lewis, *The Lion, the Witch and the Wardrobe* (New York, NY, HarperTrophy, a Division of HarperCollins Publishers, 1950) p. 86.

Chapter 18

1. www.hebrew4christians.com

Chapter 24

1. John Piper, *A Hunger for God: Desiring God through Fasting and Prayer* (Wheaton, IL, Crossway Books, 1997) p. 42.

2. Ibid, p. 43.

3. Ibid, p. 44.

Addendum 5

1. Rick Joyner *"Morningstar Daily Devotional,"* Day 32 (Fort Mill, SC, Morningstar Ministries, 2006), retrieved from https://www.morningstarministries.org/resources/daily-devotional/2006/day-32-fear#.WITQe_I97IU

2. C. S. Lewis, *The Lion, the Witch and the Wardrobe* (New York, NY, HarperTrophy, a Division of HarperCollins Publishers, 1950) p. 200.

3. Ibid, p. 86.

Addendum 6

1. Michael Sullivant, Transcribed from his message titled "Happy Holiness," Metro Christian Fellowship, Kansas City, KS, c. 2004-2005.

More about Ken Eberly

Called to pastor a small urban congregation in Reading, PA, Ken and Betty sold their home in the Lancaster Country, PA, and moved to Reading in 1979. There, for the next 20 years, they raised their five children and pastored the congregation. In addition to pastoring, Ken helped to give oversight to a number of congregations in the denomination for several years.

In 2000, after credentialing their successor, Ken and Betty were commissioned to serve an emerging regional network of churches and ministries that was focused on regional transformation. He helped to establish and direct a local house of prayer as an expression of one of the priorities of this network. Ken presently walks with numerous other pastors and leaders in the region in a desire to see them strengthened and equipped to fulfill the call of God upon their lives. He has a desire to see the Body of Messiah come together for kingdom purposes in every region.

In 2008, Ken and Betty established Behold Your God Ministries, Inc., where Ken presently serves. He now preaches, teaches and equips in the arenas of corporate prayer, spiritual maturity, biblical unity, knowing God and the coming kingdom. Ken's unique passion is teaching from the Hebrew Scriptures and uncovering how *Yeshua* (Jesus) really is the Messiah to Whom all of the Hebrew scriptures point. A key scripture driving much of his present teaching is paraphrased thus from Romans 10:4; "For Messiah is the aim (or goal) of the *torah* unto righteousness for everyone who believe. "

Contact Information

Email: ken@beholdyourgodministries.org

www.beholdyourgodministsries.org

Address: 816 North 13th Street, Reading, PA 19604

69534306R00155

Made in the USA
Middletown, DE
07 April 2018